THE MA.
BROKE THE BANK
AT
MONTE CARLO

The Man Who Broke the Bank at Monte Carlo

Charles De Ville Wells, Gambler and Fraudster Extraordinaire

Robin Quinn

The
History
Press

For Louis, Elliot, Annabelle and Oscar

Front cover illustration: Monte Carlo Casino, Monaco. (Library of Congress)

First published 2016
This paperback edition first published 2023

The History Press
97 St George's Place, Cheltenham,
Gloucestershire, GL50 3QB
www.thehistorypress.co.uk

British Library Cataloguing in Publication Data.
A catalogue record for this book is available from the British Library.

ISBN 978 1 80399 373 7

Typesetting and origination by The History Press
Printed and bound in Great Britain by TJ Books Limited, Padstow, Cornwall

FSC

MIX
Paper from
responsible sources
FSC® C013056
www.fsc.org

Trees for LYfe

Contents

France and surrounding territories, showing places mentioned in the text.

Introduction

I had never realised that there really was a man who broke the bank until several years ago, when I was researching a completely unrelated topic. I knew, of course, that there was a song called *The Man who Broke the Bank at Monte Carlo*. My grandfather, who was born towards the end of Queen Victoria's reign, used to sing it to me when I was a child. It had been one of his favourites.

A paragraph in a very old newspaper caught my eye: it was headed 'Man who broke bank at Monte Carlo dies in poverty' – or something similar. I was surprised to learn that he was a real person. And then I wondered what could have happened between breaking the bank and dying a pauper. I jotted something down on a corner of my notepad and carried on with more immediate concerns. But I never quite forgot that short article.

After I had completed my first book – *Hitler's Last Army* – I casually mentioned to my editor at The History Press that I had another vague idea in mind: a biography of the bank-breaker, Charles De Ville Wells. His immediate reply caught me unawares, 'Yes please, The History Press would love to publish the book, and the contract is in the post.'

I hesitated for a moment. No book about Wells had ever been written before, but a great deal had appeared about him in the press over the years. The only trouble was that the reports seemed to contradict one another, making it hard to separate fact from fiction. Even a picture, which supposedly portrays him as a young man and appears on many websites, turned out to be of a completely different Charles Wells – a serious-looking fellow who became mayor of Massachusetts, USA, in 1832.

No one seemed quite sure who Charles De Ville Wells was, or where he came from, and the fact that he had used numerous false identities simply muddied the waters still further. He evidently spent many years in both France and Britain, and it was not at all clear how much of his life would have been documented.

But I decided to take a chance.

Researching a man who spent most of his life keeping one jump ahead of the authorities wasn't the easiest of tasks. But tracking down his activities and sifting through the many sources of information – on both sides of the Channel – has provided me with one of the most absorbing and satisfying challenges in my life. I have been helped in my search by many generous contributors, listed in the acknowledgements. My thanks to them, and sincere apologies to anyone I may have inadvertently omitted from the list.

This new paperback edition incorporates material which had not yet been discovered when the first edition was published; it has been substantially revised and expanded.

It is not a book which will tell you how to win money in a casino – though there are plenty of others that claim to do so. Even so, there has to be *some* discussion here of casino games and of money. In these instances I have carefully avoided complex discussions of mathematics, probability theory and statistics, and have kept things simple.

One pound (£1) in the late nineteenth century was worth about £100 today. By the 1920s, when this story ends, it was worth rather less – about £80 in present-day money. In any case, such comparisons can never be more than a rough guide. Where it seems helpful to do so (which is quite often), I have placed the modern equivalent in brackets afterwards: for example, 'In one day he had transformed the £4,000 he had brought with him into £10,000 (£1 million).' Thankfully, the exchange rate between the pound and the French franc (fr.) remained rock steady at 25fr. to the pound for nearly all of the period of this book, relieving us of any unwelcome arithmetical complications from that quarter.

Although no previous book about Charles De Ville Wells has been published, he is at least mentioned in a few works, and I have used these as source material where appropriate. But, for the most part, I have relied heavily on newspaper reports of the era. In fact a new section written for this book, Chapter 18, looks specifically at the power of the press as it relates to the man who broke the bank. The press shaped public opinion, on the one hand, while reflecting the thoughts and viewpoints of their readers on the other. Sometimes we have to take what the papers said with a pinch of salt – as we do today – but on the whole they allow us to see events through the eyes of an earlier generation, while evoking the atmosphere of an era which is now long gone.

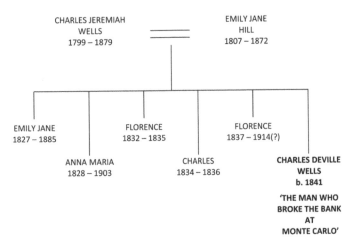

Wells family tree (simplified).

In quoting from these reports I have made minor changes to spelling, the use of capital letters, hyphens, and so on, for the sake of consistency. Where speech is reported, the actual words and expressions spoken over a century ago can sound surprisingly modern at times, but except for a few instances of slight paraphrasing for editorial reasons, the quotations are in fact unchanged from the original.

Acknowledgements

I could not have written this book without the help of the institutions and individuals listed here.

In Britain: Barclays Group Archives; British Library; Dr Francesca Denman; Simon Fowler; Guildhall Library; Jessica Handy (Unilever Archives); Hertfordshire Archives and Local Studies; Intellectual Property Office; Alan Lawrie; Lloyd's Register; London Borough of Hammersmith and Fulham Cemeteries; London Metropolitan Archives; National Archives; News UK Archives; Royal Archives, Windsor; Ben Stables; Dr Isobel Thompson (Historic Environment Record, Hertfordshire County Council); Max Tyler (British Music Hall Society); City of Westminster Archives Centre; West Yorkshire Archive Service.

The extract from Queen Victoria's journals (p. 87) was provided by the Royal Archives, Windsor, and is quoted with the permission of Her Majesty Queen Elizabeth II.

Overseas: Bibliothèque royale de Belgique; Brigitte Couplet; Bibliothèque Nationale de France; Christian Labardens; Charlotte Lubert (Société des Bains de Mer, Monte Carlo, Monaco); Martine and Joël Pairis; Father Jean-François Meuriot and colleagues, (Eglise Sainte-Marguerite, Marseille); Noëlle and Jean Pilon; Smithsonian Library (Washington DC, USA); Société des Gens de Lettres (Paris); Michel Troublé; Philippe Valcq; and the local archives in Lyon, Marseille, Morlaix and Paris.

My special thanks to all at The History Press, especially Mark Beynon who saw the potential in a story about Charles Wells. Thanks also to my editor for this edition, Chrissy McMorris, and to Lillian van Bergen for converting my text and ideas into this book. Last but by no means least, I thank my wife, Jacqueline, without whose love, support and help I could not have even considered writing this book.

Robin Quinn
May 2023

Prologue

Falmouth, Cornwall: January 1912

The elderly man with the grey beard didn't fit most people's impression of the most wanted criminal in Europe. But as Detective Sergeant George Nicholls knew full well, appearances could be deceptive. Nicholls stared into the twinkling blue eyes of the fugitive he had been stalking for the last eight months, and said, 'I am a Metropolitan Police officer. Is your name Lucien Rivier?'

'My name is Charles Wells,' the suspect replied. This came as no surprise to the lanky detective. By all accounts, this character used many aliases.

'You have passed under the name of Lucien Rivier in Paris.'

'If they like to call me Rivier, very well, yes, it's me.'

Nicholls turned to the woman. She was much younger than her companion, attractive in appearance and fashionably dressed. 'Is your name Jeanne Pairis?'

'Yes, that's my name.' She had a noticeable French accent. 'I have nothing to conceal.'

Nicholls read out the arrest warrant. With a gesture in her direction the old man said, 'It's absolutely false as to her. She's done nothing.'

'These are photographs of you?' said the officer, producing two pictures. They both answered yes. Later they were formally charged in the presence of a magistrate, whose first duty was to check that they really were the persons named on the warrant.

'Do you deny your identity?' the magistrate enquired.

'Not at all,' Charles Wells proudly replied. 'I can't deny my name. I'm the man the song was about, the man who broke the bank at Monte Carlo. You remember it?' And in 1912 there was hardly a soul alive who didn't know the most popular song of the past two decades.

Next day, Wells and his companion were taken to the railway station. A crowd of people had gathered there to wish them well. Some burst into song:

> As I walk along the Bois Boolong
> With an independent air
> You can hear the girls declare
> 'He must be a millionaire ...'

The train began its twelve-hour journey to London, rattling along the track with a clatter that was not unlike the sound of the small, white ivory ball that spirals its way around a roulette wheel. And in the long night, as Charles Wells drifted between wakefulness and slumber, he may have dreamed of that unforgettable night in Monte Carlo when the banknotes were piled a foot and a half high on the table before him. He was much younger then, and his life had taken many twists and turns since he'd staggered back to his hotel room carrying 1 million francs and slept with them under his pillow.

> You can hear them sigh and wish to die,
> You can see them wink the other eye
> At the man who broke the bank at Monte Carlo.

Yes, everybody knew the song. But what people didn't know was the incredible true story of the man who inspired it, a story which has never been fully revealed until now.

Wells had broken the bank not once, but a number of times. This was only one of his claims to fame, though. He had deceived many people and outwitted police forces on both sides of the Channel. During his lifetime he had assumed many identities. He knew several languages, and was a fine musician, an engineer, inventor, confidence trickster and fraudster extraordinaire. A man who had won several fortunes, lost them, and won them back again.

1

A Frenchman in the Making

The man who broke the bank at Monte Carlo – Charles De Ville Wells – was born at Broxbourne in the county of Hertfordshire, England, on 20 April 1841. It was not until 28 May that Charles' father finally got around to completing the formality of registering the birth. Charles Wells senior was a man who found it difficult to get around to doing anything much, except hunting, shooting, boating, catching fish and keeping bees. And he only kept bees because, as one of his friends claimed, 'while the bees were working he could be fishing'.

Charles' father – his full name was Charles Jeremiah Wells – was born in London in January 1799, the son of a well-to-do merchant. He grew into a striking young man with 'sparkling blue eyes, red curls, and bluff, rather blowsy complexion ... a bright, quick, most piquant lad, overflowing with wit and humour'.

At school, he made friends with another pupil, John Keats, who was destined to become one of the most illustrious of all English poets. Wells had literary ambitions of his own and the two young men talked incessantly about writing and poetry. Wells once sent some flowers to Keats, who responded by dedicating a sonnet to Wells:

But when, O Wells! thy roses came to me
My sense with their deliciousness was spell'd:
Soft voices had they, that with tender plea
Whisper'd of peace, and truth, and friendliness unquell'd.

As a young adult, Charles Jeremiah Wells gained a reputation as an ebullient, noisy extrovert, whose high spirits sometimes got the better of his judgement. When he was about 20, he played a mischievous trick on John Keats' younger brother, Tom. He faked a series of love letters from an imaginary girl who is supposed to have fallen for Tom. The prank backfired. Tom's disappointment on finding that there was, in fact, no female admirer upset him considerably. And there was a complication – Tom had been diagnosed with tuberculosis, and died soon afterwards. John Keats placed the entire blame for his brother's death on Wells.

'That degraded Wells,' he wrote. 'I do not think death too bad for the villain … I will harm him all I possibly can.' In an attempt to regain John's trust, Wells wrote an epic poem, *Joseph and his Brethren*. It is similar in style to Keats' own writing, and perhaps Wells had intended to flatter his friend. 'I wrote it in six weeks to compel Keats to esteem me and admit my *power*,' he later wrote, 'for we had quarrelled, and everybody who knew him must feel I was in fault.' In fact, it seems that John Keats never spoke to him or even referred to him ever again.

Although Charles Jeremiah Wells was set on pursuing a literary career, his parents forced him against his will to train as a lawyer. But he found the work dull and unsuited to his adventurous spirit. By day he worked with covenants, conveyances, deeds and affidavits; by night he caroused with new-found literary friends, who included the poet William Hazlitt. The pair 'used to get very drunk together' every night.

Around 1823–24 Wells decided to publish *Joseph and his Brethren*. But the book-buying public ignored it completely. It was a rejection that Wells never really recovered from.

In 1825, he married Emily Jane Hill, the daughter of a teacher who ran a 'boarding and day school' at Broxbourne. No description of her seems to have survived, but a letter that she wrote in later life displays – as we might expect of a teacher's daughter – beautifully formed handwriting (in contrast with her husband's spidery scrawl) with equally pristine spelling and grammar. The overall impression we gain is of a pleasant, mild-mannered, and self-effacing woman, perhaps inclined to be a little fussy and preoccupied with detail, accuracy and correctness.

Or to put it another way, she and her husband were two very different individuals. Charles was creative, lackadaisical, unscrupulous, extroverted and sometimes overbearing. Emily, on the other hand, favoured order and neatness, and made her way through life with patience and a quiet, yet strong, determination.

And, as we shall see, their son would inherit a curious mixture of these traits.

By 1831, Charles Jeremiah Wells had given up his legal practice. Around 1835 the couple relocated to Emily's home village of Broxbourne, which then had a population of about 550. They moved into an impressive house on the main street. (Plate 11)

An inheritance from his father allowed Charles to indulge his passion for outdoor activities, to which he now devoted most of his time. As well as shooting, fishing and beekeeping, he turned his hand to horticulture. According to his wife, he 'would have been a really good gardener but for his impatient habit of now and then pulling up plants to see how the roots were getting on, carefully putting them back again. He would do this early in the morning, before anybody else was up.'

The couple had three daughters: Emily Jane (named after her mother), Anna Maria and Florence. (Another girl and a boy were also born, but died in infancy.) So now all that was missing from their lives was a son. Every nineteenth-century family yearned for a male heir and they must have longed to fill the void left by the death of their first son. Charles Jeremiah Wells was, by now, around 40 years of age and Emily was in her mid-thirties. It was by no means too late for them to have a son, but perhaps they were beginning to sense that time was moving on.

The birth of Charles Wells in the spring of 1841 put an end to these concerns. They gave him the unusual middle name of De Ville, probably in honour of one of Charles Jeremiah's friends – a man named James Deville who lived on the same street. Both men had connections with the parish church in the village: Wells was one of the overseers of the poor, while James Deville served as a church warden.

On 30 May, the infant Charles, and his sister, Florence, who was now nearly 4, were christened in a joint ceremony by the Reverend Francis Thackeray (who happened to be the uncle of the author William Makepeace Thackeray). Shortly afterwards, 6-week-old Charles and the rest of the family were officially recorded in Britain's first census. This shows that Emily's brother, Robert Hill, and his family were living at the same address, and the household includes either three or four servants.

Broxbourne would have been a splendid place for young Charles to grow up, but a few weeks after he was born, the family moved out of their home and auctioned off many of their most valuable possessions. A partial list of the goods they sold gives some impression of their comfortable lifestyle up to that point: a pianoforte by Robert Wornum, the eminent maker of musical instruments, together with two other pianos; a phaeton coach with a 'handsome black pony' and harness; bees, and a beehive; a four-poster bed; other beds and bedding, furniture, carpets, 'kitchen and culinary articles ... and many other valuable effects'.

What we see here are the trappings of a wealthy family being turned into ready cash. It is unclear whether they had run short of money, or whether there was some other compelling reason to move away from the area. Charles Jeremiah Wells – although he apparently did no work – had managed to live the life of a wealthy country squire, surrounded by luxury goods which most of the villagers could never dream of owning. But after giving up this carefree existence, the family – including Emily's brother, Robert, and his wife, Mary Anne – crossed the Channel to begin a new life in France, the country where young Charles would spend most of his life.

The French *département* of Finistère – (literally, Land's End) – lies in the extreme north-west corner of France, in Brittany, nearer to the south-west coast of England than to Paris. The people's roots are remote from the rest of France, too. The railway had not yet reached these parts and communications with other parts of the country were extremely difficult. It comes as no surprise then that this isolated region had developed its own culture. The Breton language – widely spoken when the Wells family arrived in the mid-nineteenth century – has direct links to the Cornish tongue. And locally the region is known as *Cornouailles* – a name sharing the same origin as Cornwall.

The landscape is rugged, with rough, jagged summits and abrupt changes of gradient and elevation. The slopes are wild and featureless, often bare but sometimes dotted with heather. In winter storms batter the coast, and even in summer the weather can be capricious.

The region being so remote and lacking in the comforts that the Wells family had grown accustomed to, it is hard to fathom quite why they chose to move here in the first place. But Charles Jeremiah Wells and his extended family settled in the town of Quimper (pronounced 'camp-air'), the principal town of the region. What they found here was an ancient community with many mediaeval buildings, where the streets had curious names, such as Rue du Chapeau Rouge (Red Hat Street) and Ruelle du Pain Cuit (Baked Bread Alley). The River Odet flows through Quimper, and although the town is some 9 miles inland, it had a thriving fishing port based on the quay near the town centre.

By any measure, with its 10,000 inhabitants, Quimper was small. Only about 100 of the inhabitants were classed as 'foreigners' – though a good proportion of these were in fact French-speakers from Switzerland, Belgium and elsewhere. So when a complete family of English people turned up and settled in a house near the centre of town it must have caused quite a stir, as only two other English people lived in the community.

The Wells family settled in the Rue Bourg les Bourgs, not far from the river. We can well imagine father and son taking a pleasant riverside walk along the bank of the Odet, shaded by lines of elm trees. At the quay near their home the fishermen landed their catches of sardine, mackerel, anchovy, lobster and crab, while seabirds circled overhead filling the air with their shrill, persistent cries. Small merchant ships of around 100 tons sailed around the coast from other ports and came inland as far as Quimper to load and unload cargo.

Charles senior, the passionate angler and boatman, must have found it heavenly. And his enthusiasm was infectious: beginning in boyhood and throughout his life, Charles junior inherited his father's love of fishing, sailing and the sea. But there was a difference. While the father appreciated the poetic beauty of scenes such as this, the son was intrigued by how things worked. Interspersed among the many sailing ships, a few steam-powered vessels were gradually beginning to appear on the scene. These mechanical monsters, belching smoke and steam, smelling of coal and smoke and grease, their engines hissing and clanking, fascinated Charles Wells, and triggered in him a lifelong fascination with machines, engines and all things mechanical.

These, then, are the surroundings in which Charles grew up – the foundations of his first memories. At home with the family he lived the life of an English lad, while outside he was a young Frenchman in the making. And, while we cannot be certain, the *possibility* exists that this sense of 'not quite belonging anywhere' could have shaped his personality in adulthood.

We can say with rather more confidence that his father's unusual character influenced him to a great extent. Charles Jeremiah Wells had long been viewed by others as a powerful, almost intimidating, figure: 'it is probable that he had some kind of mesmeric power over people,' to quote one writer. 'He had only to see a man to make him do anything,' another claimed. And his son, Charles, certainly seems to have inherited his extraordinary powers of persuasion.

Not long after they settled in Quimper, Charles Jeremiah Wells seems to have undergone some form of spiritual conversion. The whole family relinquished the Protestant faith and joined the Roman Catholic Church. Wells senior began to make extraordinary claims that he was able to perform miracles and on one occasion, after a young woman of noble birth had died, Wells is said to have caused a great sensation among the population by raising her from the dead. On hearing this news the writer Theodore Watts-Dunton drily remarked, 'I cannot recall any other poet who has had a success of this kind … [it is] a faculty which is, I think, rare among modern poets.'

In 1846 a census took place in France, and it shows that, while the basic family structure was similar to that of 1841 at Broxbourne, some important changes had also taken place. In particular, Charles' two eldest sisters are no longer present. Emily Jane would have been 19 years old at the time. Perhaps she had already gone back to England. (It is even possible that she had never come to France in the first place. We know for a fact that she was married in London four years later.)

The second sister, Anna Maria, was 17. She became a nun at Morlaix, and, as young women were allowed to join religious orders from the age of 16 with their parents' consent, she was probably already living at a convent elsewhere at the date of the census. In their absence, Charles is likely to have become especially close to the last of the sisters, Florence, who was nearest to him in age and still living at home.

The census return also provides us with a few clues about the general language barrier experienced by this English family in France, and by the French people who encountered them. The census enumerator has evidently struggled with their names. As

Charles would find when he was a little older, he would often need to spell out his surname, Wells, because the letter 'W' does not naturally occur in French. The official has then started on the Hills, initially spelling their name with a 'W', too, before correcting it to an 'H'. Finally, Mary Ann Hill is recorded as 'Marianne', the French equivalent.

Such details may at first seem trivial, but although Charles became thoroughly assimilated into the French way of life his foreign-sounding surname must have got in the way when meeting new people or conducting business. (As we shall see, though, there were times when this apparent drawback worked to his advantage.)

Charles and Florence grew up knowing no other country than France. Charles learned to speak French perfectly, without any hint of a foreign accent, and no doubt it was the same with his slightly older sister. In these situations it often happens that the children speak French to each other, and English to their parents. In this way an exceptionally close bond was probably forged between the two siblings, while at the same time distancing them somewhat from their parents.

As an adult Charles was short in stature and this suggests that as a child he was probably of slender build, small and perhaps delicate. We know that in later life he suffered from bronchitis, and as respiratory illnesses such as this often begin in childhood, we can be reasonably certain that he had chest problems from an early age. The illness will not have been helped by the intemperate climate of Brittany, where the winters can be exceptionally cold, wet and windy. His health would have been a cause for considerable concern on his parents' part, especially as they had already lost a son and a daughter. However, his mental abilities made up for any physical weakness.

As the family's only male heir, it is probable that Charles was cosseted – 'spoiled' might perhaps be a better word. And this, again, will have had some influence on his personality in later life.

Initially Charles Jeremiah Wells seems to have spent a good deal of his time on leisure activities as he had in England. However, the family's financial circumstances forced him to earn a living and – with reluctance, no doubt – he took a job as a teacher of English at a local school. It is very likely that his son, Charles, attended the same establishment. In addition to his teaching, Wells senior wrote two long articles, 'Boar Hunt in Brittany' and 'Love-passages in the Life of Perron the Breton', in about 1846–47. Evidently he was attempting to revive his writing career, and things started to look hopeful when both works were published in Britain by *Fraser's Magazine*.

Encouraged by these small glimmers of hope, his wife Emily made the difficult journey to England, hoping to persuade publishers to reconsider his works as a whole. Emily's sister was married to William Smith Williams, the acclaimed literary editor who had 'discovered' Charlotte Brontë: her debut novel, *Jane Eyre*, was a runaway success at just that moment. However, even with such a first-rate connection, Emily found it impossible to get her husband's work published. In fact, Smith Williams regarded Wells with a certain amount of trepidation, claiming on one occasion that he was 'a most dangerous and insidious person'. Emily returned to France empty-handed.

By the beginning of the 1850s the family had left Quimper – but without Florence. Although she was only 13 they left her behind, and in the 1851 census we find her living near the quay 'in the care of' a Monsieur and Madame Bonnemaison. A little later she followed the same path as her older sister, changed her name from Florence to Marie, and became a nun at a convent at Isère, in the Rhône-Alpes region of eastern France.

For Charles De Ville Wells, now about 10 years old, it must have been a wrench to be parted from his sister and to turn his back on the town where he had spent his childhood. But now there were just the three of them – Charles, his father and his mother. Abandoning the craggy hills of Finistère, they made their way right across France to the warm breezes and calm waters of the Mediterranean and the city of Marseille.

The contrast between their former home in Brittany and this new city would have been overwhelming. With a population of around 200,000, Marseille was twenty times larger than Quimper. It was France's third largest community and the third largest port in the entire world.

The train bringing them to the city arrived at St Charles Station, high above and a little outside the limits of the city. From here the view stretched across the rooftops to the old port where the masts of the sailing ships resembled a forest on the water. Further still, to either side of the harbour mouth, stood two fortresses of cream-coloured stone – the Fort St Nicolas to the left, the Fort St Jean to the right – which looked as if they might have been uprooted from the Middle East during the Crusades and set down in nineteenth-century Marseille.

Just around the headland, beyond the Fort St Jean, vast new docks were being constructed to cope with Marseille's ever-expanding trade with the world beyond: timber from Odessa and the United States of America; rice from Italy and India; wax from the Levant; tobacco from Greece and Turkey; sponges from Tunis and Cyprus; and lead from mines in Spain. And from here commodities and finished products were sent out to every Mediterranean port, to the furthest outpost of the Empire of France and to the world beyond.

Perhaps the first difference Charles would have sensed was in the climate: the cold, damp winds that troubled the Brittany coastline never reached this far south. Instead Marseille shared sunshine and hot, dry air with the deserts of Tunis and Algeria, a day's journey across the sea. If we are correct in thinking that young Charles suffered from a bronchial illness, the warm Mediterranean climate is likely to have brought about a rapid improvement. Indeed, this may be the reason why the family moved so far south. Charles Jeremiah Wells took up another teaching post: perhaps the offer of a better paid job was another factor in their decision to relocate.

Charles' interest in boats and ships – especially steamships – was further stimulated by the sights and sounds of Marseille's docks. When the family made the city their home in about 1850, steamships were quite rare, with just thirty of them based at the port. But the next decade witnessed spectacular growth in the adoption of the new technology. By 1860, the number of steamers had quadrupled, and the average vessel was nearly three times as large. As he grew older Charles witnessed these developments at first hand, and by the time he was in his twenties, he had a job connected with engineering or shipbuilding at the local ironworks and dockyards.

He was a dark-haired, moderately handsome young man, if rather small in stature. People were drawn to this quiet – some would say very retiring – young man with his polite, gentle manner. From his speech no one would guess that he was anything but a Frenchman, and it was only his rather difficult foreign name that betrayed the fact that he was English. From his father he inherited a somewhat verbose style of writing, and a rather idiosyncratic approach to spelling and punctuation. He spoke 'with great abundance', and if he had a noticeable fault, it was his tendency to exaggerate, a habit for which the people of Marseille also have something of a reputation.

His understanding of machines was comprehensive. As an employee, he was painstaking, with a confidence in his own abilities that was amply justified by his success in practice. He never shirked from getting his hands dirty – something which inevitably happened when dealing with oily, sooty steam engines – and often he wore rather shabby clothes as a result. His leisure pursuits focussed on the sea – boats and fishing – but he also loved music and had learned to play the piano and the organ well. He very seldom drank alcohol, and never smoked.

Eventually the family had settled in the Boulevard Notre Dame, within sight of the Old Harbour. One of their neighbours, Madame Thérèse Jartoux, was a widow who had moved to that part of town following the death of her husband, a merchant, the year before. Her daughter, Marie Thérèse Joséphine Jartoux, was about the same age as Charles, and the two of them were soon engaged. The wedding ceremony took place on 8 May 1866. Their first and only child, Marie Antoinette Florence Charlotte de Ville-Wells,* was born at 4.00 p.m. on 31 March 1867.

In the register recording her birth, it appears that Charles has adopted an entirely new forename: he is shown as *Louis* Charles de Ville-Wells, and it seems that this was the name he was known by within the family. The register also shows that he has changed jobs in the year that has elapsed since his marriage, and he is now described as an 'engineer at the factories of la Nerthe' (a suburb to the north-west of Marseille). This is almost certainly a reference to the cement works, which employed many local people. However he doesn't seem to have stayed in this post for very long, and soon he was back at his old haunts in the dockyards. In common with many of his contemporaries, he almost certainly had no formal qualifications from a technical college: instead he would have learned his trade through practical experience. In France this class of engineer was called *ingénieur civil*.

By 1868 he was self-employed, selling his skills to local manufacturing companies and shipping lines. He could not have chosen a better time to go freelance. In the fifteen or so years since he had come to Marseille the flow of imports and exports through the city's docks had nearly doubled. This expansion was boosted still further by the opening of the Suez Canal in 1869, which allowed Marseille-based shipping lines ready access to ports in the Far East, such as Saigon, Hong Kong and Yokohama.

---

*   Her middle name is undoubtedly a tribute to Charles' sister, Florence. On some later documents the name is written 'Florine' but this is no doubt a mis-transcription. Incidentally, this is the first example of the family name 'de Ville-Wells' in this exact format.

Sailing ships, however, were extremely difficult to manoeuvre along the canal, which ran north–south, because the prevailing winds blew from west to east, and steam-powered vessels therefore took over quickly.

Charles worked with the largest shipping company in Marseille, the Messageries Maritimes, operators of a steamer network covering most of the globe and based at the local docks at La Joliette (Plate 2). He also carried out assignments for the Compagnie Fraissinet, a respected local steamship owner with about fifteen vessels. At the same time he invented a device which he claimed to be 'an improvement for regulating the speed of marine steam engines'. He applied for a French patent on it, and this was granted on 15 December 1868 (No. 83,451). Recognising, perhaps, that the potential for such an instrument might be even greater in Britain, he also registered the invention in London a year later. The regulator was tested on the *Durance*, one of the Fraissinet Company's steamers, and a glowing account of its performance appeared in the British publication, *Engineering*. As a result, Fraissinet bought the patent from Wells for 5,000fr. – an impressive sum equivalent to five times an engineer's annual salary.

At one point, Wells was apparently living at Nice – the centre of the olive oil industry – where he invented a device for extracting oil from the olives. His application of modern engineering techniques to the processing of an agricultural product seems to have caught the attention of Count Branicki, a nobleman of Polish origins whose family owned vast tracts of land at Bila Tserkva in Ukraine, where sugar beet was the main crop. A new factory was built to process the beet and it appears that Wells was involved in setting up the machinery. The exact extent of his contribution to the project is unknown; what is certain is that sugar production in the area increased more than tenfold over a short period.

His marriage to Marie Thérèse opened up yet more opportunities. His brother-in law, Henry Jartoux , was also an engineer, who constructed machines from Charles' drawings and sketches, including steam engines and the olive oil device. Henry had lived in Spain for a time (one of his children was born there) and it may be through his connections that Charles obtained work as engineer to a Spanish lead mine, where he stayed for a year and a half. His travels also took him to Austria and Italy, and he is said to have acquired a good command of the Italian language.

The patent speed regulator.

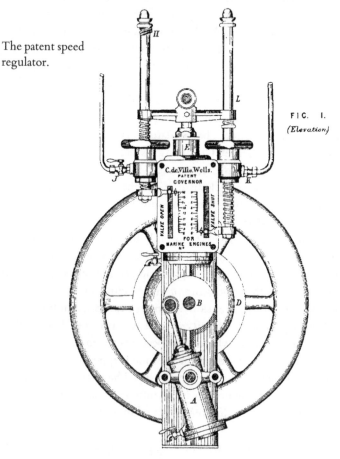

FIC. I.

(Elevation)

Scale – 3 inches to one foot

Towards the end of the 1870s, Charles must have been encouraged by the direction his career was taking: he was evidently well thought of by those who employed him, and was successful in his work. And the money he had earned from the sale of the patent had put him on a sound financial footing – if only temporarily. His parents moved to a large detached house at 2 Montée des Oblats near Notre-Dame de la Garde – the landmark cathedral which towers over the city. Their move to this property may well have been funded by Charles.

Charles himself, with his wife and his daughter, lived for a time at the home of his mother-in-law, but by the late 1870s they had moved to St Tronc, on the south-eastern outskirts of the city. From this address he applied for another patent in early 1878 – this time for a 'hygienic ice-cooled jug'.

Wells made what must have been a sizeable donation to his local church, l'église de Sainte-Marguerite, where his name is included in a list of benefactors carved on a stone tablet. It can still be seen there to this day.

Not long afterwards, Paris hosted the 1878 Exposition Universelle – the largest event of its kind that the world had ever seen. The showgrounds occupied a 190 acre site beside the Seine, a mile or so from the Bois de Boulogne, and were so extensive that a walk around the perimeter – even at a brisk pace – would have taken well over an hour. The fair opened with great ceremony on 1 May, and by the time it closed in November, 13 million visitors had passed through its gates, witnessing many stunning innovations, some of which would lead the way into a new technological era. Among them were Alexander Graham Bell's telephone; Thomas Edison's phonograph; and early examples of the refrigerator, the typewriter and the passenger lift. There was even a prototype aeroplane. The head of the Statue of Liberty was on display (this was later shipped to America with the other parts of the figure, and the structure as a whole was assembled on Liberty Island, New York).

Although there is no positive proof that Charles Wells attended the show, we know for certain that he visited Paris at this time. And for a man so closely involved with engineering and inventions it is unthinkable that he would have made the eighteen-hour journey to the capital without seeing the exposition: indeed, it was almost certainly the main purpose of his trip.

The major industrial powers, France, Britain, Germany and the United States, had all tried to outshine one another with their exhibits of engineering leviathans. Thirteen immense boilers, housed in five separate buildings, supplied steam to the static and marine engines on display. For Charles this was heaven on earth: a place where he could walk around the pavilions for hours on end, talking to the engineers and inventors, making contacts and inspecting the huge array of machinery on show.

2

With an Independent Air

The year 1879 brought Charles to a crossroads in his life. His mother had died in February 1872, leaving his father, now in his seventies, alone in a rather large house.

We have seen already how literary success had eluded Charles Jeremiah Wells as a young man. In later life he continued to write, but still no publisher showed the slightest interest in his work. After the death of Emily, depressed and disillusioned, he burned the manuscripts for all of his works, which apparently included a novel, three volumes of short stories, poems and an advanced epic.

But as long ago as the 1850s his dramatic poem *Joseph and his Brethren* had come to the attention of the poet and artist Dante Gabriel Rossetti, founder of the pre-Raphaelite movement. *Joseph* was required reading for anyone wishing to join Rossetti's circle, and his admirers were compelled to scurry along to the British Library, where the only existing copy of the book was to be found. It was thanks to Rossetti and a few other influential figures that, after a delay of many years, *Joseph* was finally republished in 1876. This time it met with great critical acclaim. One review described Wells as a 'mute inglorious Milton', while another likened his poetry to that of the young William

Shakespeare. As his entry in the *Oxford Dictionary of National Biography* says, 'for a brief period there seemed to be a chance that Wells would become a famous poet'.

But despite these plaudits, the book made no more impression on the public than it had on its first appearance, and few copies were sold. Charles Jeremiah Wells was an old man: his health was failing, and he was bedridden. Recognition came far too late to help him in any tangible way:

> I have the first society here, and the first salons open to me [he wrote to a friend] – but can't enjoy it – perfectly isolated – having nothing and wanting nothing – inhabiting one of my apartments – one bed – no servant – and *done for* by the family below. From my former habit of life it is a terrible comedown in one year.

Charles De Ville Wells must have been distressed to see his father in such a condition, and he may also have felt a sense of helplessness, as he could do so little for him. On 17 February 1879 his father died: it was seven years to the very day since his mother had passed away, and the coincidence surely felt as if fate had dealt him a double blow. And how could it come to pass that his father – once acclaimed as a genius – should die poor and unrecognised?

Anxious to avoid a similar fate, Charles determined to make a new start as a full-time inventor. With the memories of the Great Exposition still fresh in his mind, he took his wife and daughter with him to live in 'the City of Light' – Paris.

In comparison with the mighty steam engines, phonographs and electric lifts on display at the Paris exhibition of 1878, the inventions that Charles patented the following year seem fairly tame. One outlined a new kind of drill bit, while the other related to a mobile advertisement hoarding. At the time when he made these applications he was living at 34 Rue

Montaigne, a street which connects the Champs-Élysées with the Rue St-Honoré.

Within two years he relocated to the Avenue des Tilleuls, close to the Bois de Boulogne with which he would one day be associated in song ('As I walk along the Bois Boolong, with an independent air …'). From this new address he registered a patent involving 'the application of grooved rods and luminous materials for the manufacture of signs'.

There is no evidence that Charles derived any financial gain from these ideas. Luminous signs were to catch on in a big way in the age of the motor car, but in 1882 there was probably little or no demand for them. This was the difficulty facing every inventor. Some inventions were introduced years before there was any commercial need for them, while others came just too late and were pipped at the post by some rival product.

Innovations such as the phonograph and the machine gun had made their progenitors rich and famous overnight. But for every Edison and every Gatling there were scores of others struggling to make a living, their blueprints languishing in the vaults of patent offices around the globe. Ideas with great potential frequently withered on the vine simply because no industrialist could be found to take a risk and provide sufficient financial backing to turn them into marketable products. Charles Wells had overcome these difficulties with his steam regulator, and had enjoyed spectacular beginner's luck: but now – ten years later – he had not managed to repeat that early success.

Men of intelligence and ambition often reach middle age only to realise in a moment of panic that the best years of their life have mysteriously evaporated away. They become aware that they have achieved very little so far, and that there is still so much left to do. Charles Wells' father had, in all probability, counselled him long ago to avoid hard work and – so to speak – 'go fishing and let the bees do all the work'. But instead Charles had applied himself assiduously to his career as an engineer and inventor, convinced that industry and creativity would provide him and his family with a comfortable life. Yet things had not gone entirely to plan. All of the time, the care, the effort he had expended so far had achieved very little, on balance. He was now nearly 40 years of age, with a wife and a 13-year-old daughter. Would his own life be wasted, as his father's had been? Or did he still have time to make his mark on the world? And while Charles was pondering these questions his wife was hobnobbing with the countess de Janville (a celebrated writer) along with the baronesses Ordener and Saint-Amand. All indications are that by now the couple were aspiring to a lifestyle which was well beyond their means.

In his dealings with the companies which had employed him, and with people such as Count Branicki, he had seen at first hand how some individuals and businesses generated enormous wealth. Branicki and his family were among the richest people in Europe. It may have dawned on Charles at this point that while honest toil did not always pay, the financial sector seemed to be a veritable goldmine.

And so he decided to set up his own bank. In nineteenth-century France this was not as difficult as it might sound. In the laissez-faire climate of the period, the state imposed virtually no regulation on financial institutions: in fact, banks were classed not as businesses, but more as private investments by their owners. New banks seemed to open every other week, often closing again a short time later. Those who placed their funds with such institutions did so at their own risk.

In February 1882, Charles inaugurated the Banque Industrielle de France, operating from a rented office at 5 Avenue de l'Opéra – a swish address in central Paris (Plate 12). It was a new start in more ways than one. Much of central Paris had been rebuilt in the 1870s and early 1880s, and the new layout featured impressive boulevards, laid out in such a way that the eye was drawn to some architectural masterpiece at either end. The new Beaux Arts style opera house, designed by the leading architect Charles Garnier, had been constructed between 1861 and 1875

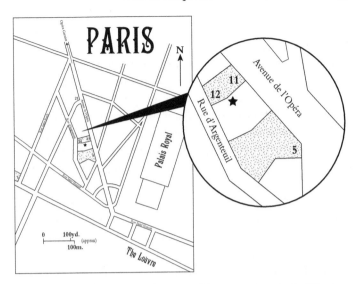

Avenue de l'Opéra, Paris, showing addresses 11 Avenue de l'Opéra and 12 Rue d'Argenteuil, which Charles Wells claimed were separate addresses occupied by branches of his company. They were, in fact, the front and rear entrances to the same building.

at the northern extremity of the avenue that was named after it. Indeed, the whole area had been completely redeveloped in recent years, and all the buildings were new, including the one housing Charles' bank near the junction of Avenue de l'Opéra and Rue St Honoré, at the opposite end to the opera house.

Charles launched his new enterprise by sending a clutch of press releases to the newspapers, explaining that the bank would invest directly in a wide variety of industries, including manganese, silver, copper and lead mines, and quarries for marble. It had a nominal capital of 5 million francs: Charles offered investors the opportunity to buy shares priced at 500fr. A brief paragraph in a newspaper, *Le Temps*, welcomed the new bank, albeit in somewhat guarded terms, stating, 'From the information to hand, we learn that the bank will not invest in the Stock

Exchange. The capital will be put to good use if it is lent directly to industry instead.'

We cannot now say what his precise intentions were: whether he believed that he was starting up a genuine undertaking, or whether he set out from the beginning to defraud investors. Dr Francesca Denman, a consultant psychiatrist, told the author of this book, 'It's quite unusual to begin a determined career of swindling people in mid-life without any previous criminality. But he may have started by sort of believing [that the scheme was genuine]. And then it becomes more convenient to swindle people.' And perhaps he was taking stock of his career so far. It was, as Dr Denman says, 'the point where he might think, "I'm not going to be another Thomas Edison", and therefore needs a shortcut to success.'

But dishonesty could equally be a trait he inherited from his father. When Charles Jeremiah Wells first decided to publish his epic, *Joseph and his Brethren*, he had approached a former classmate, Richard Hengist Horne, for financial assistance. He explained that he needed £1,000 – equivalent to at least £80,000 in today's money.* A lesser amount simply would not do, he said. And he promised Horne that he would pay interest at 5 per cent, or even more.

Horne remembered him well from their school days together at Edmonton, and recalls, 'he had no industry, nor perseverance. He was the idlest man I ever knew, and the most gifted. Nature encouraged him to live by his wit, and to do no work for himself or others.' Given his opinion of Wells, it seems strange that Horne would even entertain the idea of advancing him such an enormous loan. With remarkable generosity, not to mention

---

*   Hereafter, approximate present-day values for sums of money mentioned are given in brackets, where it is considered useful to do so. Information on how the equivalents have been calculated may be found in the Introduction.

incredible naivety, he handed the money over to Wells on condition that it must be returned when he needed it back.

Wells never repaid a farthing: in Horne's own words, 'The loss of that thousand pounds, or rather the loss of the annual interest upon it … was my ruin … My independent position never recovered [from] the shock … [and] was lost from that time forward.' Clearly, Charles Jeremiah Wells had no qualms about taking his friend's fortune. And, as later developments will show, this streak of lawlessness seems to have lived on in his son.

There were signs, even at this early stage, that the Banque Industrielle was regarded with suspicion. An unflattering article appeared in one of the financial papers, *Le Capitaliste*, claiming that the name of the new bank was too similar to that of the Banque de France (which was, to all intents and purposes, the country's national bank). 'Nothing is more suspicious,' the columnist argued, 'than arranging words in such a way as to create confusion.'

Undeterred by these criticisms, Charles then launched a second bank, which he called the Banque des Arts et Manufactures. This new institution had a nominal capital of 1 million francs. However, the only business it is known to have conducted during its brief existence was to apply for three patents: a system of coloured signs, a fast-acting brake and an energy efficient motor.

Charles, meanwhile, approached a struggling provincial newspaper, *Le Propagateur Normand*.* This journal, published in Rouen, specialised in financial matters and claimed to have a circulation of 9,000. Charles persuaded the publishers to print an article recommending readers to invest in his Banque Industrielle and – considering the parlous state of their business – they were

---

* The publication was clearly not doing at all well, as it closed down soon afterwards. (*Annuaire de la Presse Française*, 1883, p.396)

no doubt pleased to accept any cash inducement that Charles offered. Charles even saved them the trouble of writing the article by composing it himself in a heavy, convoluted and virtually incomprehensible style. He then quoted this same article in the prospectus he sent out to potential investors, making it look as if it was a flattering, unbiased, independent endorsement.

This time, though, the national press didn't pull any punches. *Le Capitaliste* said, 'To publish such gobbledygook as this *Propagateur Normand* puts out requires a kind of bravery that borders on insanity. In our estimation, nothing – absolutely nothing – about this bank can be taken seriously, and we will not waste our time going into its convoluted arrangements.' *Le Figaro*, the leading daily paper, expressed its own doubts about the *Propagateur Normand*, 'which is published somewhere – we don't know where, never having seen a copy'. The article concludes, 'This bank does not have the endorsement of any notable person and it appears to us to be a risky undertaking created by people with more daring than experience.'

Despite these scathing reviews, Wells soon found that he was raking in money from an unsuspecting public. He moved into a 'magnificent apartment' at 21 Avenue de l'Opéra, a short distance from his office. And by the end of 1882 another scheme was taking shape in his mind.

In precisely the same building where Charles had based his Banque Industrielle, a Belgian financier named Simon Philippart also had an office. He had achieved fame during the 1860s and 1870s by establishing railway networks in France, and profited from the fact that the government was legally bound to purchase them from him once construction was complete. In this way he accumulated a significant fortune, and acquired the reputation of a maverick along the way. But when he finally applied for consent to build a railway that would have competed against the state-controlled network, the government balked at having to purchase the concession from him, so he then promoted railways in Belgium, Britain and elsewhere, often amid much controversy.

Though no definite link between Philippart and Wells has been proved, the fact that they both ran broadly similar businesses as financiers and operated from the same address suggests that they had, at the very least, a nodding acquaintance with each other. Wells – fourteen years younger than Philippart – was very likely influenced and inspired by this roguish, entrepreneurial businessman. Perhaps it was Philippart who suggested to Wells that railway shares were popular with investors. We know for certain that in February 1883 Charles placed advertisements in the newspapers inviting the public to buy shares in a railway in northern France.

The small town of Berck-sur-Mer was fast becoming a popular sea-bathing resort. Publicity for the locality emphasised its many attractions for visitors, especially the fine sandy beach, 'the biggest and most healthy' in France. Berck was only four hours from Paris, an advertisement claimed. The truth of the matter is that a three-hour train ride brought visitors as far as Verton – about 4 miles inland. But the rest of the journey to the coast was sheer torture. Travellers were crammed into a slow, uncomfortable horse-drawn omnibus, 'a drive of about fifty minutes, performed under circumstances of great discomfort'.

Charles Wells capitalised on the situation by proposing to build a branch line between Verton and Berck. This would seem at first glance to have been a splendid idea, especially as all the most successful bathing resorts were already served by the rail network. He offered shares at 495fr. each, and these were often bought by people with modest savings wishing to make the most of their money. Many of the investors purchased just a single share. But others poured in more substantial sums: a ship's captain from Le Havre, seduced by Wells' promise of a 53 per cent dividend, bought thirty shares and then sat back and waited for his 15,000fr. investment to produce the promised annual profit of 8,000fr.

Again, *Le Capitaliste* expressed grave doubts about the probity of the scheme. Wells' prospectus claimed that the investment was government backed to the tune of a minimum of 5 per cent, and that under some special arrangement, subsidies would be forthcoming from the town council of Berck itself and other official sources. However, these claims were not strictly true, as *Le Capitaliste* explained. State subsidies were only available to railways which had been officially declared to be public utilities, but this was not the case here. And there were other apparent irregularities. The newspaper recommended its readers not to invest in the Berck-sur-Mer railway without completely satisfying themselves as to the truth of the claims made in the prospectus.

When the railway failed to materialise in any way, grave concerns were voiced about the investors' money. Both of Charles Wells' banks were shut down and shortly afterwards the police turned up at 5 Avenue de l'Opéra. Perhaps Wells was expecting them. But on this occasion, he was not the person they were looking for. Instead they had come to arrest his neighbour, the millionaire Simon Philippart, who was wanted in Belgium for breaking various company laws, fraud and for falsifying documents.

Shaken by these events, Charles Wells disappeared, taking the investors' money with him – a sum equivalent to about £1 million today. The Banque Industrielle was declared insolvent and the *Journal des Finances* announced that creditors would get back only 15 per cent of their investment. Coincidentally – or possibly not – the very same issue of the *Journal* stated that Philippart had also been adjudged bankrupt.

As far as the two banks were concerned, the authorities brought no charges against Charles. But the Berck-sur-Mer railway project was considered to have been fraudulent, and he became the subject of a police investigation. However, as he had seemingly vanished from the face of the earth, the police could do little more than interview his victims and hope that eventually he would turn up. He was charged in his absence – as

'Charles de Will-Wells'* – with fraud and 'misuse of funds'. Some time later, in 1885, a court in Paris found him guilty and sentenced him to two years in prison. But while his creditors and the French police vainly searched for him in Paris, he had fled the country.

As far as we know, up until this moment he had never lived in Britain, except for the first few weeks of his life. And it is doubtful whether he had even set foot in the land of his birth since then. So when he arrived in Plymouth, Devon, with his wife and daughter, they all experienced a sense of adventure.** Yet the rocky coastline was not unlike that of Brittany, and must have reminded Charles of his childhood at Quimper. And for a fugitive from the long arm of the *gendarmerie*, England was a safe haven. Perhaps, too, he had been curious to see the country of his birth, where his eldest sister, Emily, still lived.***

Charles and his family made their home at 18 Walker Terrace – not far from Plymouth Hoe, where Drake had insisted on finishing his game of bowls before taking on the Spanish Armada. Plymouth is built on hilly terrain and the city has many rows of little houses arranged on an incline: Walker Terrace is a typical example. The three-storey dwelling provided lodgings for several individuals and families, and the Wells family probably occupied one floor. It seems to have been quite a comedown from the 'magnificent apartment' in Paris. (However, it is also possible that Charles and his family lived on board one of his

---

* Note the confusion between 'V' and 'W' again. The prefix 'de' caused *Le Figaro* to assume that he was a genuine aristocrat and they named him '*Count* Charles de Will-Wells'. (*Le Figaro*, 15 December 1892)

** He claimed to have arrived in 1885, but an earlier date seems more likely. He became a fugitive from justice in about April 1883, and probably left Paris and made his way to England immediately afterwards.

*** Emily died at Edmonton, Middlesex, not very long after he moved to Britain. It is not known whether they were, in fact, ever reunited.

yachts, and used the Walker Terrace address simply as a postal address for the receipt of mail).

Just down the hill, no more than 60 yards away, were Millbay Docks, where Charles probably moored his boats. He later stated that when he came to Britain he had capital of 'about £8,000, which included floating property, consisting of steamboats, ships &c'. He said he had accumulated this money from his earnings as an engineer and from the profits of a paper-manufacturing concern that he claimed to have run in Paris. The truth was somewhat different. The £8,000 almost certainly represented the remainder of the 250,000fr. that he had obtained by fraud. But, naturally, it suited him to avoid any mention of this episode.

The waterfront was lined with engineering shops, shipbuilding yards, timber stores, warehouses, piers and wharves. Just around the corner was a convenient Great Western Railway station, from which the trains, still running on Brunel's broad-gauge track, could reach London in a little over six hours (though the slower services took considerably longer). In the distance the evening sun beyond Plymouth Sound silhouetted the craggy coastline of Cornwall.

But more importantly, as far as Charles Wells was concerned, Britain was pre-eminent in technology and engineering. Having been the birthplace of the First Industrial Revolution, beginning in about 1760, the country had witnessed a second burst of growth around the time of Charles' birth in the 1840s. This new phase saw, in particular, the application of steam power to many forms of transport and manufacturing processes. The Great Exhibition, held in London in 1851, had confirmed Britain's reputation as the world centre for technology, and inspired a generation of engineers and inventors. Engines, machines, processes and gadgets of every kind were developed at a furious pace, and we can see evidence for this boom in the growing number of patents being applied for: since the Great Exhibition, the average had increased sixfold – from 2,700 in 1854 to about 17,000 when Charles came to England.

All new patent applications were listed in *The Engineer*, a specialist magazine. A random sample, from a single issue of this periodical, can only hint at the variety of articles being developed, some of which, it must be said, seem considerably more likely than others to have succeeded: machine guns, pianofortes, velocipedes, lacings for corsets, watertight coffins, self-closing matchboxes and a combined moustache protector and cigar holder.

Having already filed several patents in France, and at least one in Britain, Charles was reasonably familiar with the procedure, and saw an opening for himself in this potentially profitable business. On 7 February 1885, he submitted a batch of four provisional applications to the Patent Office. They represent a curious and eclectic mix of subjects:

Patent No
1730 Preserving Mustard when Mixed
1731 Torpedoes
1732 Detecting the Presence of Heat in Bearings
1733 Cleaning Ships' Bottoms when Under Way

Applying for patent protection was a relatively simple procedure in the 1880s. The first stage was to file an application form together with a provisional specification. This had to be sent to the Patent Office in Chancery Lane, London, with a fee of £1 (equivalent to £100 today). A printed slip acknowledging the application was then sent to the applicant.

A provisional patent provided limited protection for nine months against another inventor copying the idea. Within that time the applicant had to submit a full specification, with a further payment of £3 (£300), or the application would lapse. If the proposal was accepted, a patent was granted, giving the inventor full protection for fourteen years. Otherwise, the application was considered 'abandoned' (though it was possible on payment of a further fee to revive a lapsed patent).

Wells' proposal for 'Preserving Mustard when Mixed' begins:

> The object of my invention is an improved method of putting up mustard when prepared for table use, and aims at replacing the ordinary and well-known mustard pot, with or without a cover, by a collapsible tube of a suitable capacity and perforated for the ejection of the required quantity of mustard.
>
> The waste as well as untidy appearance incidental to the present method of placing table mustard before anyone, especially in a certain class of restaurants, are avoided by my invention …

These are Wells' own words, in that he would have written the first draft himself. However, he used the services of a firm of patent agents, Phillips & Leigh,* who had commenced operations three years earlier in 1882. Their office was in Southampton Buildings, Chancery Lane, where the Patent Office was also to be found. Their role was to redraft the inventor's description of the article to be patented so as to prevent other inventors from exploiting some loophole, thus getting around the protection offered by the patent.

Over the following weeks and months Wells submitted a flurry of further applications for items as diverse as ships' fog horns, matches, ventilating railway tunnels, ships' anchors and linoleum. It is hard to judge, from such a distant perspective, what the potential of these inventions might have been almost 140 years ago. While some are, to all appearances, eminently sensible, others seem decidedly eccentric. In Patent No. 8229 of 1885, for a 'Sunshade or Umbrella', Wells observes that existing umbrellas and parasols suffer from the drawback that 'heat, radiated from the ground … is frequently enough to make the breathing stratum hot and stuffy …' His solution to this

---

*   The firm is still operating today from an office not far from the original one.

problem is to provide a large aperture in the top of the umbrella in question – a measure which would seem to defeat the original purpose of the item.

Wells went on to apply for provisional patents on balloons, rockets, bows and arrows, pens, matches, watches, hats and candles. Among his more startling suggestions were 'Life-saving Torpedoes' and 'A Combination Fire Extinguishing Grenade with Lamp and Chandelier'.

He also set himself up as a kind of patent agent for clients in France, and began to advertise on the business page of *Le Matin*, a Paris newspaper:

TO INVENTORS

Sale and acquisition of patents for inventions in England and America without intermediaries. Drawings and trade-mark applications filed. French firm. Messrs. Wells & Co., 132 Fleet Street, London, E.C. First-class references in Paris.

Just as Charles had persuaded the beleaguered owners of the *Propagateur Normand* to print a favourable report on his bank, he now chose a journal which had only been going for a short time in which to place his advertisements. The paper's proprietors were no doubt happy to take any advertising they could get and when Charles offered to pay for space en bloc, they were probably not too concerned about his antecedents. They even let him display the address of their London office in Fleet Street as if it was his own, and clearly he must have had an arrangement with them to forward replies to him in Plymouth. Quite how he intended to furnish the 'first-class references in Paris' is a mystery as, of course, he was a fugitive from the law in that city. No doubt, though, he would have found a way to provide something suitably convincing if the need had arisen.

Between its debut around January 1885 and the middle of the year, the advertisement was repeated about fifty times. But, eventually, it appeared less and less frequently, suggesting that Charles was receiving insufficient response to justify the expense. By October he had abandoned the idea. It was a similarly depressing story with his own inventions. Despite the large number of proposals he submitted, there is no evidence that any of them made any money. In fact he later said that, while living in Plymouth, he had taken out 'nearly 100 patents' and that this had 'practically exhausted his funds' – which he admitted were not copious in the first place, as he had spent his capital on boats.

Things were not very promising in his domestic life either. His wife, Marie Thérèse, had disapproved of his criminal activities in Paris. And south-west England must have seemed a strange, inhospitable place to those more used to Paris and Marseille. Finally, Charles' failure to generate an income must have been the last straw. Marie Thérèse went back to France with their daughter, Marie Antoinette (now in her late teens), leaving Charles to fend for himself.

Plymouth had offered him good fishing, moorings for his vessels and pleasant scenery. But there were few other reasons for him to stay there now. And, besides, it must have been inconvenient for him to practise his patent business in a town so far removed from the centre of activity.

London, on the other hand, was the world's largest city, and the hub of a global empire. It was also the busiest port on earth. And Charles was already doing regular business with his patent agents there. So he left Plymouth – probably in early 1887 – and made for the capital.

3

A Patent Fraud

At first Charles lived in a small single room in Fenchurch Street – a busy, grimy thoroughfare that had long been associated with shipping and the oceans. The headquarters of the East India Company, an organisation which had effectively governed much of the world's population, had once been based here. And it was here that ship owners and merchants had their premises, as did lightermen, engineers, tobacco brokers, boiler makers, Madagascar agents, rope manufacturers and a melange of other marine trades and industries. And above the bustling shops, warehouses and offices lived many individuals and families in impoverished surroundings.[*]

For Charles at this stage in his career, the most attractive feature of Fenchurch Street was probably the low cost of lodgings, plus the fact that his patent agents, Phillips & Leigh, were within walking distance. And it may be that Charles wanted to follow his father's lead, because Charles Jeremiah Wells had once occupied an office in the street at Langbourne

---

[*] The area was designated 'poor', with an income of 18s to 21s a week for a typical family. (Booth Poverty Map 1898–99)

0 ——————— 100yd. (approx)
        100m.

FITZROVIA, LONDON

The Fitzrovia district of London, showing addresses connected with Charles Wells.

Chambers, immediately prior to abandoning his career as a solicitor.

With so much instability, both in his domestic life and in his business, this was doubtless an anxious time for Charles Wells. But his circumstances appear to have improved quickly because later in 1887 he had already moved to more elegant surroundings in central London. His new home, 53 Charlotte Street, was situated just to the north of Oxford Street, in an area generally described as middle class and well-to-do.

At the same time as relocating his business he also changed his method of operation.

Since his arrival in Britain he had applied for many patents, only a handful of which had proceeded beyond the provisional application stage. All of them had been submitted in his sole name as the inventor. But now he decided to target reasonably wealthy individuals and offer them an opportunity to share in the proceeds of his patents. They would provide finance to enable him to develop his ideas and he, in return, would take care of the engineering side of things and obtain the patent. The plan was that his backer would be named as co-applicant for the patent alongside Wells, and would receive a quarter of all profits generated by the invention.

He first advertised for a solicitor's clerk to copy sales letters. In this era there was no quick or easy way to duplicate documents, other than to write them out by hand, a laborious and immensely tedious task. Henry Baker Vaughan, a man in his late twenties, applied for the job, and Charles Wells agreed to pay him 12s 6d for every 500 copies. With a wife and three small children to support, the young clerk gratefully accepted.

Now Wells had to find likely prospects for his scheme. He almost certainly referred to the publications of the day, such as *Kelly's Post Office Directory*, *The Army List* and *Crockford's Clerical Directory*. When Vaughan delivered the first batch of 500 letters, Wells – who was either extremely short of ready cash or in a mean-spirited mood at the time – gave him only 7s 6d, instead of the promised 12s 6d. Nonetheless, Vaughan would continue to work for Wells on and off for several years.

The initial letter sent to potential investors was only a few lines in length – just enough to tempt the recipient into asking for further information. Then, having hooked the prospect, Charles sent a more detailed proposal. In March 1887, one of the first to reply was Frederick John Goad,* who invested £25 (£2,500) as a quarter-share in a patent for 'incandescent electric lighting'. Another of Wells' early sponsors was James Thomas Pickburn, a man in his mid-sixties, who had been the publisher

---

*   Probably the Islington watchmaker and jeweller of that name. Wells could have obtained his particulars from *Kelly's Directory*, which lists the family business, Alfred Goad & Sons.

of a paper called the *Clerkenwell News* (which later evolved into the *Daily Chronicle* and, later still, the *News Chronicle* – important national daily newspapers of their time). In 1888, Pickburn financed a 'hot-air motor heated by gas'.

The impressively named Lieutenant Colonel Ralph Rhenius Evans Drake-Brockman was an officer in the Royal Engineers, and had served in India for the past twenty or so years. As he approached the age when he would have to leave the army, he was doubtless looking for a safe investment to see him through his retirement. He is listed as joint applicant with Charles Wells on a proposal for 'water-borne vessels'. For people such as these, with capital to invest, but perhaps lacking the time, opportunity or know-how to run a business themselves, Wells' inventions must have seemed attractive propositions.

Two Australian-born brothers, Montague and Richard Churchill-Shann, were already engineers and inventors in their own right.* They were co-applicants with Wells for a patent involving 'candles, wax matches, tapers etc'. It seems likely that, in this instance, Wells acted on their behalf as a kind of patent agent.

But the inventions he promoted with these partners usually fared no better than those he had put forward on his own. An exception came in December 1887, when he submitted a joint application (No. 16,711) in his own name and that of Lizzie Ritchie. The innovation this time was a musical skipping rope, and it turned out to be one of the few patents of his to proceed past the provisional application stage. Wells later claimed to have sold the patent for £50 (£5,000).

The identity of his co-applicant, Lizzie Ritchie, has never been established. In fact she may not have even existed. Her name, though, will crop up several times in Wells' story, and

---

*   The two brothers later patented inventions of their own, including several relating to marine propulsion. Decades later, one of these was cited as an underlying patent in the specification for the hovercraft.

it seems she was possibly a creation of his vivid imagination, whose presence he could magically invoke – like the genie of the lamp – whenever the need arose. Charles variously described her as his business partner and his niece. On another occasion he said he was her guardian. Of course, all of these claims could have been true, but it is unlikely.

In addition to developing his own ideas, Charles carried out many technical assignments for Francis Knoeferl, an engineer of German origin based at 100 Bolsover Street – just around the corner from Charles' own address in Charlotte Street. Knoeferl did general engineering work and had registered a few patents of his own. While Wells was there he met another German engineer, 30-year-old Hermann Eschen, who lived nearby at 142 Great Titchfield Street with his wife and two young children. In fact, it was Eschen who had earlier made the prototype of the musical skipping rope for Wells.

In late 1887, Wells and Eschen happened to meet again in the street and Wells offered him some freelance work, adding that he would give him a three-month trial initially, with the promise of more assignments afterwards if all went well. Eschen agreed to leave his job with Knoeferl and become Wells' employee for £2 12s per week. Wells would design an invention – arc lamps and hot-air engines were just two examples – and Eschen made the necessary working models. Charles Wells then moved into 115 Great Titchfield Street, almost opposite Eschen's home, and rented what were described as 'small business premises', with a workshop and a room to live in.

In Eschen's words, Charles was 'always busy, always at work … a hardworking man'. When Eschen was at home, Charles would often turn up at all times of the day or night with a roll of drawings under his arm and an idea for something new which he wanted Eschen to make. Sometimes people came to see the models. The two engineers became firm friends, and Wells later appointed Eschen as manager of his business. Later still, they submitted joint patent applications for a loom-picking mechanism and for an inkstand.

But there is no evidence that this rush of activity resulted in any significant profits for Charles. Nor is there any reason to believe that his backers received a return on their investment, since no one could be persuaded to buy the patents, except for the musical skipping rope and a few others. Clearly he was not going to make a fortune like this. According to Eschen, the preliminary models – usually made of wood – cost Wells £7–10 apiece to produce (£700–1,000). A working model of an engine in metal could cost as much as £30–50 (£3,000–5,000). Any profit from the few successes was quickly wiped out by the failures, which were more numerous.

Wells' strategy of finding a backer and taking out patents jointly with that person seems to have lasted from early 1887 to mid-1888. Then he came up with another new version of the plan: this time he advertised for the financial backing first. And it was only when he had found someone to fund the invention that he would go ahead and file the patent application – usually in his sole name. As in the past, he offered his sponsor a quarter-share in the proceeds. From early to mid-1888 he started to place frequent advertisements in the press for persons with money to invest.

In the late nineteenth century newspapers and magazines filled the role which, in future decades, would be served by radio, television and the cinema (and much later by the internet, email and social media). More than 2,500 different newspapers and periodicals were sold in Britain: 673 of these were published in the London area alone. By the late 1880s they were readily available to people at all levels of society, and they were cheap. Popular journals such as the *Morning Post* and *Reynolds's Newspaper* cost just a penny, and *The Times* was 3d. Aside from news and opinions, the press carried pages of small advertisements and announcements, some bearing poignant messages between lovers, others offering horses and carriages to buy, properties for sale or rent and job vacancies. Individuals and businesses – some of doubtful integrity – placed advertisements offering investment opportunities or asking for loans. Many people read these pages of announcements avidly from beginning to end, often responding to offers that attracted them.

Charles would become a master of the medium. His notices usually took the form of a three- or four-line classified advertisement under the heading of 'Investments & Partnerships', or some similar category. His initial efforts were of a tentative, low-key nature, providing no hard information whatsoever, and relied on the reader's curiosity to elicit a response.

Despite its cryptic nature, one of his advertisements must have elicited a satisfactory response because Charles repeated it for several years. In March 1889, it was spotted by Frances Maud Budd, a single woman, 25 years of age, living in Worthing, Sussex. She was born in Madras, where her father had been a senior officer in the British Indian Army. Her mother had died not long after Frances was born and her father resigned his post on grounds of insanity, and died a few years later.

In response to the advertisement, Miss Budd wrote a letter asking for more information. Wells replied to say that the investment 'will just suit a lady' and stated that he needed £30 (approximately £3,000 in today's terms) to develop a small motor to power domestic machines such as knife-grinders, coffee mills and boot polishers. In his words, the device was designed 'for domestic and general use, cheap, safe and desirable'.

Advertisement placed by Wells in *The Standard*, 11 March 1889.

As the offspring of a deceased British officer, Miss Budd received a pension from the army consisting of £60 per annum, paid in four quarterly instalments. She knew that she would receive £15 at the end of March, and wrote to Wells again to ask whether she could buy a half-share in the patent for that amount. Wells replied that the minimum he could accept was £30 because he 'offers the patent for security'. With considerable difficulty she managed to scrape together the additional money and sent £30 to Wells, who replied by sending her the receipt for the provisional patent application. Like most other 'clients' of Wells, she believed that this document was in fact the patent itself. Wells told her in his letter that he would begin work straight away and would keep her informed periodically as to progress. And that was the last she heard from him for quite some time.

Emily Forrester, a woman in her mid-forties, lived with her husband on the seafront at Deal, Kent. One day she spotted Wells' advertisement and wrote for further particulars. Wells sent a letter in reply in which he mentioned a German engineer, Nikolaus Otto, who had invented a pioneering internal combustion engine twelve years previously. Wells claimed that Otto was earning £400 (£40,000) per week from his discovery, adding that he, Wells, required just £30 for a quarter-share in his own patent gas engine. He assured Mrs Forrester that he would be able to sell the patent 'at once' for a substantial sum. Before parting with her money, she visited Wells in London. On seeing the model of the engine she agreed with Wells that the invention 'must be valuable' and promptly forwarded her £30 to him.

Wells became increasingly skilful in his use of the media. At an early stage he took expert advice from advertising agencies such as Brown, Gould & Co. of New Oxford Street, and – in particular – Willing's[*] of Piccadilly. James Willing claimed that his

---

[*]   The company amalgamated with a firm called May's in 1889, and for some time afterwards the names May's and Willing's were used more or less interchangeably.

company acted as 'agents for all metropolitan, provincial & foreign newspapers', and published an annual handbook, *Willing's (late May's) British & Irish Press Guide (yearly)*, which listed every newspaper and periodical available to the public. The volume is a testament to the high level of sophistication already prevailing in the advertising industry of that period.

Willing offered his clients free advice as to 'the position, importance and value as an advertising medium, of any publication'. A particular bonus was the facility for advertisers to have replies sent to Willing's offices, where they were provided with individual mailboxes. Willing's handbook emphasises that the letters 'can be retained until called for, or will be forwarded to the advertiser's address if preferred. … Strict confidence may be relied on, the names and addresses of advertisers never being communicated unless express permission is given.' This suited Charles Wells very nicely.

Each advertiser's mailbox was identified by a box number, or the person's initials, or a 'password' displayed in the advertisement instead of an actual address. Advertisers could thus conceal their true names and whereabouts, while the system also helped them to identify those advertisements generating the best response. At first, Charles simply used his own initials, 'C.W.', or a box number. He later found that the use of carefully chosen code words – such as 'Security', 'Bona Fides', 'Investor' and 'Gold Mine' – helped to instil confidence and create a powerful sense of substance and financial probity:

> FOUR HUNDRED POUNDS a YEAR. — Gentleman compelled to SELL, at inadequate price of £250, SHARE in PATENT, to bring in over above sum for over ten years. Full investigation. — Write to 'Investor,' 54, New Oxford Street, W.C.

Wells also experimented with subtle changes to the basic announcements, and from time to time he introduced completely different ones. Often he would place two advertisements side by side in the same paper – perhaps testing the relative effectiveness of each, or in the knowledge that different offers might appeal to different people. As time went by, he phased out the advertisements which relied on mystery and intrigue to whet the appetite of would-be investors: he replaced them with a more direct offer, which promised spectacular amounts of profit. Here, too, he appreciated that certain people had more to invest than others. Rewards which might seem unrealistically large to one person could be viewed by another as too paltry to bother with. Therefore he experimented by quoting different figures: £400, £750, £25,000, £50,000, £100,000 ... and, if anything, the amounts seemed to grow larger as time went by.

His annual advertising budget also increased, eventually reaching £350 (£35,000). Henry Vaughan, Wells' long-suffering clerk, later estimated that he had written 3,000 letters in response to enquiries generated by the press advertisements. Although his replies to enquirers were all broadly similar, Wells would personalise them to a small degree, to suit each applicant. If a woman wrote, for example, he would always stress that the investment was very appropriate for a lady.

Catherine Mary Phillimore, a 40-year-old spinster, lived with her two sisters and their elderly mother in a mansion at Shiplake, near Henley-on-Thames, with no fewer than eight servants to attend to their needs. Her uncle had been Speaker of the House of Commons; her late father had been a judge, politician and close friend of Prime Minister Gladstone; and her brother, Walter Phillimore, was also a senior judge.

If she had been born a few decades later, Catherine would almost certainly have attended a university. As it was, her father had arranged for her to receive a private education at home. She became an expert on Italian art and literature and by the late 1880s, when her path crossed with that of Charles De Ville Wells, she had written eight books which had been published.

She had also translated several Italian books into English, and was a contributor to *Grove's Dictionary of Music*.

In January 1889, she saw an advertisement referring to a patent. In reply to her enquiry Wells sent a letter very similar to the following:

115 Great Titchfield-street, W.,
London.

Dear Madam,
The investment would just suit a lady, as there is no further trouble than to cash the share you would have in eight weeks and the royalty for fourteen years ... As an example of the price paid in our day for inventions I may name the Gatling Gun, the price paid for the patent being over half a million sterling — £620,000 [£62 million].

Wells had clearly tailored his reply 'to suit a lady', although it is not known what effect his mention of the Gatling Gun might have had on her feminine sensibilities. His letter goes on to say that he needed an investment of £60, which he assured her would be 'bound to bring in money, even a large sum in a few weeks, and a very high yearly income'. He asked for an initial payment of £5 to take out the patent, adding that he would send the 'provisional certificate ... as a valuable security' within about five days, whereupon the balance of £55 would become payable:

With this money I would make a sample of the invention, to be ready in six to eight weeks the very outside; and then, having patent and sample, I would have no difficulty in obtaining at once a large sum for the patent; and if we take into consideration the big sums paid in our days for such patents, we might look upon £400,000 [£40 million] as a poor remuneration, and the sum mentioned to you as a yearly income is ridiculously small. However considerable the financial results may be, *I offer you a one-quarter share* of all the patent will bring in for fourteen years.

In closing he writes:

> … I am prepared to prove that I am quite certain of a wonderful success, as I am willing to repeat in your presence experiments that will prove to the most unscientific person that the saving is positive, practical, and much greater than I mention.
>
> I remain, dear Madam, faithfully yours,
>
> C. Wells.

The invention in question was a device intended to give a 40 per cent fuel saving in steamships. The Victorian world relied on steam power: every train, factory and pumping station was driven by a steam engine, and of the 170 million tons of coal mined each year in Britain, a significant proportion was used as fuel for these machines. Any invention of the kind that Charles proposed would indeed be worth a fortune.

And the idea was not as far-fetched as it might seem. Although the performance of steam engines had significantly improved over the years, there was still a long way to go. No steam engine had ever achieved much more than 10 per cent efficiency in converting the energy within the coal into motive power, and it must have seemed that there was still plentiful scope for further enhancements, if only some clever inventor could find a way to implement them.

With his letter to Miss Phillimore, Wells enclosed an elaborate prospectus about his invention, together with a long list of other inventions which had earned 'immense sums'. He neglected to mention, however, that all of these innovations had been patented by other people, not by him.

After receiving Miss Phillimore's deposit, he applied on 16 February for the provisional patent. It is impossible to say for certain what was in his mind at the time. Had he convinced himself that everything would turn out all right in the end – that he would make his own fortune and make his investors rich at the same time? Or had he already made a conscious decision to defraud his backers? Did he spare a thought for them at all?

It may be that Wells, with his unconventional upbringing, belonged to a certain group of people who have little empathy with others. Speaking in the broadest terms, psychiatrist Dr Francesca Denman says:

> Generally, if you don't belong anywhere or owe anyone a particular duty, it's easy not to think of them as people, and you might not feel bad about swindling them. … He must have been charming and persuasive. There is probably an element of anti-social personality disorder – not caring about other people and being willing to con them … He sees you can get money up front and then realises, 'why bother to do the work?'

Thus we cannot be quite sure whether at this stage he viewed Miss Phillimore and the other investors as genuine clients or as dupes. But there was something about Miss Phillimore that he did not know, and could hardly have discovered, even if the thought had occurred to him. Miss Phillimore's family owned swathes of land in London's fashionable Kensington, and when her father had died some three or four years previously, he had left a fortune to his heirs. At any time of her choosing, Catherine Mary Phillimore could dip her slender, perfectly manicured fingers into a pot of family money worth several million pounds in today's terms.

4

The Certainty of a Fortune

With money arriving in a pleasingly steady stream, and the prospect of more to come, in 1889 Charles moved into an apartment at 162 Great Portland Street – the house where Baroness Orczy, writer of the Scarlet Pimpernel novels, had once lived while in her teens. Although this grand house was only a stone's throw from Great Titchfield Street – where he retained his business premises for the time being – Great Portland Street was a much more prestigious address. In what may have been a conscious effort to present himself as a respectable, upright citizen, he made sure he was included in the electoral register and in commercial directories. And, as icing on the cake, he began to put the letters 'CE' (Civil Engineer) after his name.

In Worthing, meanwhile, Frances Budd was becoming increasingly concerned. The £30 had been more than she could really afford, and the lack of news from Wells was disquieting, to say the least. As her letters to him went unanswered she travelled to London in July to see him in person, but when she reached the Great Titchfield Street premises, he was not there. She wrote again, threatening to put a solicitor on to the case.

Wells replied that he would not try to stop her, but that he had been in Paris trying to sell the idea. Then Miss Budd received a further letter from him on 17 October. He claimed that his only fault was that he hadn't been able to sell the patent. He told her that she could not receive her money back but that he would send her a share. Although she was not satisfied with this answer and had considered taking legal action, she decided not to involve a solicitor after all, as her friends had advised her not to throw good money after bad. Finally, she contacted the Patent Office in early 1890 and discovered that only a provisional patent had been taken out, and that it had now expired.

Realising at last that the 'patent certificate' she had received from Wells was nothing of the sort, she wrote to tell him that she knew the scheme was a swindle and she would prosecute unless he returned her money. Wells politely assured her that he 'always respects a lady and regrets her action'.

Charles White, a retired doctor living at Bournemouth, had had a similar experience. In late 1889, he had consulted his solicitor with a view to getting his money back from Wells.

The lawyer responded by sending him a copy of a weekly magazine called *Truth*. This particular issue contained a damning exposé of Charles Wells and his patent schemes. Dr White, stunned by what he had read, had then made contact with the police.

Lionel William Bartram was a young man in his mid-twenties. At the age of 21 he had inherited a large sum of money from his father, who had been the proprietor of a substantial brewery business in Tonbridge. Within four years, however, Lionel had spent all of the money and was, in fact, deeply in debt. It must have seemed like a miracle when he spotted a newspaper advertisement offering a share in a 'remarkable invention' and promising £20,000 in just three months plus 'yearly revenue of £1,000 out of Royalties'. Somehow he obtained the £750 to pay for the promised share and – no doubt with a sense of profound relief – he sat back and waited – and waited – for the money to roll in. Eventually his case, too, came to the attention of the editor of *Truth*.

Truth magazine was the brainchild of Henry Labouchère, writer, publisher and Member of Parliament. He came from a privileged background and was educated at Eton. While at Cambridge University later, he had managed to run up debts of £6,000 (£600,000) and was removed by his parents. Over the next few years he travelled to Mexico, where he fell in love with a woman who was a circus performer and he even joined the troupe himself. At one point he spent six months living with a tribe of Ojibwe Indians.

But by the late 1880s, he had become one of the most distinguished journalists in Britain, with a well-earned reputation for exposing swindles, scandals and injustices. Sometimes he was sued for defamation, but in most cases he won, and on the rare occasions when he lost he could easily afford to pay damages:

> Armed at all points, he never strikes till he is certain that the blow will be crushing. Perfectly fearless, he is perhaps the only journalist for whom the law of libel has no terrors.

In early 1890, Labouchère wrote in his column that he was beginning to receive enquiries about Charles Wells, and had been prompted to investigate. His article, which stretched to a page and a half of text, quoted three of Wells' recent press advertisements in full, and listed forty-two of his patent applications going back to 1887. Labouchère informed his readers that thirty-five of them had been abandoned, and conjectured that the other seven might well suffer the same fate.

'It costs only £1 to obtain provisional protection for nine months,' he wrote. 'Any twaddle that comes to hand does for this [and] I think I have said enough to make it desirable for ladies or gentlemen eager to make their fortune rapidly to "let Wells alone".' In the next issue of his journal he writes:

I never expose a trick or a swindle without at once receiving the thanks of immense numbers of unfortunate victims. The latest case in point is that of Mr. 'C. Wells, C.E.,' with his provisional patent trick. In response to the article in last week's *Truth*, I have been favoured with several dozens of letters giving further details of Wells's operations, many of them from solicitors who have been consulted on the subject. I am much obliged for all this information, and I need not say that I shall always have C. Wells, C.E., under my eye in future.

Soon Labouchère was publishing articles on an almost weekly basis condemning Charles Wells. On 13 March he alludes to the case of Dr White (without, however, actually naming him). When White's lawyer had pursued Wells, the latter had replied that he had been 'so much frightened by the interference of the solicitor that he had not gone on with the experiments, and that the time of the provisional patent had expired'.

Labouchère added, 'I hear, however, of one case in which the victim is determined to bring the matter into a law court, and I look forward with considerable interest to that event, when C. Wells will have an opportunity of explaining his Patent Game before the Court and the public.'

Two weeks later *Truth* warned its readers, 'not upon any account to have anything whatever to do with his artful patent game, to which I think the authorities of Scotland Yard ought to direct their special attention'. We can be quite sure that Wells was following this continuing saga in *Truth*, and we know for certain that he was in possession of this very issue of the magazine.

Little by little his advertisements stopped appearing in the newspapers – including *The Standard*, which had previously carried them on an almost daily basis. Perhaps Wells himself had decided not to push his luck too far following Labouchère's exposé. But it is just as likely that the papers in question refused to print his announcements because of the adverse publicity which might arise. Others, though, continued as before:

The Times, for example, regularly carried Wells' notices for months afterwards.

Far from responding to Labouchère's call for police intervention, the authorities failed to act. In part this was because fraud was difficult to prove. Wells could have argued that he had only the best of intentions when he invited people to invest their money in his gadgets. If it turned out that some of them did not work, or if it proved impossible to find a buyer for the patent, that was not fraud – it was simply bad luck. In nineteenth-century Britain, businesses, financial schemes and advertising were largely unregulated: the responsibility to make sure that the scheme was sound rested on the investor's shoulders. And to secure a conviction for fraud, it was not sufficient to show that Wells had promised something that he later did not deliver. The prosecution had to prove that the accused had knowingly made a false claim about past events.

For example, if a man says, 'I intend to prospect for gold in Australia – invest £1,000 with me and I will make you a millionaire', it is unfortunate if investors lose their money, but no fraud has taken place. But if a man says, 'For the past ten years I have mined ten tons of gold annually: invest in my gold-mine', a fraud has been committed if that claim of past events is deliberately untrue, *and* if the investor can be shown to have relied on the claims. It can be notoriously difficult to prove intent to defraud, because who can say what a man's intent was, especially if those thoughts went through his mind some years previously?

The Metropolitan Police had better things to do with their time than pursue cases that might very well be thrown out of court. Besides, they had their own internal problems to deal with. Aside from a general reputation for inefficiency, they had suffered from bad publicity in the past when their own officers were convicted for corruption. Lately, they had failed completely to solve the infamous 'Jack the Ripper' case, after which the commissioner of police, Charles Warren, had resigned. Scotland Yard was in disarray, and it is probable that at the beginning of the 1890s the force thought it could best regain public confidence by concentrating on those cases where there was a good chance of securing a conviction.

The fact that the police ignored Labouchère's call for him to be prosecuted must have left Wells feeling that his position was unassailable as far as a criminal action was concerned. And when it came to a civil claim, the clients who had considered suing him – such as Miss Budd – often concluded that it would be a waste of time.

It is evident that the *Truth* articles had not yet come to the attention of Miss Phillimore, who seems to have been the most patient and restrained of all his investors – despite having entrusted more money to him than some of the others. Since sending her £60 for a share in the steam engine patent in early 1889, she had received nothing from Charles Wells, except for a string of empty promises. In June of that year a letter came to say he was searching for a suitable boiler for the engine, and had no doubt about the eventual success of the venture. In October, he said he had been trying to sell the patent in Paris, though without luck so far. Every day, he added soothingly, brought the chance of success. In January 1890, he had written from Paris, to express his thanks for her patience and his hope that she would 'speedily realise her desire'. After this, it would be many months before Miss Phillimore received another word from him.

Towards the end of 1890, a young aristocrat, the Hon. William Cosby Trench, of Clonodfoy Castle, County Limerick, Ireland, perused his copy of *The Times*. A classified advertisement under the heading of 'Partnerships &c.' caught his eye:

TWENTY-FIVE THOUSAND POUNDS positively paid in four months, plus large yearly income, to purchaser of share in an important patent. Price £475 down. Fullest investigation offered. Write Security, May's, 162 Piccadilly.

Trench later confessed that he knew absolutely nothing about business, or about patents, but this did not deter him from sending off for particulars. He received in return a letter from Charles Wells, C. E., of Great Titchfield Street ('established 1868') outlining proposals for an energy-saving steam engine.

Wells sent details of his latest machine, which he described as 'a most important proven invention, a new method of obtaining motive power for all purposes, but especially for propelling ships and boats, for the reason that a large amount of cold water is necessary'. The invention, he explained, could be fitted to ships like the *Rodney* – a large battleship launched two or three years earlier. The navy would pay a substantial royalty to use the patent device. As his invention would produce a fuel saving of up to 60 per cent they would recoup the costs in the first year.

Apart from knowing nothing of business or patents, Trench also knew nothing about engines. But it was common knowledge that any such discovery would be immensely valuable. Trench was interested, but was sufficiently cautious to write back to Wells for more information: in fact, a fairly lengthy correspondence ensued. Wells told him that he had conducted numerous experiments, and could fully understand that Trench might have concerns, and said, 'when a man saw the certainty of a fortune in his grasp he might be excused for being anxious.'

Trench sent off the customary £5. Wells replied, enclosing what he called 'the official certificate of patent', dated 22 December 1890. As for the £470 balance, Wells added that he 'would be very pleased if he [Trench] could arrange to let him have the money before Christmas'. However Trench was perturbed when he saw the newspaper advertisements continuing to appear, after he had agreed to fund the project. Before sending another cheque he questioned this with Wells, who calmly replied that the series of advertisements had been booked in advance and had not yet run out. Wells said the replies that were still coming in would not be wasted, as he hoped to interest the applicants in another of his inventions, which related to a new electrical discovery he had made.

On New Year's Eve, satisfied at last that the investment was a sound one, Trench sent his cheque for £470, ignorant of the fact that Wells had filed an almost identical patent application only a few days previously. In fact, during the course of the year just ending, he had submitted no fewer than nine separate patents for steam engines, three for hot-air engines and one with the vague description of 'steam and hot-air engines'.

Instead of allowing the series of advertisements to run out, as he had promised Trench, he actually inserted several entirely new ones:

MONEY MAKES MONEY.— How to earn a very large sum in a few weeks with a very small sum, by investing in a genuine, honest, reliable way. Security given. For full particulars write Bona Fides, May's, 162 Piccadilly.

And then, on 6 February 1891, Wells was back with a more generous offer than ever before:

THIRTY THOUSAND POUNDS in three months, and probably more yearly, is the certain product of a SHARE in a PATENT. Extraordinary low price, £500 cash. Write Necessity, May's Advertising Offices, 162, Piccadilly, W.

The results from this last advertisement were disappointing. For most readers the promise of a sum which would today be worth about £3 million must have seemed too good to be true, and no one was gullible enough to reply to it. No one, that is, except the Honourable William Cosby Trench.

A comical situation now arose. Trench did not realise that the advertisement had been placed by Wells. And, for his part, Wells did not immediately seem to be aware that Trench was already a 'client'. He sent Trench another letter identical to the first one except that this time £500 was requested, not £475. Then, two days later, he wrote in respect of Trench's first investment to say that the forgings and castings for the machine were nearing completion. Trench now added to the confusion by stating that a friend of his was interested in buying a share of the patent. Wells seemed glad to hear this news: he informed Trench that the ship which was to have had the new engine fitted had sunk. He, Wells, had been compelled to buy another, and thus the opportunity arose for a third party to join them. Another gentleman had applied to take a share, he confided, but Wells said he would prefer Trench's friend. The outcome was that Trench sent Wells a further £500.

During these first weeks of 1891, Wells made four new and entirely separate patent applications in respect of steam engines, and another for 'galvanic batteries'. Not one of these was ever taken beyond the provisional application stage. On 14 March Wells registered an invention for obtaining 'motive power from exhaust of steam engines', but it would be one of the last he ever delivered to the British Patent Office. He intensified his advertising campaign but, with the exception of Trench, who seemed determined to thrust large amounts of cash into Wells' hands at the slightest provocation, it was becoming evident that it was the patent scam itself that was running out of steam.

Reviewing his applications to date, it is plain that overall Wells had only ever completed one in seven of the patents he submitted – in contrast to a national average of one in two:

NUMBERS OF PATENT APPLICATIONS BY C. WELLS

	1885	1886	1887	1888	1889	1890	1891	1892	Total
Applications	22	45	9	42	54	15	5	0	192
Completed	11	0	1	7	5	4	0	0	28
Abandoned	11	45	8	35	49	11	5	0	164

Over the period in question Wells had applied for almost 200 patents, and normally each application represented another unsuspecting client. Only a small number of the victims took action against Wells – probably because they were embarrassed about having been duped. As these figures show, Wells' activities in connection with patents reached a peak in 1889, when he made fifty-four applications, but dwindled to almost nothing in 1891, finally ceasing by 1892. The character of the inventions had also changed. Whereas in the earlier years he had applied for a very mixed bag of patents – from balloons to bows and arrows – from 1890 onwards it appears that he had lost interest in dreaming up fresh ideas, and from that point his submissions were uniformly described as 'steam engines'.

Several years had passed since Charles' wife and daughter had returned to France. But in about 1890 he had met the love of his life – a striking young French woman named Jeannette Pairis[*]. She had dark eyes, 'a pretty pouting mouth' and brown hair in a long plait which reached down to her waist. According to some accounts, she was 'an artist's model from Chelsea'.

This seems to have been one of those instances where 'opposites attract'. Jeannette loved to wear new clothes, hats, jewellery and shoes, while Charles pottered around in a threadbare old suit. She enjoyed champagne and fine food, yet he was quite content to dine on a couple of boiled eggs he had prepared himself. In age, too, there was a wide gap. At 21 she was much younger than Wells, who was approaching 50.

He was old enough to be her father – he actually was born a few months before her father – and, for her part, Jeannette was several years younger than Charles' daughter. Yet they seemed oblivious to the age gap and were plainly besotted with each other. As Dr Francesca Denman explains, 'Psychologists talk about men who

---

[*]   Unusually for a French name, the final 's' in Pairis *is* pronounced. (Some French newspapers incorrectly spelt her name 'Périsse').

want to be young forever and young women are a way to do this.' And, as we shall see, he always had a penchant for 'little ladies'.

As we shall see, Charles Wells had begun to phase out his patent scam, and was already preparing for the next money-making endeavour. And it seems likely that Jeannette's arrival on the scene may have had something to do with this change of direction. Having expensive tastes, perhaps she perceived something that he did not – that his patent business simply was not making enough money. Maybe it was she who came up with the next big idea. But while his mind was occupied with future plans, Wells still had Trench as a willing backer, and made the most of the opportunity.

Wells had begun to spend more time on the Continent than in London. From Marseille he wrote to Trench to say that he was making 'splendid openings' there regarding the patent. In April he wrote again enclosing a statement from a Monsieur Georges Thibaud, whose engineer had inspected the machine and given a glowing report. On the strength of this, Wells invited Trench to take an additional share in the French patent for the sum of £1,250 (£125,000). On the sale of the patent Trench was to receive £50,000 (£5 million). Trench replied with alacrity, enclosing a cheque.

The next letter was from Paris and was dated 3 May 1891. Wells said he was setting up a Franco-Belgian company to exploit the patent, and needed £2,500 for the purpose. As he only had £500 himself he asked whether Trench would put up the other £2,000. He said Trench must not think he would be upset if he couldn't do this, as he (Wells) could easily get the money elsewhere, but he wanted to give Trench first refusal.

Up to this time the two men had never met, but later that month Trench went to the Great Titchfield Street premises, where Wells showed him a model of a steam engine, explaining that this was the invention he had put his money into. Trench seemed confident that the machine would be a success, though he said he was not sure that it would generate such immense profits as Wells had forecast. But Wells assured him that it would. This seemed to satisfy Trench, who left a cheque for the sum of £2,000.

Trench received another letter from Wells on 24 June – this time from Turin. Wells stated that he was going from there to Vienna and then Paris to form one large company. He promised Trench that for a further investment of £2,500 he would later receive £25,000 in cash, together with shares in the new company worth £50,000. Trench duly handed over the money and Wells informed him that this would bring his shareholding up to £225,000. To back this up, Wells actually sent several 'share certificates', as he described them. These showed Georges Thibaud to be the president of the company.

In July 1891, Wells invited Trench to London to watch a demonstration of his invention. The trial involved a small steam launch which Wells owned, *Flyer*, and took place on the River Thames near Charlton Pier. It was not a very salubrious setting. This stretch of the river was lined with chemical works, plants for processing guano from Peru, sewage works, refineries, as well as factories for paints, dyes, rubber and gutta-percha. Although raw effluent was no longer pumped into the river, the Thames was still a repository for all kinds of household rubbish, industrial waste and even dead animals.

Trench later recalled, 'I went on board. We went down the river for about twenty minutes. He [Wells] said he had the engines on board, but I could not see them.' It did not occur to Trench to check the most elementary piece of evidence – the amount of coal used. Nor did he question Wells about this vital point. 'I was satisfied with his assurance that it would turn out a success. I could not estimate if it saved coal, and I learned nothing from the trip.'

Wells himself gained rather more from the outing. As the diminutive craft chugged up and down the river, Trench was a captive audience. Wells regaled him with expansive details of the new French company he was setting up, for which he would need more capital. He was going to make the journey to Paris in one of his own boats, he said, and Trench asked if he could accompany him. Wells agreed to this, but whenever the subject was mentioned again he always made some excuse.

By now, though, the funds which Trench obligingly supplied were Wells' main source of income. His investment had reached £6,750 (£675,000), and he was the only 'client' to have parted with any really substantial amount of money. But still it wasn't enough to launch the project Wells had in mind. On 21 April Wells inserted his most ambitious advertisement to date, offering a larger reward than ever before: the equivalent of £5 million. But this time, it seems, he had gone too far; if anything, the advertisement smacks of desperation:

FIFTY THOUSAND POUNDS positively paid before four months to the PURCHASER of a SHARE in a PATENT. Price £1,250. Ample security given for the £50,000. Write Engineer, May's, 162, Piccadilly.

Apart from William Trench, the backers had all advanced relatively small sums to Wells: Frederick Goad had handed over £25; Dr White, Mrs Forrester and Miss Budd had each contributed £30; Miss Phillimore £60. His annual revenue – before Trench came on the scene – cannot have been much more than £1,500.

On the other side of the balance sheet, his outgoings were heavy, and he continued to take on ever greater financial responsibilities. While retaining his business premises at Great Titchfield Street, and his luxury flat at 162 Great Portland Street, he now signed the lease on a much larger commercial building, too. This imposing five-storey corner property at 154–156 Great Portland Street was just a few yards from his apartment. It had a 46ft façade on to Great Portland Street itself, with several shop windows. The ground floor was sufficiently roomy for Wells to have a very old, full-size traction engine, 'nicely painted to give it a good appearance', driven into the showroom, where it could be admired by passers-by. The rest of the building consisted of both business and living accommodation on a grand scale. But it was expensive.

Wells paid £800 for the new lease (£80,000) and was committed to an annual rent of £200 (£20,000).

Wages and salaries for Eschen, two or more other engineers and a couple of clerks accounted for at least £300 (£30,000) per annum. Expensive models were made in support of at least *some* of his patent applications, and there was an enormous advertising bill, as we have seen.

His private outgoings were also huge. From 1888 onwards, he had bought and sold a succession of boats, often owning two or more at the same time. They included: *Kettledrum* (a 55ft steam yacht); *Ituna* (a 137ft steam yacht); *Wyvern* (a 60ft steam yacht which was wrecked while in Wells' ownership); and *Flyer* (the small steam launch in which Trench had been taken up and down the river). The yacht *Isabella* was also in Wells' possession for a time. On another vessel, *Kathlinda* (a 93ft steam yacht), he already owed money for repairs, rent of moorings and so on: the outstanding debt on this boat alone eventually reached nearly £600 (£60,000).

And to add to his business worries, some of his 'investors' were becoming agitated, and wanted to know what he had done with their money. Some even called at his place of business. On one occasion Eschen answered a knock at the door, and Miss Phillimore stood there, asking to see Mr Wells. But Eschen was under strict instructions. 'When people came asking for Mr. Wells I let them in,' he later said. 'If he was not there I did not.' Miss Phillimore went away empty-handed.

And then, of course, there was Jeannette. Her shopping bills were already a drain on his finances. Yet he wanted to please her, and to impress her, and so he decided to buy another yacht. Not just an ordinary yacht like those he already owned. His new acquisition would be a truly spectacular floating palace to rival any vessel afloat. And he knew it would be hugely expensive.

Wells went to see an acquaintance, a man named Aristides Vergis, who had arrived in Britain from Egypt in the mid-1880s, and had later been involved in several high profile court cases involving ships, cargoes, and the like.

He had recently served a twelve-month sentence in Pentonville Prison, having been found guilty of obtaining a large quantity of valuable jewellery by false pretences. On his release he had set himself up as a yacht broker with upmarket offices in London's fashionable Sloane Square – probably financed with his ill-gotten proceeds from the fraud.

Vergis told Wells about a ship for sale in Liverpool. It might possibly be suitable for conversion into a large pleasure craft. The vessel in question was *Tycho Brahe*,* an iron cargo ship of 1,633 tons, built almost a quarter of a century earlier. Motive power was provided by steam, but she had two masts and a full set of sails, and, like many ships of her era, could be propelled by either the wind or by her engines, or both (Plate 5).

She had undoubtedly seen better days, having spent most of her life on the gruelling transatlantic run between Britain and South America, carrying coffee and other cargoes. But at 291ft in length she would be one of the largest and most impressive yachts in the world. In short, this was just what Charles Wells was looking for. She was being sold at the knockdown price of £3,500 (£350,000), but would need a much larger sum than this to turn her into a luxurious pleasure craft.

Charles agreed without hesitation to buy the ship. At the same time, he appointed Vergis, the professional yacht broker and fraudster, as his agent for all maritime matters.

A new money-making scheme was taking shape in his mind – one which would eclipse all of his previous schemes. In late July in that year of 1891, he packed his bags and set off for the destination with which he will be forever associated – Monte Carlo.**

---

*   The vessel was named after the Danish astronomer Tycho Brahe (1546–1601).

**   On the very day that Wells arrived in Monaco, Lionel Bartram – the young man who had invested £750 in one of Wells' patents – was served with papers as the first step in bankruptcy proceedings.

5

Breaking the Bank

The famous *Casino de Monte-Carlo* stands on a hill overlooking the principality's small harbour, where millionaires' yachts line the quayside. The building itself is a creamy-yellow – almost white in colour and in the midday sun it shines out against the blue Mediterranean beyond and the lush green of the surrounding gardens, where orange trees, palms, eucalyptus and jasmine grow. The casino, with its *faux* bell towers, sweeping balustrades and statuary, is unique in appearance. Influenced by Italian architecture of the sixteenth and seventeenth centuries, it could easily be mistaken for a glittering European palace, an embassy, or some important religious building.

In 1891, summer was the off-season in Monte Carlo. Between May and August the heat was unbearable – especially for the overdressed Victorians. And while the principality already had an enviable reputation as a *station balnéaire*, or sea-bathing resort, sunbathing was unknown in the 1890s: indeed, the very idea of baring one's flesh in public would have been unthinkable.

Consequently few people were around, on 28 July 1891, when Charles Wells trotted across the Place du Casino, and up the steps leading to the entrance. Two commissionaires with gleaming brass buttons on their uniforms observed him as he passed. They had seen hundreds of thousands of gamblers before, and prided themselves on being able to ascertain each person's nationality, social status and approximate wealth with a single glance. The fact that he was there at all in July marked him out as a person of indeterminate breeding, an eccentric or an Englishman – or possibly all three. Besides, respectable people would not dream of visiting during the day, and preferably would only go there in the late evening after dinner and perhaps a visit to the theatre.

These considerations did not trouble Charles Wells in the slightest. He had a strategy, the result of much deliberation on his part, and intended to follow it through. His plan required him to play for the longest possible time without interruption and this, in turn, demanded as early a start as possible.

He entered an interior 'as gorgeous as money and art can make it', crossed the gleaming floor of the atrium with its twenty-eight Grecian pillars made of marble and stepped into the Salle Mauresque, the Moorish Room, with its eastern flavoured decor and its five gaming tables. It was a room to rival the Palace of Versailles, a 'dazzling place', as the author Mark Twain remembered, with walls which seemed to be 'papered with mirrors'. Five magnificent chandeliers, fitted with the astonishing new electric lamps, hung from the gilded ceiling. The walls of the salon were decorated with pastoral scenes, and with bas-reliefs of the female form, all set among velvet drapes, classical columns and ornate carvings of chocolate-coloured wood.

The thick piled carpet deadens Charles Wells' footsteps as he crosses to one of the roulette tables, selects a chair, and sinks into the velvet covered cushion.

The roulette tables of the era are about 16ft in length and 6ft wide, with a narrower 'waist' in the middle, where the highly polished roulette wheel is mounted (Plate 7). Two croupiers sit on each side of the table in the central position, nearest to the wheel, where they can rake in the losses and pay out the winnings. Another croupier is stationed at each end to keep an eye on the game and prevent cheating. Finally, in charge of the table, the *chef de partie*, or supervisor, with overall responsibility for the team, sits in a raised position behind one of the pairs of croupiers. The players occupy a row of chairs along either side.

As Wells takes his seat the croupiers eye him with the silent disdain of a waiter who spots a customer using the wrong fork. The game of roulette begins, and the croupier says in an expressionless voice, '*Faites vos jeux, messieurs* [Place your bets, gentlemen]'. (Women may play, but they are never addresssed as such.)

Charles takes several *louis* – small gold coins worth 20fr. – and places them carefully on the numbered squares marked on the green baize of the roulette table. Chips are not used: all bets must be made in cash – either gold *louis* or banknotes.*

The croupier reaches for the handle at the centre of the roulette wheel and, with a little flourish, gives it a spin. He takes the small, white ivory ball and expertly throws it in the opposite direction to that of the wheel – or *cylindre*, as the croupiers always call it. The wheel begins, almost imperceptibly, to slow. In a firm voice the croupier says, '*Les jeux sont faits* [The bets have been placed]'. And, as if responding to his words, the white ball begins its downward spiral. '*Rien ne va plus* [No more bets will be accepted]'. With a faint rattling sound the ball meshes with the wheel, finally settling into one of the numbered pockets. The whole cycle takes about sixty seconds, and will be repeated over and over again by the time the casino closes late that night.

---

* At the time, tokens – or 'chips' – had been tried experimentally, but it was found that they were too easy to counterfeit. By the time of Wells' visit, the casino had gone back to using cash only. Today, each gambler is issued with chips of a different colour or pattern to help the croupier to distinguish where each player has placed his or her stake.

The stake money of £4,000 that Charles had managed to amass fell short of the £6,000 that he had reckoned to be ideal. But circumstances had forced him to compromise. And he proceeded to bet 'with a recklessness that suggested a mad millionaire endeavouring to get rid of his capital'. Within a short time, the banknotes piled in front of him on the table were evidence that, whatever method he was using, it was working so far.

People seemed to appear from nowhere. The casino – empty a short time earlier – was suddenly teeming with humanity. With a murmur here, a whisper there, finally an outbreak of animated chatter, a crowd formed around Wells' table to observe this unassuming little man with the bald head and dark moustache and beard. The seats around the table, beside and opposite Wells, were all occupied now. Standing behind them, sometimes on tiptoe, sometimes squeezing forward for a better view, a crowd of onlookers grew steadily. From the back it was hard to see what was going on and even harder to participate in the play: and so the spectators jostled and shoved one another in an undignified *mêlée* as they tried to get closer.

'The worst thing was the greed that his success aroused in the other guests,' said the *chef de partie*, a man named Bertollini:

> In a few minutes the table was six or seven deep with people attempting to play with him, and the croupiers were overwhelmed with men and women crying in French, German English and Italian, in Hindu and Urdu and every known language for their stakes to be placed on the same number Wells backed. In the course of two hours he had won the hundred thousand francs with which each table starts out every morning, and it was necessary to send to the office for more.

Since all stakes had to be in cash, it could be hard at busy periods for even the most experienced croupier to be sure where each player had placed a bet. But this was no ordinary busy period: it was a near riot. Dozens of people pushed and shoved to put their money on the same squares that Wells had chosen, or called on the bewildered croupier to 'do the same as this monsieur'. Amid the mayhem it was soon impossible to tell who had won what.

For hour after hour Wells played on despite the hubbub, coolly following the strategy he had worked out over the preceding months. For many of the other patrons, the heat in the *salle* became oppressive, the air fetid and unbreathable. But where others had to go outside for a breath of fresh air, or to refresh themselves with something to eat or drink, Wells never left his seat.

Camille Blanc, a distinguished looking 45-year-old, had for the past ten years, been chief director of the company that owned and operated the casino. He could feel any tiny fluctuation in the pulse of the business as surely as a sea captain can discern the slightest alteration in the sound of his ship's engines. From a small room overlooking the gaming hall, he often watched the play in progress through a peephole concealed among the mirrors and gilded carvings. Unseen by the clients and his staff, he spent hours here watching the ebb and flow of thousands of francs being won and lost. An immense crowd had gathered around just one table. At the centre of all the activity was a rather ordinary looking man, who appeared to be the only one in the room who was not in a frenzied state of agitation.

It was nearly thirty years earlier that Camille's father, François Blanc, had rescued the casino from bankruptcy and turned it into the multi-million franc business it had become. As young men, François Blanc and his twin brother, Louis, had frequented the gambling dens of 1830s Paris, before realising that it was not the players who made the most money, however lucky or skilful they might be: it was the organiser of the games who won in the long run. The twins were resourceful young men. 'If we cannot earn a good living as gamblers we shall start our own casino,' they agreed.

Their first difficulty was a lack of capital, and they overcame this hurdle in an inventive way that Charles Wells himself would have been proud of. They discovered that news of fluctuations in the price of shares on the Paris stock market could take as long as twenty-four hours to reach a city on the other side of the country, such as Bordeaux, 310 miles to the southwest. This was, of course, long before the introduction of telegrams and telephones.

Suppose a stock increased in value by 10 per cent in Paris. If the brothers could immediately buy shares at the old price in Bordeaux, they had only to wait a few hours to resell them at a significant profit. But how could this be achieved?

They soon realised that the French government had a system for communicating information very quickly. Messages of national importance could be sent all over the country by means of visual semaphore signals relayed from one hilltop station to another. The only difficulty as far as the Blanc brothers were concerned was that this network was strictly reserved for official business only. So they bribed government employees to transmit their coded messages for them. The escapade succeeded and in a short time they had increased their small capital to 100,000fr. (£400,000 in Sterling today).

It was only when one of their accomplices fell gravely ill and made a deathbed confession that the scheme fell apart. The Blanc brothers were eventually both found guilty of corrupting government employees, but when the court gave its verdict it must have seemed as if the telegraph employees were not the only ones to have been bribed. Instead of receiving a stiff sentence the brothers were merely ordered to pay the court costs and were then set free. It had been such a good scam that a few years later the famous novelist, Alexandre Dumas, copied the plot in almost every detail in his novel, *The Count of Monte Cristo*.

Meanwhile, gambling had been outlawed in almost every European country. But with the capital he had earned from the share swindle, François Blanc set up a casino in Bad Homburg, a small, self-governing enclave in what is now Germany. Blanc split the profits with Count Ludwig, the head of state, and a mutually profitable business partnership was born. Well-heeled visitors flocked to the tiny domain in the hope of gaining dizzying sums of money. But the only real winners, most of the time, were François Blanc and the count.

Although the laws of chance dictated that the casino would always be the overall winner, there were some visitors who enjoyed spectacular gains. Prince Charles Lucien Bonaparte – the nephew of Napoleon Bonaparte – made the journey to Bad Homburg in 1852 and was so successful at the tables that he nearly bankrupted the casino. He sensibly left with the cash he had won, instead of being tempted to play on and possibly lose it all again. In 1860, a Spaniard named Tomás Garcia was a consistent winner, and profited to the tune of 800,000fr. (about £3 million). Although these impressive wins temporarily dented Blanc's profits, he came to the realisation that the publicity attracted many more gamblers to his casino and, on balance, this more than compensated for the bank's short-term loss.

At the start of each day every gaming table was provided with a cash reserve or 'bank'. From time to time a gambler might have such a large win that this money was insufficient to pay out all of the winnings, and when this happened extra cash had to be sent for from the casino's vaults. This is what is known as 'breaking the bank'.

To heighten the drama of such occasions, Blanc invented a ceremony which was enacted by casino staff when the bank was broken. The table in question was temporarily closed down and, with all the pomp of a state funeral, a black crêpe cloth was spread over it. Play was suspended while more cash was brought in from the reserves. During this ritual, the patrons would generally drift away to play at other tables. And then, after a decent interval, the table would reopen.

François Blanc prospered, and so did the ruler of Bad Homburg. Indeed, the whole principality received a welcome boost from its share of the casino profits. This cosy arrangement lasted until 1866, when the enclave was about to be absorbed into the Prussian Empire. As gambling was illegal in the rest of Germany, the days of the Homburg Casino were numbered. But as luck would have it – and Blanc had always been a very lucky man – an opportunity in the tiny principality of Monaco presented itself at just that moment. A casino had opened there as early as 1856, but it had failed to take off because Monaco was not yet served by the railways, and was simply too out of the way for most tourists. Between 15 and 20 March 1857, 'only one visitor entered the casino, where he won two francs! On the 21st two more arrived, and lost two hundred and five francs.' Business was so slack that the croupiers would stand around outside the building, taking it in turns to peer through a telescope and try to spot any visitor who might be coming down the road.

After a long struggle the original promoters became insolvent. The prince – who also teetered on the edge of bankruptcy – searched for someone who could turn the failing enterprise around. He contacted François Blanc and they signed a binding agreement in April 1863, giving Blanc the exclusive right to run the casino for fifty years. In return, Blanc was to pay an annual sum of 250,000fr. (£1 million) to the royal household. The casino would also meet all of the public expenses of the principality, maintaining its small army, its roads, schools, hospitals and police. Thus the prince would henceforth enjoy a rich lifestyle, and the people of Monaco would never again have to pay any taxes.

In order to downplay the gambling aspect, which many people regarded with disdain, François Blanc set up a holding company to run the casino, and euphemistically named it the SBM, which stands for *Société des Bains de Mer* (Sea-Bathing Company). Blanc and his family owned nearly all of the shares in this body.

Under Blanc's management the business went from near collapse to unprecedented success. In fact, his wealth reached such huge proportions that on one occasion he bailed out the French government when it was short of funds. The project in question was Charles Garnier's opera house in Paris. Work had begun in 1862, but it had ground to a halt during the Franco-Prussian War of 1870–71, and the partly completed building was temporarily used as a warehouse, a hospital and then a barracks. Instead of the elegant theatre of Garnier's dreams, the unfinished structure became a blot on the landscape for several years. Garnier feared that his association with the ill-fated venture might end his career.

François Blanc was the kind of man who knows that money can buy anything – including respectability. He also recognised the cachet to be gained by being associated with such a prestigious cultural project. Blanc offered to lend the government some 5 million francs to finish the opera house. In return, the state was to repay the loan with interest – at an exceptionally high rate of 6 per cent. A further condition imposed by Blanc was that a railway was to be constructed to connect Monaco with the French transport network.

Paris got its opera; Blanc finally got a rail link which enabled far more clients to visit his casino than ever before; and Garnier was so grateful that he publicly declared his indebtedness to François Blanc. So when Blanc asked Garnier to design a new concert hall to be built next to the casino, the architect could hardly refuse.* The theatre opened in 1879, and the greatest French actress of the era, Sarah Bernhardt, recited a specially written monologue as part of the inaugural ceremony.

With one foot now firmly planted on the ladder of French society, Blanc consolidated his position by arranging for his elder daughter, Louise, to marry into a distinguished but cash-strapped family. She became the wife of Prince Constantin Radziwill, whose family were Polish exiles.

---

* Garnier was also responsible for some subsequent alterations and additions to the gaming rooms in the casino itself.

His second daughter, Marie, married Prince Roland Bonaparte – a great-nephew of the former Emperor Napoleon. She died in childbirth the year after, but the child lived. Thus François Blanc's grandson was born a royal.* But Blanc did not live to see it. He had died three years earlier. He left a fortune of 88 million francs (about £300 million), and on his deathbed he bemoaned the fact that he had not been able to leave even more money to his family. His widow took over the casino for a few years until her death in 1881, and then his two sons, Camille and Edmond, inherited the business. The company was now restructured so that its capital was 30 million francs, and the Blanc family owned no less than 87 per cent of the shares.

At the time of Charles Wells' 1891 visit to Monte Carlo, the casino there was the only place in Europe where gambling was still permitted. The contract between the Blanc family and the Prince of Monaco was as good as a licence to print money. But,

---

*   As a result of this alliance, our present monarch, King Charles III, is
      related – albeit somewhat distantly – to François Blanc.

Monte Carlo croupiers watching for the arrival of players (from a
contemporary drawing).

as Camille Blanc was well aware, the casino had many enemies, and its survival could never be taken for granted.

Nineteenth-century society, with its strict morals, considered betting to be a vice, on a par with sexual impropriety and drunkenness. It was believed that temptations such as these, if left unchecked, would lead the working classes into a life of sin and erode the moral fibre of the nation. Newspapers such as *The Times* frequently referred to the Monte Carlo Casino as a 'blot on civilisation', a 'plague spot' and a 'gambling hell'. The Vatican and the Church of England organised petitions demanding the closure of the gaming salons, and at various times the British, French and United States governments had expressed their disapproval in the strongest terms (though it has to be said that none of these protests had so far had any effect in practice). Still, the casino remained a popular destination for some well-known pillars of society, including Baron Rothschild, Lord Randolph Churchill (father of Winston), Sir Arthur Sullivan (of Gilbert and Sullivan fame) and W.H. Smith (bookseller, MP and philanthropist).

These opposing viewpoints are perhaps best illustrated by the example of the British royal family. Queen Victoria herself thought that the casino was an abomination. When she visited the principality in 1882 she wrote in her journal, 'The harm this attractive gambling establishment does, cannot be overestimated. The old Prince of Monaco, derives his income from it and therefore does not wish to stop it, though efforts are being made to do so.' But the efforts were always in vain. And, although the queen disapproved of gambling, her eldest son, Bertie (later King Edward VII), frequently travelled to Monte Carlo, where he was a popular guest at the casino. However, only a few weeks before Wells attained Monte Carlo fame, Bertie had received scathing criticism in the press for gambling with a group of aristocrats in London.

The British newspapers constantly reported on gamblers who, having lost all of their money, finished up in the bankruptcy courts. Or those who, seeing no hope, had committed suicide. *The Times* claimed:

> Another victim of Monte Carlo is now lying at the hospital of the Principality. A young man … lost all his money at the tables, and as he went through the hall attempted to blow his brains out with a revolver, but the bullet passed through his cheek and lodged in his palate. He is in a critical condition.

When Sarah Bernhardt appeared again some years after her Monte Carlo debut, she gambled away most of her fortune, until one evening she was down to her last 100,000fr. In a final attempt to recoup her losses she staked this money, too, only to lose every centime within three hours. She took an overdose of a sleeping powder in her room at the Hôtel de Paris, where she would have died if she had not been saved by a friend, a wealthy duke. He subsequently lent her enough to clear her 300,000fr. debt.

To keep scandals like these out of the press, the casino allotted up to £20,000 (£2 million) each year for what it coyly termed 'publicity'. This was, in fact, the hush money paid to newspaper editors to turn a blind eye to the more unsavoury aspects of the casino's affairs, a practice which had been going on for years.

But lately a shadow had fallen over the very existence of the casino, and this new threat seemed alarmingly real. Two years previously, in 1889, Prince Charles III of Monaco, the ruler who had first made a pact with François Blanc, had died, and was succeeded by his son, Albert. Camille Blanc expressed his condolences by sending wreaths to be placed upon the late prince's coffin. But Albert returned the flowers with neither comment nor explanation. As far as Camille Blanc was concerned, it was hardly an auspicious start to the new prince's reign. Albert despised the casino, and resented the influence its money-grabbing owners had exerted over his late father and the state in general. And the fact that most of his personal income was derived from other people's losses at the tables troubled his conscience. He allegedly said, 'I'd shut it up tomorrow. I hate the corruptions of it ... I loathe the place.'*

Within weeks of becoming the ruler of Monaco, Albert had married American-born Alice Heine, widow of the Duke of Richelieu. With her wealth at his disposal, Albert was no longer dependent on the money being paid to him by Blanc. Would the prince break the contract their fathers had signed over a quarter of a century earlier, and have the casino shut down? It was a question that undoubtedly gave Camille Blanc sleepless nights, especially when he read press reports of the following kind:

> There is a very considerable chance of the gaming tables at Monte Carlo being closed for good. The fact is the Prince of Monaco is anxious to secure friendly relations not only with our Queen but with other European sovereigns who have not smiled favourably on the enterprise. (Clifton Society 23 July 1891).

The article goes on to say that there was a proposal to relocate the casino in the principality of Andorra, on the border between France and Spain. Others claimed that negotiations were taking place concerning a move to Liechtenstein. Neither of these places, however, had the rail links that Monaco possessed, and it might be argued that neither was quite as attractive a destination.

As he pondered on these matters, Camille looked down through the spyhole on to the gaming tables in the room below. The ordinary-looking man was still winning.

---

* Ironically it was Albert who, as a 10-year-old boy, had laid the foundation stone of the original casino in May 1858. (Smith, A., p.302.)

Many observers have put forward their own theories to explain how Wells could have been so successful at the gaming tables. Some claimed that he was simply very lucky. A few suggested that he had used an infallible 'martingale' or system. Others wondered whether he had somehow cheated the casino.

The author of this book has conducted extensive research on this topic and – in one of the later chapters – offers an alternative explanation.

By eleven o'clock in the evening – closing time at the casino – Charles Wells had broken the bank. In one day he had transformed the £4,000 he had brought with him into £10,000 (£1 million). He left with his winnings, felt the cool breeze on his face and breathed in the evening air, laden with the scent of oleanders, tangerine trees and other fragrant plants in the casino gardens – a welcome change from the stuffy, ill-ventilated gaming halls.

In the morning Wells went to Smith's Bank – a British-owned establishment at the Galerie Charles III, overlooking the casino gardens – to transfer the previous night's proceeds to his own bank in London. He went to the casino again at opening time, and sat at the tables until late at night, never taking a break, never pausing for food or drink,* and this was his routine for the next few days. By the end of his five-day stay he claimed to have won no less than £40,000 (£4 million).

The first news of Charles Wells' success at Monte Carlo reached Britain in the form of a very brief report which appeared in several newspapers:

---

* These long stints must have been exhausting. The previous year a man had tried to gamble for long periods at the casino. He stated, 'The third day I felt ill – nine hours or so a day in the hot rooms, without a break, would kill anyone in time.'

LUCK AT MONTE CARLO – Reuter's Telegram
An English visitor, after playing continuously at the roulette tables here during the last four days, has just won a sum
of £20,000.

By the following day a few more details had begun to
trickle through:

GAMBLING AT MONTE CARLO
MONTE CARLO, JULY 31.
An Englishman named Wells, who is staying here, has just
had a run of luck so extraordinary as to be the chief topic of
the hour, not only with those who frequent the Casino, but
among the residents of Monte Carlo generally ... He won
several stakes of 26,000 *f*, and twice consecutively backed the
number one 'en plein' successfully for 8,000 *f*, the *maximum*
amount allowed. He also frequently backed with similar good
fortune the even chances ... and more than once won all these
stakes at the same time. (Reuter's Special Service)

A follow-up report appeared on 3 August, Bank Holiday Monday:

MONTE CARLO, AUG 2.
Mr. Wells ... continues to be favoured by the same good
fortune. Finding the luck turning against him, he had the
prudence to quit the table at which he had been assiduously
playing day after day from the opening of the Casino till its
close. Before leaving the building, however, he risked a few
stakes at another game, trente-et-quarante,* and, winning
each, continued to play till he had further increased his gains
by the sum of 160,000 *f*, or close upon £6,400. Mr. Wells at
trente-et-quarante follows the same system that proved so
successful at roulette – the famous 'coup des trois' – that is

---

*   A casino game played with cards.

to say, following the luck till he has won thrice in succession, and then withdrawing the accumulated stake. People here and at Nice are talking of nothing but his marvellous success. (Reuter's Special Service)

A further account described how the table where Wells was playing 'was surrounded by a large crowd, and intense excitement prevailed, such persistent good fortune having never been witnessed before'. Wells' winning streak was beginning to have an adverse effect on the bank, the paper claimed, adding that Wells 'keeps two secretaries to assist him in his transactions'.*

---

*   It is possible that the 'secretaries' were in fact his wife and daughter. It is known for a fact that they accompanied him on a later visit.

6

The Infallible System

Most readers enjoy a happy, good luck story, especially on a summery holiday weekend, and the reports struck a chord with the public. Charles Wells, 'the lucky Englishman', was both envied and admired. People reading his story would have loved to have accomplished what he had just done: but as they were unlikely ever to have a chance of doing so, they imagined what it must be like to be in his position, and admired him for having beaten the system. It was evident that his wins were not due to good fortune alone, but to his own strengths as an individual: his stamina, his cool-headed manner and his tenacity. And, unlike many other gamblers, he had been businesslike and had sent his gains home instead of running the risk of losing them again. Because luck was only part of the winning formula, he was seen as having *earned* his reward.

His reputation was by no means confined to Britain. Within days his name appeared in newspapers around the world, particularly in the United States of America and in Australia. Wherever his story was told, people wondered how Charles Wells had beaten the bank: had he really invented a foolproof system for gambling? Had he cheated? Or simply been incredibly lucky? Or was there some other explanation? Almost everyone had a different opinion, but no one actually knew. And before anyone had the opportunity to quiz him on his triumph he had left Monte Carlo.

His success at the gambling tables enabled Charles Wells to close the lid on his moribund patent business. He had submitted only five applications that year and did not complete any of them.

In contrast, his plan to break the bank had achieved everything he had hoped for, and more. The money was welcome, but there were other advantages, too. He was praised in newspapers around the world, and within a few days he had achieved far greater recognition than his father had earned in a whole lifetime. And he was determined to return to the casino before very long. There was just one sobering thought. Even with his newly acquired wealth he could not afford to complete the purchase of the ship, and put his business affairs in order at the same time.

But in a flash of inspiration, he realised that there was a way to expand on his recent attainments, and during September and October he placed a new advertisement in high-circulation newspapers. It bears a passing resemblance to his earlier publicity, with its headline promising a large amount of cash. But this time, the offer was not a quarter-share in a patent. It was instead the opportunity to back him in his future gambling activities at Monte Carlo. And with this new scheme came the promise of a substantially larger reward than before: £30,000 – £3 million in present-day terms – *every month*.

The password, 'Perseverance', seems particularly appropriate in the case of Wells, who had plotted, schemed, worked and waited so long for success and fame to come. Wells now had a reputation as the gambler who had broken the bank, and was determined to exploit it to the full.

The idea was inspired. It remains to this day the perfect money-making scheme. Wells is saying, in effect, 'give me £6,000 [£600,000] to gamble with using my "infallible system". If I win I'll give you a return of £1,000 a day [£100,000]. If I don't, the most you will lose is the £6,000 you have invested.' Whatever happened, Wells himself could not lose. And the beauty of the stratagem was that – although it was distinctly shady – no one could possibly point to anything about it that was illegal.

We can picture him as he eagerly makes the 1-mile trip from his office in Great Portland Street to Willing's Advertising Office at 162 Piccadilly – a 1s ride in a hansom cab. He is not expecting a flood of replies, as only a very small number of people have £6,000 in ready cash to invest. But on this particular day he finds an envelope waiting for him in his mailbox, and his pulse quickens.

Yet something about the letter seems familiar: the handwriting, the stationery, a faint hint of perfume, perhaps. As he tears open the envelope the truth slowly dawns on him. This is not something he has reckoned with at all. The sender of the letter is none other than Miss Catherine Mary Phillimore.

Not a single word had passed between Charles Wells and Miss Phillimore for almost two years. Having received her investment of £60, Charles had virtually ignored her, save for his letter of January 1890, in which he hoped she would 'speedily realise her desire'. Since then, with so many other things on his mind, he had virtually forgotten her.

Miss Phillimore also had more pressing concerns. Her ageing mother, who was nearing the end of her life, doubtless took precedence over Wells, his inventions and the relatively small sum she had invested with him. In short, she had probably forgotten him, too.

But now she had answered his new advertisement, Wells' interest in her was reawakened. This, he realised, could only mean that she must have £6,000 at her disposal – a thought that had never previously occurred to him. The very idea opened up distinct new possibilities.

The correspondence between them recommenced, with Wells enthusing in a letter about his recent Monte Carlo success. But Miss Phillimore seems to have been quite unaware of these exploits. Far from being impressed, as Wells had expected, she was horrified. She was a devout Christian who took a dim view of gambling, and she told him so.

Neatly side-stepping her objections, Wells then explained that he needed the money to finance new projects, cheerfully adding that he 'couldn't have got through if the Monte Carlo affair hadn't turned up'. Realising, though, that Miss Phillimore was unlikely to finance his future gambling activities, he skilfully changed tack, and sent her a long, highly detailed letter bearing his new business address of 154–156 Great Portland Street. He told her how successful he had been in other matters and said that he had invented another new device for saving fuel in steam engines. He forecast early results, explaining that he already spent 'thousands' on his present venture, and complimenting Miss Phillimore on her good fortune in being in a position to back his idea by purchasing a quarter-share.

He then went on to describe in rapturous terms the lavish new business premises and listed the various departments: 'machinery in all its branches' on the ground floor; offices on the first floor; a 'chemical laboratory and testing department' on the second floor; a 'tracing room for models and patents' on the third floor; and, lastly, an 'electrical department' in the basement.

He also wrote about the ship that he proposed to purchase once he had raised the money. The vessel would be used as a kind of travelling demonstration of his fuel-saving devices. A cargo worth £2,000 was already promised, he claimed, and in a single voyage the ship would earn £150. He added that he had thirty ships under his control, and claimed that by fitting his patent engine to all of these he would make a profit of over £1 million in just the first year. He told Miss Phillimore that he could have offered a share in this new invention to a company, but he would rather offer it to her, as a company might fail and that would be 'an everlasting stain' on his name.

He promised her a quarter-share of the revenue in exchange for an investment of £6,000, and assured her that 'as for the

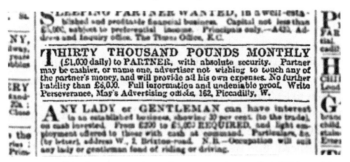

Charles Wells' advertisement in *The Times*, 7 September 1891, inviting readers to back him at Monte Carlo.

£1,000 a day [as projected in his advertisement] it was the least part of the anticipated return'.

Miss Phillimore considered his offer. It sounded as if the ship represented good security, and she agreed to advance the sum that he needed – but on one condition, namely that the 'loan of £6,000 was made to him on the distinct understanding that he never resorted to that mode of raising money [gambling] again'.

At almost exactly the same time Wells received another surprise in his mailbox at Willing's. The Honourable William Cosby Trench – surely the most loyal reader *The Times* ever had – spotted Wells' new advertisement. Unlike Miss Phillimore, Trench was fully aware of Wells' gambling achievement – he had, of course, devoured every word of the recent press coverage. But although the notice in the classifieds bore a marked resemblance to those he had previously replied to, it did not dawn on him that Wells was behind it. 'The advertisement I answered gave the address of Willing's office,' he said later, 'and I had no idea I was communicating with Wells when I answered it. He wrote saying the matter was in connection with his scheme at Monte Carlo.'

Since Trench already knew about his gambling activities, there was no reason for Wells to beat about the bush. He told Trench he wanted a backer to put up £6,000 for him to gamble at the casino again, and wondered whether Trench was interested. He explained in glowing terms how he had devised a system which enabled him to win with certainty. While he was recently 'in Italy' to promote the patent machine that Trench was already ostensibly financing, he had spent six days at the gaming tables financed by a person who had put up the stake money. He was at pains to let Trench know that his winnings had been £40,000. Although the profits had been so huge, he informed Trench that he had left Monte Carlo to perfect the invention that Trench had financed. But Trench was alarmed at the thought of Wells gambling with his money and – like Miss Phillimore – refused to entertain the idea. 'I sent him no money to play the scheme with,' he later emphasised.

As his two biggest 'investors' had both refused to back his next gambling expedition to Monte Carlo, Wells now had to rethink his approach. He decided that when he next received a response to his announcement in the paper, he would first send a letter describing in very general terms the fortune that could be earned by investing with him, but carefully avoiding any mention of Monte Carlo or of gambling for the time being.

It is believed that, to prove his bona fides, he sent his bank passbook to each applicant, together with a polite request in the accompanying letter for its prompt return.* This was a gesture calculated to engender mutual trust between Wells and his prospect. Following his win at Monte Carlo, Wells' account at the London & South-Western Bank in Sloane Square showed a healthy balance, with large sums credited since July. There can be little doubt that this was the 'undeniable proof' mentioned in his advertisement.

A few other replies did come in, apparently, but no further subscribers are thought to have signed up to Wells' new project. In fact, this is where his planning went off the rails completely:

---

* Although such an action would be most unusual today, Wells is known to have done this on at least one occasion, as described below. In an era long before photocopying had been invented, it was common enough for valuable original documents to be sent back and forth via the postal service – which was, incidentally, both quick and secure.

several people, on receiving his first letter outlining the scheme in the most general and non-committal terms imaginable, had reservations about the business. Instead of writing back to Wells accepting his offer of an explanatory brochure, they forwarded his letter to Henry Labouchère at *Truth* magazine.

With the proceeds of his Monte Carlo adventure, Wells completed his acquisition of the ship *Tycho Brahe*. The mountain of other debts probably swallowed up any remaining cash. On 15 October 1891, he engaged Captain George Samuel Smith to take command of the vessel for a salary of £180 per annum (£18,000) with food and uniform provided. He told Smith he intended to sail to places such as Monte Carlo, Nice, Cannes, Menton and other Mediterranean ports, and promised him an extra 7s (£35) a week when the ship navigated these foreign waters.

Smith – a man about the same age as Wells – was born in the coastal town of Exmouth, Devon. He went to sea at an early age and, in 1869, while still in his mid-twenties, qualified as a ship's master on sailing vessels. Two years later he earned his ticket to command steam-driven ships. Then he sailed for years on the lucrative South American run, between Liverpool, Brazil, the River Plate, the Caribbean and the eastern ports of the United States. These were the very routes that *Tycho Brahe* had been built for, and certainly there were few captains with more experience of this kind of vessel than George Smith. By the time he crossed paths with Charles Wells he had undoubtedly been around the world many times.

When he was not sailing on the ocean waves, Captain Smith lived in Redesdale Street, Chelsea. Charles Wells and Jeannette are believed to have lived in the neighbourhood for a time, and the estranged wife of ship-broker Aristides Vergis resided in the same street. Vergis himself had an office not far away and it was he who had probably introduced Captain Smith to Wells. At first Smith was cautious. It was well known among mariners that passengers were far more troublesome than cargoes, and besides he was not sure quite what to make of Wells. To Smith, who was a man with both feet firmly planted on the ground, the scheme to create a luxury yacht out of an old rust bucket like the *Tycho Brahe* seemed quite preposterous. He certainly would not have paid as much for her as Wells had. And, as for the intended improvements, only 'a mug' would spend £20,000 (£2 million) as Wells proposed to do. But he conceded that she must have been a beautiful ship when new, and that she was seaworthy. And after some deliberation he decided to give it a try.

A few days later, on 22 October, the purchase was completed and the official register of shipping was amended to show Charles Wells as 'managing owner'. Wells immediately changed the vessel's name from the obscure *Tycho Brahe* to *Palais Royal* – an inspired choice, which perfectly evokes the floating palace that he had in mind.

The new name was fitting for several other reasons, too. The Palais Royal in Paris had been, from 1642 onwards, the king's official residence: it is situated at the southern end of the Avenue de l'Opéra, where Charles had his offices a decade earlier. Lastly, as Charles almost certainly knew, it had once been renowned as a gambling centre, where games such as roulette were played before being outlawed in France. It was in this very place that the rules were first established for the principal casino games.

The old cargo ship was moved to the Herculaneum Docks beside the River Mersey. Wells found a nearby shipwright, John J. Marks ('Ship and Anchor Smiths; Shipwrights, wood and iron'), to transform the decrepit old steamer into a pleasure craft of the most lavish kind. As both Marks and Wells were early subscribers to the new telephone system, they could conduct long-distance discussions between London and Liverpool about the progress of work on the ship.

An important task for Marks was to alter the arrangement of the accommodation below decks so as to provide a saloon, as well as opulent cabins for Wells and his travelling companions. But the *pièce de résistance* would be the ballroom, 50ft long and extending the entire width of the ship, 32ft, with room for fifty or sixty people to be entertained in comfort. An organ, a grand piano and a harmonium would be provided for the delight of the guests, and for Charles to demonstrate his keyboard prowess.

At that time only a very small number of individuals were privileged enough to own a yacht. With his existing 'fleet' of smaller vessels, Charles Wells was already a member of this elite community: but when the conversion had been completed, the *Palais Royal* would be something quite out of the ordinary. According to *Lloyd's Register of Yachts* for 1892 (which lists 'all yachts the particulars of which are known') the *Palais Royal* would be the seventh largest vessel of its kind in the entire world: Charles Wells Esq., of Portland Place, would soon find himself among some extremely distinguished company. After all, he reasoned, if Queen Victoria and the Emperor of Germany could have gigantic luxury yachts, why should he and Jeannette not have one too?

PRIVATELY OWNED YACHTS IN ORDER OF SIZE, 1892

	Name of Yacht	Tons	Owner
1	*Mahroussa*	3,359	His Highness the Khedive of Egypt
2	*Poliarnaia Zvezda*	3,034	His Imperial Majesty the Czar of Russia
3	*Derjava*	2,753	His Imperial Majesty the Czar of Russia
4	*Ceylon*	2,360	Mr Drury-Lavin (private owner)
5	*Victoria & Albert*[*]	2,243	Her Majesty Queen Victoria
6	*Victoria*	1,692	Steam Yacht Victoria Ltd.
7	**Palais Royal**	**1,633**	**Charles Wells C.E.**
8	*Osborne*[**]	1,490	Her Majesty Queen Victoria
9	*Hohenzollern*	1,439	His Imperial Highness, the Emperor of Germany

[*]   The royal yacht.

[**]   The tender to the royal yacht.

While work on the ship proceeded, Wells paid regular visits to Liverpool, staying at the North-Western Hotel, beside Lime Street Station. In many cities the area around the principal rail terminus becomes the red-light district, and Lime Street was no exception. Its reputation for 'ladies of the night' had never been more lurid than in the 1890s.* And whenever Wells turned up at the docks to see how work on his ship was progressing, he was invariably accompanied by young women. He explained their presence to Captain Smith by saying that they were his 'nieces' – an assertion which no doubt caused some amusement among the crew of worldly mariners. Smith later said that he saw champagne being drunk, though Charles Wells, who seldom took alcohol, did not have any.

At other times Wells turned up with Jeannette – also described as a 'niece', predictably. The crew naturally noticed that when she and Charles spoke together it was always in French. By way of explanation, Wells told them that she was of Swiss nationality, and was from Zurich. In this, as we shall soon discover, Wells was not quite telling the truth.

---

* The old folk song about a Liverpool prostitute, 'Maggie May', popular at the time, includes the line, 'She'll never walk down Lime Street any more'.

7

Monte Carlo Wells

For the next few months Charles Wells was to lead an extraordinary double life: as Charles Wells the cool, calm, courageous gambler, and as Charles Wells CE, patentee and rogue. On 2 November, or thereabouts, he reappeared at Monte Carlo. As before, he brought with him £4,000 in stake money.

This time the atmosphere was noticeably different from his previous visit. The season had begun and the casino was much busier than on his previous trip in the summer. And Wells himself had changed. He was no longer the anonymous Englishman. Instead he was famous as one of the most successful gamblers the world had ever known. Everyone wanted to know how he had done it, and as if they might fathom the secret of his success by merely watching him, their eyes never left him from the moment he entered the building. It would seem, though, that he might have been put off his stroke by this intense scrutiny. Certainly it seemed as if the luck he had enjoyed in the summer had deserted him.

RETURNING TO BE PLUCKED
Mr Wells, the English gentleman who had the good fortune to win the sum of £32,000 some months ago at the gaming tables at Monte Carlo, has returned thither, and is once more

playing heavily. So far, however, his luck has failed him, and he has opened his campaign by losing £4,000.

When he returned two days later, inquisitive eyes followed his every move. Perhaps he had been trying to acquire another £4,000 to replenish his stake money. If so, it seems that he did not succeed.

His first stake showed extreme caution, as if he was dipping a toe in the water to see whether his luck – or his 'system' – had deserted him. He started by carefully placing six gold *louis* on the table. Once again, he played for eleven hours without a break. In that time he magically transmuted six gold coins amounting to about £5 (£500) into a pile of banknotes to the value of £4,000 (£400,000). Now he had regained his earlier position.

On the second day, 'an excited crowd gathered round the tables', *The Times* reported. 'Mr. Wells made a vigorous attack on the bank, and at the close of play had amassed a pile of 70,000 *f*, bringing up the total of his winnings since his arrival in Monte Carlo to over 250,000 *f*. [£1 million].'

His technique was to watch for 'runs' or 'series': that is, when the same colour – black or red – came up several times in a row. He always gambled the maximum stake of 12,000fr., and on Thursday and Friday he broke the bank several times. On Friday night, 'Mr. "Bonne-Chance Wells"' had before him on the green tables a pile of 1,000 f notes a foot and a half high, [but] he never lost his head at play, and afterward slept soundly with them under his pillow at the Hotel de Paris, overlooking the Place du Casino'.

On the Saturday he played *trente et quarante*. He bet 12,000fr. maximums thirty times in a row and won twenty-three. Then he broke the bank again at the roulette table. By one o'clock he had cleaned the bank out of 10fr. and 1,000fr. notes, and the croupiers had to pay out the amounts he won in odd notes and rouleaux* of gold coins until a further 'float' of 100,000fr. was delivered to the table. 'All this naturally afforded splendid sport for the spectators, who rejoiced at so successful an attack upon the enemy,' the *Pall Mall Gazette* told its readers.

However, he was unable to make any further progress that afternoon, and decided to leave. Just as he had done previously, he sent his profits – amounting to nearly £20,000 (£2 million) this time – back to London. This policy removed any temptation to gamble away the money he had already won.

In contrast with his previous visit, when the press had not learned of his exploits until he was about to leave, this time Reuter's Agency had sent a cable to the major newspapers immediately on his arrival. Consequently, British journalists were able to get there in time to quiz him on the spot. He comes across as a reluctant and decidedly publicity shy interviewee. Naturally, reporters were anxious to establish who he was, since his background had been something of a mystery up to now. He told them his name was Charles Hill Wells – Hill being his mother's maiden name. No doubt this was a ploy to avoid being identified with either 'Will-Wells', who was still a wanted man in France, or as the perpetrator of the patent swindle who was currently acquiring an unsavoury reputation in Britain through the frequent articles in *Truth*.

He told newspaper men that he had developed an infallible gambling system, but – unsurprisingly – he declined to say what it was. He did reveal, however, that he followed the table, watching for recurring numbers or sequences of numbers – as he had done on Friday. If other gamblers wanted to see how he played they were welcome to do so, but he felt that most of them would not have the courage to do what he did, nor would they risk the amount of capital that he was ready

---

*   A number of coins to a specific value encased in a tube of rolled-up paper.

to stake. His system, he claimed, needed £6,000 capital as he always staked maximums.

One of the journalists challenged Wells to explain why he did not carry on winning until he had brought the casino to its knees. He replied:

> Because the physical strain is beyond my strength. I have been sitting daily from twelve noon till eleven at night, playing without a break, and I am worn out. But I have decided to come again shortly. I have implicit faith in my system, and am perfectly sure I can win again.

The man from *The Times* was somewhat sceptical, and observed Wells at play:

> After watching the game of this gentleman for some hours, it does not seem to me that he has made any very novel discovery in the science of playing roulette and trente-et-quarante. The secret of his success rather seems to be in the courageous way in which he attacks the tables and his cool-headed manner of treating either great success or any rebuff which may be encountered. Most men get excited in either event and lose control over their play … [and] few have had the courage to risk repeatedly for 11 hours a day close upon a thousand pounds at almost every coup.

Wells went on to say that he had no complaint about the way the games were run, but he was annoyed at the way in which casino 'detectives' followed him around outside the gaming hall in an attempt to find out who he was, where he was from and who his friends were. He was troubled by numerous people pestering him for gifts and loans, and had received hundreds of begging letters. A man who had gambled away his daughter's dowry pleaded with Wells for its return. And a woman demanded that Wells give her £6,000: she had watched as the croupier scooped up her losing stake and handed it to Wells as part of his winnings. Applying her own brand of logic to the problem, she was now asking him to give back what she still perceived as her money.

Wells told the reporters that he had bought £2,000 worth of casino shares – a wise move as the casino had just enjoyed its most profitable year ever. Reports of Wells' good fortune that summer had indisputably contributed to these record results. Wells said the shares were a good investment: he felt that the house would always win when pitted against *ordinary* gamblers.

Since Wells' last visit Camille Blanc and the Prince of Monaco had come to a mutually acceptable agreement. One of the prince's favourite occupations was research into marine life, and he dreamed of opening a prestigious oceanographic museum in Monaco. It would have been an enormously costly project, and was well beyond his present means. Acting as intermediary, the father of the princess, a businessman with impressive powers of persuasion, approached Blanc and secured a new deal. Blanc was virtually blackmailed into handing over an immediate payment of 10 million francs to the state treasury, a further 12 million for harbour improvements and charitable works and a percentage of the casino's future profits. All of this was in addition to the annual 'retainer' already paid to the royal household. In return the prince graciously allowed the casino to continue to operate. The future of the business was guaranteed. In fact, things had never been better.

Now that Blanc had renewed his contract with the prince, plans for the enlargement of the casino, which had been put on hold for the summer, were being dusted off again. Days after this most recent visit by Wells, a new gaming room, the *Salle Touzet*,* reopened for the first time that season. Some of the older rooms were extensively cleaned and re-gilded.

---

* After its architect, Jules Touzet.

'The cost of these alterations', a journalist wrote, 'is a sign that the directors have a good deal of confidence in the future, and that they do not anticipate any intervention ...'

With the extra space, the casino now had about twelve tables in all. These additional facilities came not a moment too soon because gamblers were already making their way to Monaco in droves. And, according to a report on 18 November, Wells was almost single-handedly responsible for the bonanza:

RUSH TO MONTE CARLO

The recent reports of enormous gains at the tables at Monte Carlo have produced their inevitable consequence in attracting to Monte Carlo swarms of visitors from every part of Europe, most of whom frequent the Casino with the one dominant idea, that of 'breaking the bank.' ... A good many hundreds have attempted the exploit within the last week or two, to the no small profit of the Casino shareholders. Several well-known English ladies and gentlemen have made themselves conspicuous by the persistence with which they have endeavoured to work out to a successful issue the infallible system which Mr. Wells confided to the correspondents of certain London journals. The shares of the company ... now realise 2,000 francs.

At the end of the month the publicity surrounding Wells' good fortune was still in evidence:

The hotels are already well filled. Play at the tables has been high. There is no doubt that much of this is due to the reports which were so extensively circulated concerning large winnings made by Wells, for it is certain that at no time within the history of the Casino have the tables been so well patronised at such an early period of the season.

Wells must have looked back on his recent triumphs with pride and satisfaction. Within a matter of a few days he had achieved far greater recognition and earned far more money than ever before. No longer was he dependent on the moribund patent business; instead he was praised in newspapers around the world for his prowess as a gambler.

In the pages of *Truth* back in London, however, Henry Labouchère's campaign against Wells continued tirelessly. As mentioned, several people had responded to Wells' advertisement promising '£1,000 a day' and on receiving his reply had forwarded it to Labouchère. On 5 November – the very day that Wells had been in Monte Carlo adding another 70,000fr. to his fortune – Labouchère threw down a fresh challenge to the authorities. 'If it is worth while for a detective to hunt down an "astrologer" who advertises for shillings, why is this Wells left free to defraud the public year after year?'

Soon afterwards Labouchère became aware – rather belatedly – that the patent scam had involved much more than obtaining an initial £5 from each victim. It had come to his attention that Lionel Bartram had sent to Wells £750 (£75,000 in today's terms), and was facing bankruptcy. Labouchère's new discovery showed the swindle to be 'of a far worse character than anything that has yet been disclosed respecting Wells'. But if Labouchère suspected that Wells of Monte Carlo and Wells the patent agent were one and the same person, he was keeping his suspicions to himself for the present. He even mentions 'Wells of Monte Carlo' – as though he were an entirely different person – in a separate article, in which he dismisses the 'infallible system' as a fiction. 'The Nice correspondent of *The Times* seems … to be now hoodwinked by Mr. Wells in respect to an infallible system …' (It is odd that Labouchère should ridicule gambling systems in this way, as he had adopted one himself in the past: it is known to this day as the Labouchère System – or 'Labby'.)

It was left to the *Evening News* to put two and two together and reveal that Wells of Monte Carlo and Wells the fraudster were one and the same person. 'Wells of Monte Carlo is clearly and unmistakably *my* Wells,' Labouchère wrote a few days later, 'the lying, swindling, bogus patentee …' We can almost picture Labouchère rubbing his hands with glee, as he throws down a challenge. 'I therefore appeal to Mr. Wells again,' he writes a week later, 'to let the public hear from him.' Wells did not respond, of course. Yet it should be mentioned that other publications still referred to him in glowing terms:

> Mr. Charles Hill Wells, the hero of Monte Carlo, is a civil engineer and inventor, who has been in business for about 23 years. He is a well-known figure in City circles, and is spoken of as being a very smart man. His coolness under all circumstances is proverbial amongst his intimate acquaintances. Nothing seems to disturb his equanimity whether good fortune or bad pursues him, and the fickle goddess has not always smiled upon his efforts. Indeed we may say that, like most of us, he has met with reverses, but has always, by indomitable pluck, overcome them.
>
> Whatever Mr Wells' secret is, it is evident he is a surprisingly acute man, and the only question is, Will he know when to stop, or go on until he has lost it all?

Charles Wells found himself in the unenviable position of continually having to fend off anxious enquiries from investors and creditors, while at the same time trying to generate fresh funds. Immediately before Christmas in that year of 1891, he sent a letter to Miss Phillimore – apparently from Great Portland Street – in which he wrote that he was ill and feeling 'very week [*sic*]'. He would send her a cheque very soon, he promised, and closed by wishing her the compliments of the season. On 6 January he wrote to her again, stating that he was making up for lost time and hoped to send the cheque shortly. This letter had a Liverpool address, but like the preceding one was probably written in France or Monaco and reposted in Britain to cover Wells' tracks – something he could have arranged with relative ease. Given her earlier reaction to his request for funds to gamble with, he was evidently at pains to keep her in the dark about his latest expedition to Monte Carlo.

Having told reporters that he had every faith in his 'system' and that he expected to be back soon, he kept his promise and reappeared on the evening of 7 January. Surprisingly, he turned up at the casino in the company of his wife, Marie Thérèse, from whom he had been estranged for several years. His 25-year-old daughter, Marie Antoinette, was there too. A press report of the time states that he had been staying since November at 1 Rue Saint-Roche, Paris (near where his wife lived around the time in question). The inescapable conclusion is that he had spent part of the Christmas or New Year holiday with them, and it is possible that, after a separation of some six or seven years, there was talk of a reconciliation. If so, Marie Thérèse is likely to have told him that she would only consider having him back if he gave up his dishonest activities. And perhaps, given his successes at Monte Carlo, this was a condition he could afford to agree to. But at some point in the discussions it was inevitable that the subject of Jeannette would crop up. Marie Thérèse must surely have insisted that he sever all connections with his mistress –

something that Charles found difficult even to contemplate. For the moment, he and his wife had reached an impasse.

On the evening of his arrival Charles went straight to the casino after dinner, and began to play *trente et quarante* 'with a big pile of notes'.

"Monte Carlo" Wells.

Charles De Ville Wells.

January and February were the height of the season and the salons were crowded. 'Every movement of his is watched with the greatest curiosity, and his play excites much interest,' a news agency correspondent wrote.

One account claims that Camille Blanc himself acted as *chef de partie*, and watched over the table where Wells was seated. This could have been an unnerving experience for Wells, who already found himself at a disadvantage. With his wife and daughter present, he had been obliged to abandon his habit of spending eleven solid hours at the tables. Instead he divided his time between his loved ones and the game, dropping in to the casino now and then for a few hours at a time. But the change of routine had serious consequences. 'Mr. Wells started backing both chances for one, two, and three thousand francs each, but immediately began to lose,' *The Standard* reported. 'He tried all the dodges of his famous system, but the cards kept beating him mercilessly, and when the tables closed at eleven o'clock he had lost two thousand pounds.'

On the following day he did not go to the casino until late afternoon. He had some minor wins at first, but every time he amassed some money he lost it again. 'Before the dinner hour he was cleared out of all his capital, and left the building.'

'He has several times reached the maximum amount permitted,' another report explained, 'but has invariably lost his biggest stakes. Mr Wells has now lost seventy-thousand francs since his arrival on Thursday.'

Next day he tried again. 'Mr Wells has been playing all day, but he has made no headway. On the contrary, he continues to lose,' the correspondent for *The Standard* disclosed. 'I had a conversation with him this afternoon, and I asked him how it was that the famous system, of which he boasted to me on the occasion of his last visit, had now broken down so ignominiously.'

'Oh, I am very much fatigued, and I cannot play with that care and persistency which are necessary. I have had some domestic troubles since I was last here, and I do not feel equal to sitting for twelve hours continuously at the tables.'

It seems certain that these 'domestic troubles' were to do with Marie Thérèse. He later admitted that he had lost between £3,000 and £4,000 (£300,000–£400,000) on this third visit to Monte Carlo, and explained that 'he had his wife and family there worrying him about his meals, and so preventing him from working on his usual system'. The journalist remarked that Wells looked careworn and was much thinner than before (perhaps because of the illness he had suffered around Christmas time which had made him 'very week [*sic*]').

Having breathlessly eulogised Wells when he previously broke the bank, *The Times* reverted to its customary moral stance:

> The return of Mr. Hill Wells to the gambling rooms of Monte Carlo is scarcely worthy of notice as an event of extraordinary import, because his case is simply the repetition of that of thousands of others who have had the good fortune to win large sums and then come back again to win a little more. This is only human nature, and particularly is it the nature of those under the insatiable influence of the gambling passion.

The newspaper hit back at Labouchère's accusation that its Nice correspondent had been 'hoodwinked' by Wells and his 'infallible system', adding in rather sniffy terms:

> Mr. Hill Wells is not a very fascinating personage, but he is a *bona fide* player for all that, and one doing his best to beat the bank. He came to Monte Carlo in August last and again in December*, and certainly won the large sums as telegraphed at the time ... All the [gaming] rooms are now in use, and this week another table has been added, making eight for

---

*   Actually November.

roulette and three for trente-et-quarante. They are all crowded, though there is a remarkable falling-off in the social standing of the Englishmen who frequent the rooms, which seems to be declining year by year.

The implication that Wells was of inferior breeding gave rise to a number of inaccurate and prejudiced accounts. Author Charles Kingston characterises Wells as a vulgar, scruffy, Cockney nonentity, and even tries to assert that his command of French 'was confined to the more obvious parts of the menu card' – an absurd claim, since Wells was bilingual and spoke perfect French. He may have been lacking in the finer social graces, and was sometimes rather neglectful of his appearance; however, he came from a genteel background and fully appreciated the value of being well groomed and smartly dressed when the occasion required.

But the slurs did him no harm. If anything, the description of him as an uneducated Cockney merely strengthened his growing reputation as a hero to the common man.

Charles De Ville Wells may have captured the public imagination for a few months with his gambling conquests, but he might have been quickly forgotten had it not been for Fred Gilbert – a relatively unknown 40-year-old Londoner. Gilbert was the son of a music hall comedian and had entered the entertainment business in his own right as a theatrical agent. As a sideline he also wrote songs, none of which had ever been successful enough for him to give up his day job so far.

He happened one day to be walking along the Strand, not far from London's theatre land, when he spotted a newspaper vendor's placard, which read:

THE MAN WHO BROKE THE BANK AT MONTE CARLO

Something about the phrase enthralled him: he repeated the words to himself, over and over again. And on the following day he wrote a song to fit the headline.

Gilbert was convinced that he had a hit on his hands, but now it was a question of persuading a music hall singer to take it on. He hawked it around London, offering it to some of the leading performers. Through family connections and his own contacts in the industry, he knew some of the big names, including Albert Chevalier and Walter Munroe. But they rejected the song. Gilbert then decided to send a copy to another famous singer, Charles Coborn.*

Coborn later said:

> [I] liked the tune very much, especially the chorus, but I was rather afraid that some of the phrasing was rather too highbrow for an average music hall audience. Such words as 'Sunny Southern Shore', 'Grand Triumphal Arch', … etc., seemed to me somewhat out of the reach of say Hoxton.

Coborn was, after all, an East Ender himself, and liked to think that he understood his audiences. He turned the song down, but began to have second thoughts a few hours later when he found it impossible to get the chorus out of his head. On an impulse he rushed back to Gilbert, and snapped up the singing rights for £10 before the composer had a chance to sell them to anyone else.

His initial qualm about the song was proved to be wrong: audiences in Stepney, Limehouse and Hoxton might never have been to the places mentioned in the lyric, nor were they likely to go. But the man in the street was better informed and better educated than ever before. Schooling had been compulsory for twenty years, and literacy was becoming the norm; public libraries and lectures were freely available and newspapers were cheap and ubiquitous. It was true that most of Coborn's music

---

*   Not to be confused with Charles Coburn, the American actor.

hall followers would never see the marbled halls of the casino for themselves. Many would not earn £10,000 in the whole of their working lives, let alone acquire the unimaginable sums that Wells had won in just a few days.

But they could dream about the money, the luxury and those 'sunny southern shores'. And because they could vicariously live those dreams through the medium of Charles Wells, so to speak, they held him in awe – a mythical figure who had gone to Monte Carlo as if on their behalf, a man who had sat at the tables amid the royals, the aristocrats and the millionaires *for them*. He knew how to play this role to perfection, yet he was 'not very fascinating' – a regular fellow, in other words – just like themselves.

They knew little or nothing about Wells as a man, but Wells the legend earned a place in their hearts. The song based on his adventures was rapidly adopted as a music hall standard, and was assuredly the number one hit of a generation. It earned what one commentator called 'the supreme compliment' when it began to be played on the barrel organs of London.*

The phrase that Fred Gilbert had spotted on a newsboy's placard entered the English language in mid-February 1892, when an announcement in a show-business paper, *The Era*, said that Mr Charles Coborn would be introducing a new song in his act: 'The Man Who Broke the Bank at Monte Carlo'. As far as can be ascertained, this is the first time the expression ever appeared in any newspaper, journal or book. It certainly would not be the last. Gilbert's composition helped to immortalise Charles Wells. Others before him had won fortunes at Monte Carlo (though probably not on such a large scale), but the song transformed him from just another lucky gambler into a lasting legend.

---

*   The song was popularised in the United States by vaudeville artiste Bill 'Old Hoss' Hoey. According to his obituary in the *New York Times* of 30 June 1897, many Americans believed that Hoey was the man who broke the bank – an impression he did nothing to dispel.

Ironically, just at the point where he was becoming a household name, Wells faced serious new obstacles. The losses on his last visit to Monte Carlo had severely depleted his finances. The *Palais Royal* was nearing completion at Liverpool, and was soaking up alarming amounts of money. Even as his fame was spreading through the power of the music halls and the press, Wells needed all his ingenuity to secure the cash flow that he would require in the coming weeks and months. In a letter to Miss Phillimore, he said that the English patent on his invention now had to be completed, and a French patent taken out. He offered a 'guarantee' that the ship would be floated within two weeks and asked for a further £1,500: if she could let him have this sum now she would receive at least £10,000 a short time later. As her mother had died just a few days previously, perhaps Miss Phillimore simply wanted Wells to leave her in peace. She sent the cheque.

Wells then went to work on the Honourable William Cosby Trench. He told him that the ship had been fitted with the new fuel-saving engine and would be operational within a week. In addition, a French company was to be launched to promote the invention. Trench advanced £1,500, followed by another £450.

In Liverpool, meanwhile, rumours had spread that the man who broke the bank was having an old cargo ship transformed into a splendid yacht:

> There is now lying in the Herculaneum Dock the steam yacht *Palais Royal*, belonging to Mr. Wells, of Monte Carlo fame. The yacht ... has been most elaborately fitted up with a ballroom, a dining room, a smokeroom, several state rooms, and every comfort and, indeed, luxury which could be thought of. All the fittings in the vessel are electro-plated, and the electric light is laid on throughout. The cost of the alterations has been, roughly speaking, £10,000 [£1 million], and it is estimated that the expenses of the yacht's annual maintenance will be £15,000 [£1.5 million] ... The *Palais Royal* will leave for Monte Carlo in about a week.

THE MAN WHO BROKE THE BANK AT MONTE CARLO

(Words and Music: Fred Gilbert, 1891)

I've just got here, through Paris, from the sunny southern shore;
I to Monte Carlo went, just to raise my winter's rent.
Dame Fortune smiled upon me as she'd never done before,
And I've now such lots of money, I'm a gent.
Yes, I've now such lots of money, I'm a gent.

> *As I walk along the Bois Boolong*
> *With an independent air*
> *You can hear the girls declare*
> *'He must be a millionaire.'*
> *You can hear them sigh and wish to die,*
> *You can see them wink the other eye*
> *At the man who broke the bank at Monte Carlo.*

I stay indoors till after lunch, and then my daily walk
To the great Triumphal Arch is one grand triumphal march,
Observed by each observer with the keenness of a hawk,
I'm a mass of money, linen, silk and starch -
I'm a mass of money, linen, silk and starch.

Chorus

I patronised the tables at the Monte Carlo hell
Till they hadn't got a sou for a Christian or a Jew;
So I quickly went to Paris for the charms of mad'moiselle,
Who's the lodestone of my heart - what can I do,
When with twenty tongues she swears that she'll be true?

Chorus

While work was being carried out in the dockyard, the ship became a kind of tourist attraction. A journalist wrote:

> Many visitors inspected the *Palais Royal* while she was in dock at Liverpool, and were struck with the beauty of the fittings and the completeness of the appliances. On more than one occasion Wells was to be seen reclining in luxurious ease on the comfortable lounges of the cosy saloon.

The article went on to stress that Wells' ordinary appearance gave little or no clue to the 'alertness, skill and tact which naturally go to constitute the professional gambler and successful plunger who can break a bank at roulette'.

In February, Trench went to view the *Palais Royal* for himself, and saw workmen putting the finishing touches to the elaborate decorations. As Trench later recalled, Wells was going to 'receive company promoters and Government officials on board, and show them his invention, and entertain them in the ball-room and the concert room – he offered to take me to France in her'. But, as before, Wells never kept his promise.

A few days later disaster struck. At about 1.45 in the morning of 23 February, a stove in the ballroom of the *Palais Royal* overheated and the vessel was set ablaze. Someone phoned the police station in Dale Street, and the fire brigade was sent to the Herculaneum Dock. By 2.20 a.m., the flames had been doused, but considerable damage had been done by the fire itself, and by the large quantities of water used to extinguish it.

Wells was not there at the time. In a letter to Miss Phillimore written two days after the blaze he described what had happened and told her he had lost £6,000. The insurers, he said, would not meet his claim until they had completed a full investigation. Three days later he sent a telegram to Trench: 'Sad disaster. Ship gutted by fire. All insured. Am writing. Wells.' It is not known whether the ship actually was insured, or whether anything was ever received from the insurance company. Later he wrote to Trench again asking for more money – this time promising a return of £100,000 (£10 million).

The year had hardly begun, but 1892 was already turning into a catastrophe for Charles Wells. And he experienced a further difficulty in early March. Emily Forrester, who had invested in one of Wells' patents more than three years earlier, began legal action against him in the Bloomsbury County Court. Mrs Forrester was now a widow, her husband having died since she was first in contact with Wells.

Her lawyer told the court that she had 'foolishly' replied to the advertisement in late 1888, and invested £30. Since then she had received letters from Wells which had been posted from Paris and Marseille. This, the advocate said, was when he was breaking the bank at Monte Carlo. He considered that if Wells went into the witness box the scheme would be unmasked as a swindle.

The judge did not quite agree. Inventors always had high hopes for their ideas, which could sometimes take longer than expected to bear fruit. It would be a different matter, he admitted, if it could be shown that the money had been spent on riotous living. Mrs Forrester's lawyer quickly responded. 'Perhaps I *can* prove that,' he said. Mrs Forrester herself was then called upon to give evidence. She was certain that the whole thing was fraudulent, she said, and that Wells had gambled with her money at Monte Carlo. She did, however, admit to having seen a model of the invention, and to having said that she thought it must be valuable.

Wells reserved his right not to enter the witness box. The judge said that the action had been brought prematurely. He hoped that the plaintiff had not lost her money, and perhaps the day would come when she would recover it. If not, she would not be the first person to lose money by speculation. He then dismissed the case. It was a victory for Wells, but not a resounding one: he had a number of other investors, most of whom were growing impatient, and knew that any one of them might follow Mrs Forrester's lead and take him to court. Most of them had read about his Monte Carlo exploits, and they probably all believed that he 'must be a millionaire' and therefore well worth suing. And another judge on another day might come to a different decision from the first one.

Incidentally, the *Yorkshire Evening Post* had published its report on the case under the heading, 'ACTION AGAINST MONTE CARLO WELLS'. The name stuck. Thereafter, he was almost invariably called 'Monte Carlo Wells'.

8

The Biggest Swindler

The fire on board *Palais Royal* had been a greater setback than Wells cared to admit. Repairing the damage would take a long time, and he found himself once more in serious financial difficulties. Despite this, he put on a brave face and contacted Trench again to say he was going to install new engines in a larger vessel. 'Now all is right and our harvest is here,' he wrote. However, the true situation must have been dire because in April he sold the casino shares he had purchased only a few weeks earlier.

Although he had promised Miss Phillimore the enormous sum of £10,000 by mid-March, this sum did not materialise. Instead, using the same tactic he had previously employed with William Trench, he persuaded her to part with a further £1,300: in return he undertook to send £11,000 within a month, plus a £100,000 share in the patent. Miss Phillimore trustingly posted another cheque to him. But instead of cash, Wells sent a bundle of 'share certificates', as he called them, in an envelope with a Paris postmark. The shares, he informed her, were in a new company he had formed to promote his inventions – Charles Wells & Co.

Next, he sent a telegram from Menton requesting another £2,000. This time he said he was carrying on important negotiations with the Italian government regarding the sale of an invention. There can be little doubt that he was actually at Monte Carlo and, to cover his tracks, was writing from other nearby towns, Menton being only 12 miles from Monte Carlo. Around the end of April, Wells asked for yet more money, promising a return of £25,000 by the end of the month. For the first time Miss Phillimore appears to have hesitated. However, Wells evidently came up with a convincing response, because in a letter of 9 May she agrees to pay £3,000 into his bank, and virtually apologises for having had misgivings. She emphasises that she has 'full confidence' in him, and is 'sure he would fulfil his promise to pay the £25,000 at the end of May'.

A flurry of letters and telegrams went to and fro until 20 May, when Wells asked for a further £1,200 and promised £150,000 'from Russia'. He was now, he said, only short of the 'miserable amount' of £500. Although her confidence in Wells was starting to fade again, Miss Phillimore grudgingly paid that sum into his account.

When he did not send any of the money he had promised, Miss Phillimore did what she should have done a long time previously: she consulted her brother, Sir Walter Phillimore, the judge. He advised her to see her solicitor, James Sykes. He, in turn, tried to call on Wells at Great Portland Street. Mr Wells was not in the office, he was told.

On 20 June, a writ was issued against Charles Wells on Miss Phillimore's behalf, and judgement was obtained for £18,860 (about £2 million). Wells replied three days later to say that he regretted being away at this important time. The attempt to serve him with a summons was ill-conceived, he claimed, because the publicity would be harmful to them both. Soon afterwards he sent another letter in his own handwriting, but on paper headed 'Wells, Phillimore & Co.' He addressed her as 'madam and honoured partner' and stated that all of the members were liable for any debts of the company, and claimed that if they ruined him they would ruin Miss Phillimore, too, 'unless she had many millions'. No one could deny that Miss Phillimore had received the shares, he said, and the value of those shares was beyond his control. All shareholders were equally liable, especially 'founders'. He closed his letter with a jibe at Sykes, the solicitor, claiming that lawyers always tried to make money out of their clients: 'Very scarce are solicitors who impress upon their clients the wisdom of an arrangement instead of a costly law suit.' They seemed to think that Wells was a silly fool and that they could get hold of his property. Wells said he knew little about the law, but he had a certain dose of common sense.

For the next part of the intrigue Wells went back to the legal clerk whom he had employed previously – Henry Baker Vaughan. Wells explained that he had won a fortune at Monte Carlo and that he was starting a company in France. He had hinted for some time that he would give Vaughan some kind of administrative role in his affairs, and said the time had come to appoint him company secretary. But Vaughan was not to discuss the matter with Wells' manager, Hermann Eschen, who might be jealous. Wells offered to take Vaughan on an expenses paid trip to Paris, and promised to give him £1 per day for the duration of the visit. In the event, this was hardly a crippling financial burden for Wells, as they were not gone for more than two days. In fact, the whole expedition seems to have been conducted at whirlwind speed.

On arrival in Paris they first went to the Hôtel Terminus. Wells dashed out on some errand leaving Vaughan on his own, but he returned later and gave him a document to copy. This was an affidavit to say that he, Vaughan, was the company secretary of Wells, Phillimore & Co., which had offices at 16 Rue de Surène. Later, Vaughan asked if he could see these offices and, as they sped through the city in a horse-drawn cab, with an airy wave of his hand Wells pointed out the street where the company was allegedly based. Conversations with various people took place in French, which the bewildered Vaughan did not understand. They drew up outside a building which turned out to be the British Consul's office, and once inside Vaughan was instructed to swear the affidavit. Caught up in this frenzy of activity he did so, against his better judgement.

On his return to Britain, Wells decided that it was time for the Honourable William Trench to make another contribution. On 13 July, he wrote to the young aristocrat saying that yet another new company – 'Wells, Phillimore, Trench & Co.' – had been formed in Paris to exploit the invention, and that the further sum of £1,500 was urgently needed, as otherwise the partners would all be ruined. The company was not limited, he claimed, and therefore the shareholders were fully liable for any debts.

Trench must by now have had his own doubts about Wells. Before handing over the money Trench arranged to meet Wells at Drummond's Bank – an institution patronised by the elite of British society, including members of the royal family. This was where Trench's account was held. Trench insisted that he would only advance more funds if Wells could provide security. Wells offered three of his boats: the small steam launch *Flyer*, in which Trench had travelled on the Thames, and two yachts, *Isabella* and *Ituna*. Apparently satisfied that these assets were good collateral for a loan, Trench then handed over the £1,500 that Wells asked for.

Soon afterwards Wells sent a telegram: 'Bad news from Paris. Company not being limited all shareholders are responsible.' He wrote:

> I must explain what I thought you knew very well. A shareholder is liable to pay up to any extent – even millions, as the company is not limited. Each shareholder is liable to pay the whole. If a shareholder prefers to go bankrupt, then the liabilities fall on any other shareholder. You are a shareholder for the moment. You seem to have taken the matter very coolly, but it is very grave, I assure you.

He ended by saying that Trench must stump up another £10,000 (£1 million) or else they would all be liable for debts of £50,000 (£5 million) in a few days. Finally the truth dawned on Trench. What Wells had told him must be wrong. Although the young aristocrat was inexperienced in these matters, he did not believe that the law could be so unfair, and he consulted his solicitors, Hughes & Gleadow. Trench and Wells went together to the firm's offices in Gracechurch Street. Wells gave his version of the situation, emphasising that Trench was liable for the company debts, and offering to free him from his obligation in exchange for the sum of £2,500. When quizzed by solicitor Paul Gleadow, Wells said that the company of Wells, Phillimore, Trench & Co. had no books of account and no list of shareholders. Only he, Charles Wells, knew the value of the shares.

At one point Trench lost his temper and threatened to punch Wells, who begged Trench not to hit him, as he was 'a family man'. He didn't mind being 'punched by the law', he said – with a sly glance at the solicitor, no doubt. He 'had had encounters of that kind and had come out of them successfully'. The meeting produced no useful result, and Trench and Wells went their separate ways.

Trench next received a notice from Wells inviting him to a company meeting in Paris. Trench's lawyer, Gleadow, decided to look into the matter further and went to Paris to make enquiries. First he went to 16 Rue de Surène, the supposed offices of Wells, Phillimore, Trench & Co. There was no trace of the company, not even a brass plate at the door. The concierge told him that Wells had once lived in a room there, and had then reserved some office space in the building, but when his furniture was delivered it was of such poor quality that the concierge declined to accept Wells as a tenant.

Paul Gleadow then made his way to the Hôtel Terminus, where the company meeting was due to take place. On reaching Wells' room he heard women's voices from within. Wells came to the door. He seemed shocked to see Gleadow and was dumbfounded when the lawyer told him that he had been to the place where the company's office was supposed to have been. Recovering his poise, Wells said that Gleadow was too late: the meeting had already ended. As Gleadow later recalled:

> I asked him where the meeting was held ... who attended it, and what was done. He declined to tell me. I said the whole thing was a fraud, that the patent was invalid, and I had the proof – the certificate of abandonment, that is, that the patent had been abandoned. ... I said the whole thing was a swindle and a fraud. There was a somewhat heated argument – he said he would have me thrown out of his hotel [and] I then left.

With both Miss Phillimore and the Hon. William Trench firmly out of the picture as far as funding was concerned, Wells was forced to look elsewhere. Reluctantly, he fell back on the old patent scam again and began to advertise. This time the promised rewards were more generous than ever before.

Wells was growing desperate, and it showed. The offer seemed far too good to be true, and only one investor is known to have come forward. Frederic Hooper Aldrich-Blake was a young clergyman, not quite 30 years of age, who had graduated from Pembroke College, Cambridge, with a master's degree. In contrast to the stereotypical nineteenth-century vicar, he had been a keen sportsman and a particularly talented tennis player. Three years earlier he had been appointed vicar of Bishopswood, near Ross-on-Wye, Herefordshire.

Wells proceeded to give him the usual sales pitch about an improved steam engine with a fuel saving of at least 50 per cent. He said he needed £1,500 to develop it, and undertook to provide a steamboat for demonstrations. As was his custom, he offered Blake a quarter of all profits, and he would retain the rest himself. Wells said he was an experienced engineer, '45 years of age' (he was actually 51), who would not take his clients' money without being quite sure of the results. He posted his bank passbook to Blake to prove the large sums passing through his hands, and to show himself as 'a man of position'.

Blake confessed that he knew nothing whatsoever about steam engines, but offered an investment of £750 – half the amount that Wells said he needed. Wells agreed to this, adding that he guaranteed a return of £50,000, and if this result was not achieved he, Wells, would refund all of Blake's outlay. On the strength of these representations Blake sent a cheque.

On 25 July Charles Wells filed Patent No. 13,545 of 1892 (under the now predictable heading of 'steam engines'). The Reverend Blake seems to have been his only 'catch' on this occasion, because this was the only patent Wells registered in the whole of that year. In fact, it was the last British patent ever to be recorded in the name of Charles Wells.

Blake later met Wells at Great Portland Street, and was introduced to Eschen. Wells assured him that work was proceeding and the machinery would shortly be installed on board a ship at Liverpool. Blake could not help noticing that the office was empty, but Wells explained the absence of any clerks by saying that he had given up his ordinary business for the time being so as to be able to concentrate on the present invention. Blake must have been satisfied by this explanation, as he then gave Wells another cheque for £750, on the promise of a further £100,000 which would be paid when the invention was sold.

Wells reported on progress from time to time. Things were going splendidly, he said, and there were good prospects in Germany and Italy. Large sums of money would be on their way to Blake within the month. Wells generously offered to let Blake have his money first as he, Wells, could wait. On 12 September he wrote, 'Herewith I have the pleasure to send you £3,000' as the first instalment of the profits. This was only a start, he said. There was just one slight drawback: as before, the payment was in 'shares'. Wells said he would soon be able to exchange these for cash. And the cash payments would begin at the end of the month, by which time the shares would have doubled or trebled in value. He then asked for a further £500, but Blake declined.

In Liverpool remedial work on the fire-damaged yacht was well advanced. Wells had even engaged a specialist to carry out repairs to the piano – 'to the tune [!] of £69', according to one source.

It was time for the yacht to make its first voyage since its reincarnation as *Palais Royal*. In mid-August Wells came to the docks with Jeannette, and Vergis, now described as his agent, was there to see them off. Wells ordered Captain Smith to make the vessel ready to sail. However, Smith had been growing deeply disillusioned with the job. He had been captain of the ship for ten months and Wells had told him they would be going to Monte Carlo, Nice and other exotic places. Instead he had sat around commanding a vessel which had not so much as moved out of its dock in Liverpool and the only excitement had been when the ship caught fire. It was, he said, 'too easy a berth' for him. He had repeatedly asked Wells to sign his contract of employment, but for some reason Wells would not do so, and now his patience was at an end. An argument started between the two men: Smith called Wells a rogue, refused to sail the ship out of Liverpool and, despite Vergis' attempt to pacify him, quit the appointment.

First Officer Thomas Johnston was now instructed to take command of the vessel. On Saturday, 20 August the *Palais Royal* sailed majestically down the River Mersey and out to sea, with Wells and Jeannette on board. The newly refurbished ship must have been a magnificent sight with her eighteen-man crew smartly turned out in their brand new uniforms, which had cost Wells no less than £10 (£1,000) apiece.

The sea was smooth and the winds light as the ship steamed southward along the coast. Next morning they awoke to a fine, very warm day as they rounded the south-western tip of Cornwall, and finally reached Plymouth. Here the vessel was moored in the

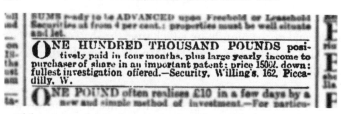

Blake answered this advertisement in *The Standard*, 16 June 1892.

Great Western Docks, near where Charles Wells had lived with his wife and daughter some seven or eight years earlier.

Wells engaged a prominent local engineering firm, Willoughby Brothers, to finish the alterations, reconstruct the saloon and provide new machinery – a contract worth several thousand pounds, on which numerous men were employed. Wells and Jeannette lived on board while this work was being carried out. He spent much of his time supervising the project, but sometimes he indulged his passion for fishing. At other times he was away for several days on end. One of these trips was to Paris, where he called on a Madame Bichet, who ran a lodging house at 35 Rue de Londres. He took a room there, either to provide himself with a bolthole in France for when things became too hot for him in England, or as a convenient address in France for receiving mail.

Since the Reverend Blake had been so reluctant to part with any more money, Wells resorted to blackmail, adopting the same tactics he had used on Miss Phillimore and Mr Trench. He told Blake that the company was not limited, that all shareholders would be ruined unless Blake paid. He even threatened to contact Blake's father, a senior churchman. On the other hand, he wrote, the small sum of £1,000 (£100,000) would prevent disaster, and all would be 'bright and happy forever'. But the clergyman was made of sterner stuff than Wells had realised, and refused to pay. Instead, he returned the shares, and sent a letter to Wells at the Rue de Londres address, informing him that he no longer wanted anything to do with him or his inventions. This letter was subsequently returned via the Dead Letter Office.

Wells had already defended himself successfully in a civil action, when Emily Forrester had taken him to court. But now much more serious criminal proceedings appeared inevitable. If he was arrested, his world would rapidly fall apart. He instantly realised that he must have an escape plan, and that the *Palais Royal* would play an important part in this. But first the work to the ship needed to be finished, and he was running out of money again.

In a desperate move, on 3 October he borrowed £1,535 (about £150,000) from a finance house in the City of London, pledging the Palais Royal as security. In doing so, he surrendered his outright ownership of the vessel, something he was doubtless very reluctant to do. And the fact that he agreed to pay interest at the exorbitant rate of 20 per cent simply underlines the seriousness of his situation. Then, when it seemed that things could get no worse, a new article from Henry Labouchère appeared:

THE BIGGEST SWINDLER LIVING

Readers of *Truth* are familiar – too familiar, I fear – with the name of 'C. Wells,' the fraudulent patent-monger, who carries on business in Great Titchfield Street,[*] London, W. For nearly three years past I have been doing my best to warn the public against the machinations of this unscrupulous villain. But there are certain members of the great British public who, unfortunately for themselves do not read *Truth*, and from among these Wells continues to find victims. Encouraged by the impunity which he enjoys, and the co-operation of some of the leading London papers, he has grown even bolder, and some of his latest coups have been on such a scale that I am quite prepared to find the facts received with incredulity.

---

[*]   Labouchère overlooks the fact that Wells' headquarters were now in Great Portland Street.

The article then goes on to mention – without disclosing their names – a lady who had entrusted Wells with £18,000 (doubtless Miss Phillimore), a gentleman who had invested £10,000 (Trench) and another (unknown) who parted with £4,000–5,000. Labouchère asks, firstly, how it could be that 'Wells of Monte Carlo' needs to continue with these frauds if he did in fact win 'the large sums which he was credited with in sensational telegrams emanating from unknown sources at Monte Carlo'. And, secondly, he asks why Wells has not yet been prosecuted, and urges any of Wells' other victims to come forward and testify in the interests of justice.

A pivotal moment followed on the morning of 16 November in the High Court of Justice, when a man named Harris, who had invested £240 in one of Wells' patents, finally brought civil proceedings. Harris claimed repayment of the £240, with an additional £1,000 in damages. Wells had made fraudulent misrepresentations, he claimed, and there had been a breach of contract. It may be that Wells could have avoided a great deal of trouble if he had made an out-of-court settlement. But clearly he did not have the money to do so or decided to take a chance and contest Harris's claim.

Harris' counsel described how Wells had obtained funds 'mostly from widows and unprotected ladies'. There were, he added, 'a large number of people who had been victims of this heartless swindle', and he said the public should be made aware of it.

Wells was present in the courtroom, but – once again – took no part in the proceedings. His lawyer tried to argue on his behalf that as the sum of £240 was not disputed, there was no need to go into the alleged fraud.

The judge disagreed. If the allegations were true it was a matter for the criminal courts, and the Public Prosecutor should be informed. The barrister representing Harris left the public in no doubt when he said, 'I think it should be known that the address of Mr Charles Wells is 154 and 156 Great Portland Street.'

Charles realised that the game was finally up and hurried out of the courtroom. It seems that one or more of his opponents were waiting for him: at any rate, Wells was apparently punched. Nursing a swollen eye, he dashed round to his bank in Sloane Square and withdrew £5,000 from his account, leaving a balance of 5 shillings. Finally, at Paddington Station, he caught the overnight train to Plymouth, where Jeannette anxiously awaited him on board the *Palais Royal*.

The train drew into Millbay Station just before 5.00 a.m. Charles 'instructed the cabman to drive with all speed to the yacht, where he told the engineer to get up steam to be away as quickly as possible' and sail to France. Workmen scrambled to gather their belongings together at such short notice. Some reports suggest that the ship left so abruptly that some of the workers did not even have time to disembark and had to remain on board for the journey. Another, more plausible, version of this story is that Wells had intended to make London his first port of call before proceeding to the Continent. He had at first offered to give two workmen who lived in the capital a lift home. However, as he risked being arrested, he seems to have had second thoughts about the stop in London, and the ship sailed straight to France instead.

Alexander Ferguson, a Scotsman in his early thirties, was second engineer on board. 'There was a small leak in the boiler at the back of the furnace leading into the combustion chamber,' he later recalled. 'Wells said he did not intend to do much to the boilers as he intended to take the fronts out altogether when he got to Marseilles.' As trivial as the exchange may seem, it demonstrates Wells' confidence in engineering matters, even when the task ahead was a difficult one. And with remarkable sangfroid for a man on the run, Wells calmly informed Ferguson that he also intended to complete the alterations to the ballroom once they reached Marseille.

The ship stopped at Brest, then went on to Cherbourg, where five of the crew left. 'We remained in Cherbourg about a week,' Ferguson said. '[Wells] was going to meet a friend, but I do not know that anyone came.' Ferguson heard some talk of proceeding to Lisbon. This would have been a shrewd move on Wells' part, as Britain and Portugal did not have reciprocal agreements on extradition. However, the crew's articles* would not permit them to go any further than Brest.

'We could not go to Lisbon,' Ferguson explained. 'We were under coasting articles, and if we had gone beyond the coast we should have had the Board of Trade after us, and had no protection from the English Consul.' Instead, they proceeded eastwards to the port of Le Havre.

A few days later, Detective Inspector Charles Richards went to 154–156 Great Portland Street to search the premises. Just inside the front door stood a large cannon, he noted. In the office upstairs he found a copy of *Truth* from March 1890, in which Wells was mentioned (see page 65). There was also a quantity of the headed paper Wells had used for his letters to Miss Phillimore. Printed down one side was a list of the various departments supposedly located at the property, but, on looking around, the officer could see no evidence of the 'electrical department', or of the 'chemical laboratory and testing department', or 'machinery in all its branches' – unless, by some stretch of the imagination, this description extended to the old traction engine, a weighing machine, two pumps and a few lengths of pipe.

What he did find, though, was a large quantity of papers, which he collected together and took away with him as evidence.

It was a dull November day with temperatures hovering just above freezing point when the *Palais Royal* moored alongside the Quai de la Seine at Le Havre. Charles Wells was so short of ready cash that he made it known in the town that he was

---

*   In effect, their contracts of employment.

prepared to sell 100 tons of coal from the ship's bunkers. When two smartly dressed gentlemen came marching purposefully along the quayside and boarded the vessel he assumed that they were coal merchants who had come to make an offer. He was mistaken. Britain had applied to France for his extradition. The men were French detectives and brought with them a warrant for his arrest.

The exchange that followed was farcical. The individual who greeted them matched a description of the man wanted by the British authorities: 'age 50, height 5 feet 4 inches, hair whiskers and moustaches dark (turning grey), very bald, supposed black eye'. There was one discrepancy, though. The fugitive was described as an Englishman, whereas this character insisted that he was French. Indeed, 'his French was so pure that the detectives were for a moment half inclined to imagine they had got hold of the wrong man'. The ensuing conversation did not exactly clarify matters.

'Who am I? It's not my business to find out, it's yours,' said Wells.

Charles and Jeannette were placed under arrest and taken to the local jail. The Public Prosecutor ordered his men to search the *Palais Royal*, and maritime police officers were left to guard the vessel. Under questioning, Wells admitted his true identity, and boasted that he had recently broken the bank at Monte Carlo. At the time of his arrest, though, he had only 24fr. (less than £1) in his pocket.

The story of Wells' exceptional success at the gaming tables had so far attracted little or no attention in the French press. But the arrest of this mysterious Englishman and his 'niece' on a yacht of gargantuan size set the pages of the Paris newspapers ablaze. Motivated more by sensationalism than by any quest for accuracy, *Le Figaro* claimed, 'The magnificent English yacht *Palais Royal*, well known on the shores of the Channel and the Mediterranean, having moored more than once at Nice, arrived yesterday at Le Havre from Cherbourg'.[*] According to the article, Wells was 'one of the richest men in England'. Other dispatches claimed that he had been on the point of leaving for Lisbon, and was only waiting for the tide to turn before doing so. 'Wells is the man who twice broke the bank at Monte Carlo,' declared an overexcited columnist. 'He owns several yachts known as "the Monte Carlo Fleet".'

The fact that he was accompanied by an attractive woman half his age added spice to the story. 'Charles Wells, the adventurous man whom *Truth* has pilloried and assailed with vigour, bids fair to provide us with a romantic titbit for conversation at Christmastide,' a British journal, the *Penny Illustrated*, reflected, adding that 'a young woman who appeared greatly attached to him was found in his company on board the *Palais Royal*'. Jeannette's identity remained a mystery until a resourceful journalist probed a little more deeply than his rivals had done, and revealed that 'she is the daughter of a railway employee from Reims, who recently died'. But this was only part of the story.

Marie Jeanne Pairis was born in 1869 in the Alsace region of France at Mulhouse, an industrial town on the French–German border. Culturally and linguistically, Alsace had always been heavily influenced by its immediate neighbour: most people spoke German as their first language and many had German surnames.

---

[*]   In reality, the only journeys Wells ever made in the ship were from Liverpool to Plymouth and then from Plymouth to Le Havre via Brest and Cherbourg. (*Financial Times*, 4 April 1893.) Many accounts in books and periodicals describe imaginary voyages with prominent guests being entertained on board. One describes a glittering, but wholly fictitious, dinner attended by 'five British peers … with their wives, and a German millionaire, three American millionaires and a distinguished French diplomat'. (Fielding, p.95.) But no doubt this is the sort of thing Charles Wells had in mind when he bought the ship.

Jeannette – as she was generally known – was the second of eight children born to Georges Constant Pairis and Marie Pairis (née Busch), who had married in 1867 when he was 26 and she was only 16. Georges secured a job with the Eastern Railway of France as a kind of travelling deputy stationmaster. If a local official at one of the smaller stations was indisposed or on leave, Georges was sent there to stand in. The company controlled a railway line extending from Paris to Basel, via Strasbourg, and the family's life was mapped out between points on this line as Georges was dispatched from one place to another.

All was well until the eve of Jeannette's first birthday, when the Franco-Prussian War began. The Prussians invaded Alsace and absorbed the region into the German Empire. The invaders had believed at first that the local population would welcome them as liberators, but in reality – despite the people's strong Germanic roots – very few welcomed the Prussians. Along with some half a million others, the Pairis family became refugees, scrambling and jostling at the railway station and fighting for a place on one of the trains leaving for the unoccupied parts of France. The family settled near the city of Reims, an important route centre on the Eastern Railway some 80 miles to the northeast of Paris.

A law was passed to the effect that any former inhabitants of Alsace who had migrated in this way could retain their French nationality provided they pledged their allegiance to the country, and undertook not to return to Alsace. In July 1872, 3-year-old Jeannette, her elder sister Léonie and a younger sibling, were taken to the *mairie* by their parents, who completed the formalities enabling them all to remain French citizens.

By the time Jeannette was 10, her mother was about to give birth to her eighth child. However, some grave complication must have arisen, as the baby lived for only one day and the mother died three weeks afterwards. Jeannette's father remarried a year later, and it seems that he still preferred younger women, as he was now 40 and his new bride was only 20. This meant that only about ten years separated Jeannette and her stepmother. Friction can often exist between children and a step-parent, but in this case the situation was serious. Georges' new spouse had eyes for him alone – not for his brood of seven children. And to make things worse, as far as Jeannette was concerned, a new stepbrother and stepsister promptly came along.

All of the children of Georges' first marriage were then split up and farmed out to various families. The details are unclear, but it is quite likely that Jeannette and her older sister became little more than unpaid servants to their new hosts. Anxious to escape this loveless, Cinderella-like existence, Jeannette eventually made the daunting journey to London on her own – an extremely courageous and possibly dangerous move in those days for a young woman in her teens or early twenties.

While contact with the rest of her brothers and sisters appears to have been sporadic, she seems to have been in regular communication with her elder sister, Léonie. In letters from Britain, Jeannette wrote that she was engaged to an English aristocrat; that he had unexpectedly died just before the wedding; and that his family had rejected her, and left her to fend for herself in a foreign country. The story seemed highly implausible, but it was all Léonie and the others had to go on.

Jeannette was an attractive young woman with remarkable strength of character and a keen sense of adventure. Yet she desperately needed love, stability and material comfort. When Charles De Ville Wells came into her life around 1890 he was able to provide her with these advantages, and a passionate love affair developed between them. There would be times when Charles was on top of the world; and times of great hardship, too. The bond between them survived these extremes of fortune – even though their life together was not always plain sailing.

9

The Darling of the Hour

The arrest of 'Monte Carlo Wells' at le Havre was received in Britain with shock, dismay and disbelief. Headlines in the papers such as, 'SENSATIONAL ARREST FOR FRAUD' and 'THE HERO OF MONTE CARLO' trumpeted the news:

> Monte Carlo Wells was for the time the most famous man in Europe. He eclipsed every other social notable. His wealth was supposed to be immense, and everything he touched turned into gold. He became the theme of every music hall and pantomime ditty. No comedy of the day was complete without a reference to the man who broke the bank. ... Suddenly there came the crash, and the public learned *with pain and surprise that the darling of the hour had been arrested ...'* [Author's italics]

Readers were reminded of Labouchère's repeated attacks on Wells in the pages of *Truth*, and there was much conjecture on the outcome of any prosecution, which now seemed inevitable. 'Perhaps Mr. Charles Wells will emerge triumphant from the web which Mr. Labouchère has been weaving for so long. The man who broke the bank at Monte Carlo ought, at

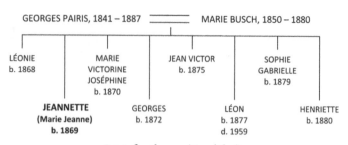

Pairis family tree (simplified).

all events, to make a good fight even against so redoubtable an antagonist.'

Wells initially tried to prevent his deportation to Britain by declaring that he was a French subject. However, since he could not possibly substantiate this claim, he later retracted. In his prison cell at Le Havre, he had plenty of time to reflect. At any time someone might discover his crimes in Paris a decade ago, when he had fled the country and been sentenced in his absence. He weighed up the odds, as any gambler would: wait around and serve a two-year prison sentence in France – or stand trial in Britain with a chance of being acquitted. After some thought, he agreed to being handed over to the British authorities without the formalities of a long-winded extradition procedure.

On 9 December, Wells was led into a Le Havre courtroom by two gendarmes. He walked unsteadily and appeared to have suffered a wound to his head. Since arriving in France he had incurred debts, and a Cherbourg businessman had applied for the *Palais Royal* to be impounded until Wells had settled his account. A large unpaid invoice from the shipbuilders in England had also caught up with him. Today he was to be examined over these liabilities.

While giving evidence he replied in a faint voice and appeared somewhat confused. In answer to the judge's questioning, he said he had spent £20,000 on repairs to the *Palais Royal*. He was rather hazy about the vessel's present value, however, and also neglected to mention that the ship was already mortgaged in Britain. He told the court:

> I recognise the debts contracted by me at Le Havre and Cherbourg, particularly to M. Martin of Cherbourg, but cannot accept the English ship-builder's invoice. As it is necessary for you to appoint an administrator for my yacht, choose a competent person, because the vessel needs skilled care. In addition, the ship has on board numerous valuable objects, including statues. I insist that an inventory of these goods be made, and a copy given to the captain.

The wound to his head prompted claims that Wells had tried to commit suicide by banging his head against the wall of his cell. However, this rumour was dispelled by a report in *Le Temps*:

> Since his arrest, and contrary to reports, Charles Wells has shown himself to be in good spirits, and, last evening, when officers told him that it had been announced that he had made a suicide attempt he burst out laughing. The owner of the 'Monte Carlo fleet' never considered suicide.

It was Jeannette, the newspaper claimed, who had threatened suicide, as she was now left high and dry in France with no funds whatsoever. The Public Prosecutor eventually accepted that she had not participated in any of Wells' frauds, took pity on her, and gave her the fare back to London.

Shortly afterwards, Wells wrote two letters from his cell. The first was addressed to his agent, Aristides Vergis, asking him to take care of Jeannette. The other was to Jeannette herself, telling her that she could have certain articles at the house in Great Portland Street. He ended by saying, 'Don't forget anything. Remember the desk with pigeon-holes.'*

He told reporters that he was sanguine about his return to Britain, and had nothing to fear from the British judges. After all, he said, he just owed some debts, which he would easily be able to repay at some convenient time in the future.

He was due to be handed over to the British police on 12 December, but the documents from London were not delivered in time for this to take place. Then, on the very next day, a local man turned up at the jail and asked if he might be allowed to see the prisoner in his cell. Of all the ports he could have picked, Wells had made the worst possible choice. The man in question was the sea captain from Le Havre who, almost ten years earlier, had invested in the phoney railway at Berck-sur-Mer. He identified Wells as the man who had absconded with his 15,000fr.

British detectives arrived, meanwhile, expecting to take Wells back with them. But this most recent development forced them to return empty handed. The French authorities debated whether to enforce the prison sentence which had been imposed on 'Will-Wells' in his absence years ago.

Christmas came and went, as did New Year. Wells remained in his cell while his fate was decided. France's statute of limitations extended for ten years from the date of the crime. But although, strictly speaking, this period had not quite elapsed, it was clear

---

* The precise contents of this desk were never revealed, but one item it almost certainly contained was the key to Wells' safe deposit box in Chancery Lane. This key never was found. As bailiffs were in attendance at the same time as Richards was conducting his search, it is quite possible that they had already removed the desk and its contents. Wells had probably intended to go to Great Portland Street to remove any incriminating items, but – as mentioned above – he evidently decided against returning to his London office and running the risk of being apprehended. (Bankruptcy, 1893, opening remarks (probably read out from Wells' own statement of affairs).)

that *some* of the crimes had taken place months earlier, and could not therefore be introduced as evidence. Since a conviction was by no means certain, the French authorities decided not to proceed. Besides, the prisoner was proving to be a nuisance and they were finally 'only too glad to get rid of Wells'.

Appallingly bad weather marked the beginning of 1893. In Paris the thermometer fell to 6 degrees below freezing and the River Seine froze. Snow fell all over northern France. Life in a prison cell is not conducive to the health of a bronchitis sufferer like Charles Wells at the best of times, and the intense cold and damp, combined with the grey skies, must have added to his misery.

Palais Royal was moved to an immense dock close to the town centre, the Bassin du Commerce, where it was moored near the *Velléda*. This vessel was owned by Henri Menier, vice president of an important French yacht club and heir to a renowned chocolate manufacturer. A press report declared that *Velléda*, one of the most beautiful – and largest – of all French yachts, looked insignificant beside Wells' ship. The *Palais Royal* would probably be sold at Le Havre, but it was recognised that its immense proportions might make it an unattractive proposition for ordinary yachtsmen. To make it a little more appealing, all of the furniture and fittings were stripped out to be sold separately.

Wells' dreams were crumbling and he was powerless to prevent it. To add to his problems, a bankruptcy petition was served on him while he was in the prison. The tailor who had made his crew's new uniforms, a man named Jupp, had still not been paid for them, and could no longer afford to wait for his money. This action had an immediate and devastating effect on Wells: with a pending bankruptcy he could no longer borrow money to cover his needs, or even access any funds of his own.

On Saturday, 14 January, two British detectives disembarked at Le Havre for a second time with twenty-four warrants from the Bow Street Court. They planned to take Wells back with them on that evening's ferry, but Wells was said to be 'seriously ill' with bronchitis, and their departure was delayed another two days. Finally, French police took Wells to the harbour, and handed him over to detectives Dinnie and McCarthy of Scotland Yard, along with a large bundle of papers which had been found on *Palais Royal*. After they had boarded the steamer, Dinnie formally read out to Wells the twenty-four warrants – some for fraud, some for theft.

Wells was shaken. 'I knew of the cases of fraud,' he replied, 'but not the larcenies.'*

The overnight ferry *Wolf* left Le Havre around 10.00 that evening with Wells and the two detectives. The ship 'had nothing about it in terms of elegance or comfort to remind him of his beautiful yacht the *Palais Royal*, currently surrounded by ice in the Bassin du Commerce'. Had it not been dark as they pulled away from the quayside, it is just possible that Wells might have glimpsed the very top of his yacht's masts above the rooftops of the town. The reality was that he would never see his beloved ship again.

Wolf had made this same journey countless times, but after thirty years of service she was nearing the end of her days. Her antiquated engines battled against violent winds and massive waves. Inspector Walter Dinnie, Detective McCarthy, and Charles Wells settled down to the long overnight crossing. Dinnie and Wells were ill-matched travelling companions: both were sons of poets, but they had nothing else in common.

Dinnie was almost ten years younger than Wells, having been born in Aberdeenshire, Scotland, on Boxing Day, 1850. His eldest brother, Donald, a renowned gymnast, was variously described as the 'greatest athlete in the world' and 'the world's strongest man'. Walter was also a keen sportsman, though he never matched his brother's prowess in that sphere. Instead he joined the Metropolitan Police in 1876 and became an inspector

---

*	Larceny (theft) carried a maximum sentence of fourteen years, and was usually easier to prove than fraud.

in 1889. He was a hard-working, straight-laced egotist, who did everything by the book and took an exceptionally dim view of gambling. Quite what he made of Wells, the bank-breaker of Monte Carlo, we can but guess. Nevertheless, Wells was reported as being 'lively and talkative' during the voyage. Polite as ever, he thanked the detectives for allowing him time to recover from his illness before making the journey.

Finally, the ferry reached Southampton at 8.00 a.m., over an hour late. The detectives had to help Wells walk from the quayside to their reserved second-class compartment on the train. Detective Inspector Richards – the officer who had searched the Great Portland Street building – met them at Waterloo Station and they all went by cab straight to Bow Street Magistrates' Court where, again, officers helped him to alight. A little crowd had gathered outside, but no one seemed to recognise 'the Monte Carlo Hero', as some newspapers still called him.

This comes as no surprise. If they were expecting to see the debonair young blade described in the music hall song they would have been disappointed. Wells was dressed in a shabby blue overcoat, so long that it reached his ankles. He wore a soft Alpine hat, pulled down over his eyes so that his face was hardly visible. He looked extremely ill and dishevelled. In the words of one onlooker, he was of 'somewhat common-place appearance, apparently rather over middle age, somewhat under average height ... somewhat stout ...'

> He was somewhat unkempt in appearance, his linen being stained, and his clothes having none of that exquisite fit with which the Wells of a more prosperous period was associated. He looked ill and miserable [and] walked lamely ...

A few weeks in a French jail, followed by a return to the cold, damp, smoke-filled air of London had aggravated his chest condition and his cough was 'quite painful to listen to'.

The mysterious wound to his head was still clearly visible and prompted much speculation. In France he may have scoffed at the suggestion that he had attempted suicide, but now an even more implausible explanation was offered by the press. While on *Palais Royal*, they claimed, 'he was firing a cannon on board,* which, being overcharged, recoiled in an unexpected manner and grazed his forehead. Had he received the full force of the blow he would certainly not have lived ...'

At this preliminary hearing in the magistrates' court, the task of the prosecution was to present a sample of the evidence against Wells. Then, if the magistrate determined that the case was sufficiently strong, Wells would stand trial in the Central Criminal Court. If not, he would walk away a free man.

Charles was led into the dock, clutching his hat and avoiding the inquisitive glances directed towards him. At first he looked depressed and downcast, as if he had no fight left in him. Sir John Bridge, Chief Magistrate for London, read out the charges and named some of the alleged victims. As he did so, Wells slowly regained his usual poise. 'His confidence returned and his demeanour changed to one of apparent bravado. As the charges were read out he appeared unconcerned.'

Sir John asked him whether he was represented in court by a lawyer. When Wells replied to say he was not sure whether his representative was in court, it was the first time the public had heard him speak. 'It was curious to note that the prisoner's Continental sojourning had lent him quite a foreign accent.' Those present in the courtroom also noticed his unusual mannerisms, which included a typically French shrug of the shoulders.

After formal evidence of the arrest had been given by Inspector Dinnie, the hearing was adjourned so that the other

---

*   Perhaps the twin of the weapon found by Inspector Richards at Wells' London premises.

witnesses – who were said to be 'all over England' – could be rounded up, and to give Wells time to recover from his illness.

The hearing resumed eight days later, and as one observer put it, 'While the streets of London are still echoing with the glorious achievements of the "man who broke the bank at Monte Carlo" and his "independent air", the original of the song, Charles Wells, again made his appearance today at Bow Street to answer the charges ...'. There was a brief moment of drama. Seated in the room was Catherine Mary Phillimore. Beside her sat her brother, Sir Walter Phillimore, the eminent judge. It had been almost exactly four years since she had first answered Wells' newspaper advertisement. Four years, in which time she had handed over to him the equivalent in today's money of about £2 million. And the only time they had even come close to meeting in person was when she had become concerned about her money and made the trip to Great Portland Street. This was the occasion when Eschen, the manager, had informed her that his boss was not there, and would not let her in.

Now, in the confines of the crowded courtroom, Miss Phillimore and Charles Wells exchanged glances for the very first time. It must have been a heart stopping moment for them both. A second or two passed as if in slow motion. And then it was back to reality as the hearing began in earnest. Prosecuting counsel Charles Frederick Gill, a barrister of twenty years' experience, outlined the substance of the case. Since 1888, Charles Wells had done 'absolutely nothing but defraud people', he declared. Wells had pretended that his business was established in 1868, and had called himself a civil engineer; he had even put the letters CE after his name but he was not entitled to do so, Gill alleged, as he was not a member of the Institute of Civil Engineers.

However, in reality Wells *had* become a self-employed engineer in France around 1868. And furthermore, he was considered to be an *ingénieur civil* in France, as previously mentioned. Besides, there were many people in Britain who claimed to be civil engineers without being members of the Institute of Civil Engineers.* All of these points should have been challenged by the defence barrister later, but were not.

Gill went on to say that Wells had gone through the motions of patenting everything imaginable – including electric baths.

Sir John Bridge peered over the top of his pince-nez. 'There was a musical skipping-rope, was there not,' he enquired.

'Yes, Sir John – and that was the only patent on which he proceeded so far as to get a patent.** The prisoner applied for such things as navigable balloons, sunshades and foghorns ... signalling fires ... bows and arrows, and spring guns.' Gill accused Wells of having used the huge sums of money he had obtained in this way 'for gambling'.

Wells was represented by 34-year-old Edward Abinger, who had been a barrister for about five years, and was renowned for the distinctive habit of tapping his snuffbox as he was putting a searching question to a witness, or submitting a difficult argument to a judge.

Miss Phillimore was sworn in and began to tell her side of the story. Looking younger than her 45 years, and clad 'in deep mourning' (her mother having died twelve months previously), she soon won the sympathy of the onlookers. Though nervous, she gave a long and detailed account of her dealings with Wells: the many letters and telegrams, the increasingly urgent requests for more funds, the ever larger cheques. Wells had never sent her a penny of the promised returns, she told the court.

---

*   The list of civil engineers in the 1892 *Kelly's Post Office Directory* – which, incidentally, includes Wells – clearly shows which of these persons belong to the Institute of Civil Engineers. About one-third of those describing themselves as civil engineers do not belong to the Institute. After the Wells case, Kelly's Directory made the distinction between those who were members of the Institute and those who were not.

**   This statement was also wrong, and should have been rebutted by the defence. Twenty-eight patents had in fact been completed.

Abinger, with snuffbox at the ready, pointed out that although Miss Phillimore had not received cash, Wells had sent her a parcel of shares instead.

'They are pieces of paper,' the magistrate snorted. 'To call them shares is nonsense.'

'They are for a larger amount than the capital of the company,' Gill added, which raised a laugh in the courtroom.

The Honourable William Cosby Trench entered the witness box next. Contemporary accounts portray him as a 'gentleman of youthful appearance' with considerably more money than sense. In his testimony he admitted that he had answered no fewer than four separate advertisements, all placed by the same person – Wells. Although the notices all looked remarkably similar, it had simply never occurred to him that they all emanated from the same source. And, every time he responded, Wells offered him a fresh 'business opportunity'. Then, after Wells had sent him what purported to be the 'official certificate of patent', Trench failed to notice that it was only a receipt. This comment met with another outburst of laughter. (But, as we have seen, Trench was certainly not the only one who failed to notice this crucial point. In fact, there is no evidence that *any* of Wells' victims realised that the 'patent certificate' was no more than an acknowledgement for the application.)

Trench recalled his meeting with Charles Wells at Drummond's Bank, when he advanced the sum of £1,500 against the security of three of Wells' yachts. When Wells had failed to repay the money, Trench had taken possession of the boats. However, when they were auctioned off to settle the debt, the amount realised was only a fraction of what Trench had handed over. Between them, the *Isabella* and the *Ituna* raised only £90, while *Flyer* was nowhere to be found.

'It flew away!' Sir John Bridge said with glee. 'Had you no one to whom you could go for advice?'

'I did not ask anyone.'

'How old are you?'

'Twenty-four.' Trench had no experience of London, and said that the people in the south of Ireland were all honest. He admitted, too, that he had not received a college education. He had seen the enticing advertisements but did not think the profits would be nearly as great as forecast. In fact he had said as much to Wells himself.

As it was now late, the magistrate asked whether the prisoner had any objection to the hearing being continued next day.

'Please yourself,' Wells replied nonchalantly, 'I don't mind.' And he was taken back to the cells.

When the next session began, however, Wells was in a despondent mood again. His lawyer was late and missed the start of the proceedings. Sir John asked Wells whether he was represented. He was not, he answered. He didn't think it was any use being represented after what had happened on the previous day. He would take some notes himself, he said.

A few days later, when Wells appeared in court for a fifth time, it was reported that he had 'considerably improved in appearance during his incarceration. He now looked in good health and spirits, and watched the case with interest and occasional amusement.'

A woman in her seventies, Caroline Eliza Davison from Paddington, testified that in 1889 she had agreed to invest £100 in a fuel-saving device invented by Wells. She called on him repeatedly to check on progress, and on each occasion he made excuses, blaming the delay on both the Patent Office and the ironworkers who were making the parts. On one occasion he offered her a £50 note and had the gall to say that she could keep it if she would write a glowing reference for him to give to another prospect. She naturally declined to do so, and put the banknote down on the table. Wells snatched it back in the blink of an eye and replaced it in his pocket. Laughter again echoed around the courtroom. Mrs Davison added that she had subsequently sued Wells, but the case had been thrown out on the grounds that the evidence against him was not strong enough.

Sir John Bridge
"What was the Prisoner
doing at Monte Carlo?"

The magistrate, Sir John Bridge.

George Samuel Smith, former captain of the *Palais Royal*, appeared next. After Smith's falling out with Wells the prosecution very likely expected his evidence to help clinch the case. He described how the ship had been converted by constructing a saloon, a ballroom and a ladies' cabin. The ladies in question were described as Wells' nieces, he added.

'I don't suppose there were any uncles?' Sir John enquired, raising a further laugh. But it is safe to assume that Jeannette – who was in court that day – failed to see the funny side of this particular exchange. As the prosecutors had hoped, Captain Smith's account of a bevy of young females strengthened their case considerably. It would suggest that Wells' alleged businesses were actually nothing more than schemes to raise money which he subsequently squandered with abandon.

But then Second Engineer Ferguson was sworn in. He had joined the ship shortly before she sailed from Liverpool to

Plymouth, he explained. He recalled Wells coming aboard with Jeannette. In contrast with the captain's version of events, Ferguson said that he had only ever seen *one* woman on board, and that he recognised her in court today.

It was clear that Captain Smith had fallen out with Wells. Could Smith's word be relied on? Perhaps the living was not so riotous after all. And Ferguson's replies under cross-examination did more good than harm to Wells' case. He was 'a very plain-living man,' Ferguson declared, 'in fact he lived more plainly than we did.' If this was the best the prosecution could deliver there was a chance that Wells might be acquitted. But Wells did not have it all his own way. His insistence that the *Palais Royal* had been bought and fitted out with the sole purpose of demonstrating an improved steam engine was seriously undermined when both Captain Smith and Ferguson testified that the ship's engines were very old. Neither man had seen any alteration being made for the purpose of saving fuel, or heard of any such plan.

The preliminary hearings at Bow Street dragged on into March, by which time Wells was beginning to look ill and worried again. Miss Frances Budd was one of the last of his 'clients' to give evidence at this stage, and she explained how she had, with difficulty, raised £30 to invest in the small motor for coffee grinders and other household machines. As he had done with other backers, Wells had referred her to his patent agents, Phillips & Leigh, who had told her that he conducted his business with them in an honourable manner. But time passed and she received nothing for her money. She had accused him of being a swindler and would have sued him there and then, she told the court, but friends had advised her that it was not worthwhile.

By an extraordinary coincidence, she later visited Monte Carlo and was taken aback to see none other than Charles Wells at the casino.[*]

'What was he doing?' Sir John Bridge enquired.

'Gambling,' Miss Budd replied.

'Breaking the bank, Sir John,' interjected Wells' defence lawyer. [Laughter.] The magistrate pointed at Wells. 'Is that the man you saw playing at the table?'

'Yes.'

'Did you follow his luck and get your £30 back?' Abinger asked.

---

[*] In early 1891 she had gone on holiday to the south of France with her sister and a female cousin and the cousin's husband. Her grievance with Wells, however, still rankled. She wrote to Henry Labouchère of *Truth* fame to say that, as a single woman, she was 'unable to undertake the punishment of this scoundrel single-handed' but was prepared to co-operate with other victims to bring him to court. Labouchère wrote, 'If any more of Wells' victims will favour me with their names, in confidence, I shall be happy to put them in communication with each other.'

Miss Francis Budd

'Well, I watched him playing *trente et quarante* for about half an hour, but I didn't play.'

Sir John Bridge said that after hearing all the testimony and legal arguments he found evidence of false pretences in all of the cases. He then formally committed Wells for trial.

10

An Accomplished Scoundrel

Charles De Ville Wells appeared on 9 March 1893 before a judge and a jury at the Old Bailey – or Central Criminal Court, to give it its proper title. According to a contemporary account, 'His trial excited an enormous amount of interest. A crowd assembled in front of the Old Bailey, and the court was packed with people drawn thither merely by a desire to see the notorious adventurer.'

A string of witnesses would give evidence over the next few days, but Charles Wells himself would not be one of them: court procedure at that time dictated that the accused could not be questioned or cross-examined.[*]

Wells sat in the dock, 'dapper, quick, and alert in his manner, incessantly watchful and clever'. The judge, 75-year-old Henry Hawkins, opened the proceedings, and the barrister for the prosecution, Charles Gill, outlined the case against Wells, repeating essentially the same arguments he had used at the preliminary hearings. As he did so, Wells' lawyer, Abinger, listened and absentmindedly doodled on a piece of blotting paper.

---

[*]   It was not until five years later, in 1898, that the accused would first be allowed to testify on oath. (Williams, p.12–3.)

'I didn't brief you and pay you a substantial sum of money to amuse yourself by sketching,' said Wells. 'Kindly attend to what Mr. Gill is saying.'

The court usher stood just in front of the dock with his back to Wells. Occasionally Wells dashed off handwritten notes to Abinger. According to one account, Wells then tickled the usher's bald head with the feathered end of his quill pen to attract his attention, and the usher would in turn pass the note to Abinger.

As first witness, Miss Phillimore had to relive her ordeal again. Abinger recalled, 'The poor lady was dreadfully nervous and, of course, she did not want it blazoned forth that she had been a victim of a specious adventurer.' It took a considerable time for her to recount all of her dealings with Wells, and many of the letters and telegrams which had passed between them were read out in court. The dismay in her voice still echoes down the years as she describes the outcome of these transactions:

> I never received a farthing. All the £18,860 that I parted with was lost ... When I got his letters describing the kind of business he was carrying on, and the different departments, I believed it was a genuine description of his business. I believed I was helping an honest, clever inventor to promote an invention which would be of general benefit to the world.

'And to some extent to yourself in particular,' Judge Hawkins interjected. 'Was this your first speculation?'

'Yes – my first and last.'

One by one, Wells' clients told their story again. Edward Abinger asked the Honourable William Cosby Trench whether Wells had informed him that the *Palais Royal* would be used to entertain financiers, company promoters, government officials and judges.

'He didn't include judges,' Trench replied.

'I should think not,' retorted the judge.

The Reverend Blake said he initially believed Wells was an honest man; Dr White, the Bournemouth medic, had considered him 'honest, but poor'. Henry Baker Vaughan, the clerk who had copied thousands of letters, spoke of an occasion when Wells was expecting a client to visit him at the office. Wells had given him a magazine to copy out – presumably for no other purpose than to further the impression that a business was being carried on.

Edward Towers, one of the four principal clerks at the Patent Office, testified that any invention could be registered in outline form for £1. His establishment would grant a provisional patent 'for making eggs out of sawdust, if you showed a way of doing it'.

'You take the patentee's sovereign and he takes his chance?' the judge said.

The next witness was Alfred Edward Green, a 30-year-old Australian. He was the manager of the London & South-Western Bank at 34 Sloane Square, where Wells had an account. He read out a long and rather confusing list of deposits, withdrawals and transfers. He then said, intriguingly, 'I should say we remitted more money to Monte Carlo than we received back.'

Abinger pounced on him at this point: was it a statement of fact or simply Green's impression?

The witness became indignant, and snapped back, 'I did not state it as my decided opinion – I will not contradict what I have said.'

Captain Smith and Second Engineer Alexander Ferguson both reiterated their previous evidence that Wells had shown no sign of personal extravagance.

'Wells of Monte Carlo once more bared his bald scalp at the Old Bailey,' a newspaperman scribbled in his notebook on Monday, 13 March. The court had already heard three days' worth of prosecution evidence: now it was time for Abinger to try to convince the jury of his client's innocence. Hermann Eschen was the first defence witness. The young German's testimony was both detailed and compelling. There *had* been as many as four engineers working on Wells' inventions at any one time, and the departments at 154–156 Great Portland Street really *had* existed. When Wells was in town he was always busy, always at work:

> He came at all times of the night. He would sometimes fetch me out of bed if he wanted something done all at once. He would make a little sketch, and I did it there and then. I should describe him as a hard-working man, and nobody could do otherwise.

This was exactly what Wells and his defence lawyers wanted to hear. Wells 'fairly danced up and down the dock in his excitement all the time the German was giving his evidence'. According to Mr Wells' explanation, he said, the fuel-saving engine 'must be valuable – it must work, it cannot do otherwise'. As for the steam engine he had made for *Flyer*, he added, 'in my opinion this is a feasible invention for saving coal'. Using diagrams and models, Eschen proceeded to describe the workings of one of Wells' fuel-saving inventions, although his strong accent, combined with the technical nature of the subject matter, left most of the listeners in a daze:

> Here comes a triple crank shaft about three inch and another with three inch so as the middle one is acted with the piston and by working him down the power is gained ... so as you get so much more power as with the double size of engine.

'Quite so,' said Abinger. [Laughter.]

Eschen explained how, from Wells' drawings, he had constructed models for arc lamps, a hot-air engine and electric railway signals – but not for the 'inflammable balloon'. [Laughter.]

'Then I will take it generally that you made models for many useful inventions?' said Abinger.

'Including the musical skipping-rope,' said the judge, to renewed laughter.

Abinger had one of the musical skipping ropes with him, and – taking this opportunity to show that Wells really had invented something – asked if he might demonstrate it to the court. 'You can do anything you like,' replied the judge with a deep sigh.

The prosecution now attempted to discredit Eschen by suggesting that he had offered a £5 bribe to some unnamed person to find out whether there was a warrant out for Wells. He had then allegedly written to Wells in Plymouth to warn him. It was also insinuated that he had advised Wells to go to Lisbon as he could not be extradited from there. However, Eschen succeeded in fending off these questions. It was Vergis, apparently, who had given the £5 bribe. Under further questioning, Eschen admitted that he was on 'very friendly terms' with his employer, which may have led the jury to suppose that he had deliberately portrayed Wells in a favourable light. Even so, his testimony seems, in the main, to have cast real doubt on the validity of the prosecution's case.

An engineer named Oliver Hollingsworth was the next witness to testify. In about 1889 he had worked for Wells for three weeks without wages, just to gain experience. At the time he knew nothing about engines, but he apparently learned a great

'The Man Who Broke the Bank at Monte Carlo'. Charles Wells, his lawyer and one of his victims, sketched at the Old Bailey.

deal since he appears in the 1891 census as a 'Steam Engine Maker'. He stayed in the job for about 18 months. There were, he said, four other men working there, and Wells was present most of the day, working on drawings and experimenting.

It appears that Aristides Vergis was due to be called for the defence. As other witnesses took the stand, they were asked whether they had seen him in court. Apparently there had been a brief sighting of him in the morning but he had disappeared again, no doubt fearful that he would be asked some awkward questions about the £5 bribe, and that the inquisition would uncover his unsavoury past, including his criminal record. Moreover, on his brief attendance that morning, he had no doubt recognised the lawyer, Gill, who had been the prosecution barrister at his own trial in connection with the jewellery scam some seven years earlier. Vergis could not be found anywhere in the building, and thus never testified.

A whisper went around the Old Bailey that a very important witness – from overseas, it was rumoured – was scheduled to appear. As he could not be found either, the hearing was adjourned until the morning.

On the next day, Tuesday, 14 March, the judge was asked how long the trial was likely to go on. 'This case may last for ever,' he groaned. The spectators laughed. 'I may be dead before it is over,' he added to further laughter. He went on to complain about the enormous volume of papers which had been put in evidence by the lawyers. 'There has been so much confusion in the whole case that it has been with great labour that I have been able to separate the documents, and I find that there is ... a hundredweight of letters and documents which are absolutely useless to the case.' A small sample of charges against the prisoner would have sufficed, he said, not the twenty-three which had been brought.

The day's session got under way with evidence from Eschen's landlord, George Langford, a man in his late seventies, originally from Manchester. He confirmed that Wells had called on Eschen:

He came on business with drawings in his hand, perhaps a dozen times a day, from 1887 up to 1891. Wells came frequently at all hours, early in the morning and late at night. I have heard him come to give orders for work, in the morning, I suppose.

Walter Mynn* – an electrician who had installed the lighting on the *Palais Royal* – had attended one of the trials of the fuel-saving device on the River Thames, and had taken the *Isabella* to Gravesend and back. The fuel consumption had been 'very small'.

'Where is the *Isabella* now?' Gill enquired.

'In the hands of the Official Receiver in Bankruptcy,' Abinger replied.

'Are they cruising about?' the judge quipped. 'Are they all at sea?' Now even His Lordship was playing for laughs.

At last, the mystery witness from overseas appeared – Charles Wells' brother-in-law, Henry Jartoux. Speaking through an interpreter, he explained that his sister, Marie Thérèse de Ville-Wells, had asked him to go to the hearing in London to testify on behalf of her husband. He had known Wells for about twenty-five years, he said, and in that time Wells had been an engineer in Marseille working for large shipping companies. He had also been employed at Count Branicki's sugar processing plant in Ukraine; at the Spanish lead mine; and at Nice, where he had invented a machine for purifying oils. When questioned about his brother-in-law's aliases, Jartoux said that in France he had always been known as Wells – Jartoux never knew him by any other name.

Summing up the case for the defence, Abinger said that if a man claimed to be conducting a valuable business and it was not valuable, that was not a criminal offence. Wells had suggested that at his premises there were departments which did not really exist. That was not criminal: something of the sort went on in

---

* Mynn was a nephew of the famous Kent cricketer, Alfred Mynn.

all businesses, and was no worse than a barrister smoking his pipe in his chambers and keeping a solicitor waiting half an hour in order to give the impression that he was busy.

'I hope that sort of thing does not go on now,' the judge declared. [Laughter.]

Abinger said that Miss Phillimore and the others had parted with their money in the hope of making vast profits, but Wells' only failing was that he had been born a century too late. If only he had lived a hundred years earlier he would undoubtedly have been the inventor of the steam engine or the electric motor: but because of this cruel trick of fortune he had had to confine himself to 'such small devices as musical skipping-ropes and sardine openers'.

He suggested that Wells' difficulties had begun when he broke the bank. From that moment on, Abinger contended, his client had become a gambler and everything else was forgotten, including his inventions. He was now known everywhere, 'even on the street organ', as the man who broke the bank at Monte Carlo. Sensing that this oration had by no means won over the jury, Abinger then tried to distract them in the hope that they might disregard the evidence they had heard during the trial:

> The prisoner is a man of a wonderful brain. He has won forty thousand pounds in five days, and anyone in possession of this very simple system of his can make eight thousand pounds a day as long as they like. ... And now ... I am going to tell you what this system is! ... Now, gentlemen of the jury ... this is the system!

Abinger paused for effect. Complete silence descended on the courtroom, as all eyes and ears focussed on him. After a few seconds he continued:

> No, gentlemen of the jury, I will not tell you this system. If I were to do so, you may desert your wives and families,

my learned friends might sell their wigs and gowns, and even my lord who adorns the Bench might suddenly desert it to make a vast sum of money. No gentlemen … I will not tell you.

Abinger had hoped that this theatrical gesture might at least help to reduce Wells' sentence. But instead it would rebound on him, as he was about to discover. The court adjourned for lunch. Abinger saw Judge Hawkins, still in his scarlet robes, beckoning him with an imperious forefinger. 'Do you know that system?'

'No, Judge.'

'I thought not,' said Hawkins with a look of disgust on his face.

When the hearing resumed, the prosecuting counsel, Charles Gill, acknowledged that Wells had a gift for invention. It was a pity that his fertile brain had not been applied to some genuine scientific discovery instead of being used to deceive and defraud people, he said. He reminded the jury that Wells & Co. was a fake company, and that the 'shares' he had sent to several investors were worthless. Wells' threat to Miss Phillimore and Trench that they would be ruined unless they stumped up more money amounted to blackmail.

The judge said that William Trench was still a young man who – he hoped – would become older and wiser. He had no knowledge of machines and would have been better off if he had stayed in Ireland. [Laughter.] His Lordship referred to the weakness, credulity and carelessness of the victims. Nevertheless, Wells was not justified in trading on these faults.

The jury took only one minute to find Charles Wells guilty. The judge sentenced him to eight years' penal servitude, adding that it had been a 'very cruel, very wide scheme'.

'It was easy to see, from the expression of his face, that the sentence took him (Wells) aback,' an onlooker observed. 'He looked wildly round the Court and wanted to speak, but the Judge would not hear him.'* Abinger wrote in his memoirs:

> I had been hoping to get the prisoner off with a light sentence, but I am very much afraid that the Judge had not got over his disappointment. ... It was a sadly disillusioned man who went to Dartmoor** to serve his punishment, and I don't suppose anyone will blame me for saying that I felt very sorry for him.

It is clear that Wells succeeded in patenting at least some of his inventions, otherwise there would have been no need to employ Eschen and as many as three other engineers. This, perhaps, should have been emphasised more strongly by Abinger. The biggest flaw in Wells' defence was that, despite all the advertisements and all the money he had received from would-be investors, he was not able to produce a single satisfied client to vouch for him in court. Far from condemning him, the *London Daily News* expressed grudging admiration for Wells, describing him as 'a great advertiser. In one year he gave as many as three hundred and fifty orders to Messrs. Willing. They showed imagination of a high order.' The newspapers had not yet caught on to the fact that Charles was the son of a widely praised poet but, with admirable insight, the commentator added, 'If poetry paid, Mr. Wells might have made his fortune in epics. There was something quite epical in his cast of character, and in his scheme of life. He knew nothing of half measures, in his promises, or in his demands.' The piece concluded, 'He had a note of greatness in the extreme simplicity of his methods. For years and years he kept afloat by devices

---

*   Although the accused could not testify during the trial itself, judges could
       at their discretion allow prisoners an opportunity to speak after sentence
       had been passed – but Wells was not invited to do so. (Williams, p.71.)
**   In fact it was Portland Prison.

that most men would have trembled to use before the bumpkins of a country fair.'

Other newspapers, though, condemned him as 'one of the most accomplished scoundrels of his time. Gifted apparently with a fair share of inventive genius, he applied it to the most wicked purposes.' His victims came in for a share of the criticism, too. The same article referred to them as 'guileless simpletons who become the dupes of swindlers'. Some commentators felt that the victims' shortcomings went further than naivety:

Suppose Mr. Wells could have fulfilled his promises and given in hard cash £100,000 in four months and a large yearly income in return for the modest investment of £1,500, would it have been moral to accept such terms? Gains such as these could not be honestly made, and the person who was tempted by them must have let his cupidity get the better of his judgment. It is the old vice of over-haste after riches. ... It is idle to sympathise with such. Theirs has been no honest investment, but a bit of greedy gambling, and they deserve all the trouble that falls on them.

The Times suggested that Wells had contributed to his own downfall. 'It is true that the breaking of the bank at Monte Carlo was the beginning of the end for Mr Wells. It lifted him into notoriety – a thing which every judicious swindler ought to avoid.' But his gambling exploits and the bogus patents were not really separate facets of his life. In his mind, they had been two inter-twined threads within the same plot.

The guilty verdict in Charles Wells' trial seemed to have little adverse effect on his public image. On the contrary, his transformation from man to myth simply gained momentum, especially among the masses. Readers of the popular press were reassured to learn that, like Robin Hood, Dick Turpin and other icons, he only robbed the rich.*

The class divide was a major talking point in that era. Socialism had become a powerful political force, thanks in part to the writings of Dickens and Marx. Yet the 'man in the street' had few rights or privileges and in many cases was not even entitled to vote. This is not to say that most people would have approved of Wells' behaviour – the majority certainly would not. But for the public generally, the upper classes were considered fair game. People such as Miss Phillimore, whose family owned a large slice of London, or Trench, who lived in a fairy tale castle in Ireland, could afford to lose a few thousand pounds and be none the worse off for it.

People were more concerned with the mystery of Wells' true identity and his past. 'What has he been about since the age of one-and-twenty?' *The Times* asked. 'Was he ever an honest and hardworking member of society?' He was said to be British, yet his speech and mannerisms suggested otherwise. The *New York Herald* claimed he was really Emanuel Edgar Albo de Bernales, a newspaper editor. The real Bernales sued the *Herald* and won. British journalists indulged in similar guessing games. '"Monte Carlo Wells" was educated as a solicitor, and practised for a short time in Tenby [Wales], but he left hurriedly,' one mistakenly claimed. Finally an enterprising newshound discovered the truth:

> It appears that the convict Wells, 'the man who broke the bank at Monte Carlo,' is a son of the late Charles Jeremiah Wells, the author of *Joseph and his Brethren* ... a work of consummate genius ... Wells, of Monte Carlo, appears to have

---

*   Not *all* of Wells' victims were rich. As mentioned previously, Miss Budd lived on an allowance of just £60 a year and there were others in similar circumstances.

inherited some of his late father's imagination, but unfortunately he turned his gifts to swindling instead of to literature.

The public demand for information about him never flagged. A man named James Anderson Peddie, who wrote about sports and gambling, produced a pamphlet called *All about Monte Carlo: Extraordinary Career of Charles Wells, the Man who Broke the Bank at Monte Carlo*, and sold copies for 1*d* each. It was a curious publication, cobbled together from articles which had appeared in the *Daily News*papers and in *Truth*. The same author later published a more substantial booklet about Wells. He claimed to have been given access to Wells' diary, and quoted what he said were extracts from it:

Saturday—My luck continues, netted £1,500. This is even better than the patent business.
Sunday—Took yacht to Genoa ...
Wednesday—A climax arose at last. When I had netted about £16,000 the table was shut up for the night; it was covered with a green cloth and I had *broken the bank*.

In reality, it is most unlikely that Peddie had ever met Wells, and even more improbable that Wells would have kept a written record of his exploits, and then shared it with a stranger. But the interest in Charles Wells was such that people paid a shilling a time for this second booklet, many believing it to be a genuine autobiographical work by Wells. No fact about him was too trivial to be quoted and requoted. While Wells was temporarily held at Holloway Prison, a reporter discovered that he was one of a number of inmates who enjoyed the privilege of ordering their meals from outside the jail. The journalist went to the Holloway Castle Tavern where these dishes were prepared, and revealed that Wells' favourite choices were 'sole, soup, and fowl'.

Wells was later transferred to Wormwood Scrubbs Prison.[*] On 22 May – a public holiday – crowds of people congregated around the prison walls and sang 'such music-hall songs as appear applicable to the case of the better known among the prisoners. Monte Carlo Wells is one of the prisoners, and they, of course, sang "The Man that Broke the Bank".' The writer condemned their behaviour as 'cruel fun', but Wells probably revelled in the adulation.

On 13 July 1893 – some four months after being convicted on the fraud charges – he was brought from prison to the bankruptcy court in order to give an account of his finances. First, a list was read out of all the claims against him, which amounted to more than £30,000 (£3 million).

Miss Phillimore and the Hon. William Trench accounted for most of this sum – roughly £29,000 between the two of them. Miss Budd, who was owed £30, was prominent among the claimants, which suggests that with Labouchère's help, she had – as promised – brought together a group of people whom Wells had defrauded. Other creditors included former clients Frederick John Goad (£25) and Mrs Forrester (£45). The tailor who had made the uniforms for the crew of *Palais Royal*, and who had first petitioned for Wells' bankruptcy, was owed £191. The smallest claim was that of Henry Baker Vaughan, Wells' long-suffering clerk, who was due £8 10s in unpaid wages.

During the preceding criminal trial Wells had been given no opportunity to tell his side of the story: in the civil court, however, he could speak on his own behalf, and made the most of it. He was in fine fettle and seemed to have a ready answer to every question that was put to him.

One of the Registrars in Bankruptcy for the London District, Mr Herbert James Hope, presided over the hearing. Most of the detailed questioning, however, was carried out by his colleague, the Assistant Official Receiver – whose name,

---

[*]   Now usually spelled 'Scrubs' with one 'b'.

confusingly, was Mr *Pope*. And thus the double act of Messrs Hope and Pope set about the task of unravelling Charles Wells' complex finances.

They began with the fundamental question of Wells' identity. Although everyone else seemed to know exactly who he was, since the information had been in all the newspapers, the legal system had evidently not yet caught up with the facts. His real name, he told them, was Charles De Ville Wells, but when he had arrived in Plymouth in 1885 he had 'altered it to Charles Hill Wells, to prevent confusion, there being several Wells in that town'. In truth, Wells was a singularly uncommon name in that part of the country, and in any case his real middle name, De Ville, was much more distinctive than Hill.

The examination soon turned to the *Palais Royal*. The Official Receiver in Bankruptcy asked him, 'Have you not expended about £20,000 on the ornamentation of the yacht?' If he expected Wells to deny this, the answer must have come as a surprise.

'I have spent about £22,000 on her altogether,' Wells said with pride.

'From what source did you obtain so large a sum of money?'

'From the profits from my transactions at Monte Carlo.'

'Will you undertake to swear that no part of it was money entrusted to you by different persons for investment in your inventions?'

Again, the answer was unexpected. Wells said he could make no such statement. He had spent about £5,000 of the funds obtained from his investors. He was asked about his speculations at Monte Carlo, but he denied that he had gambled. It had taken him six years to develop what he called an infallible system for gambling. He had won a total of £60,000 (£6 million) at Monte Carlo, of which his share was £20,000 (£2 million). The reason for the heavy loss on one visit was that his family had been with him, and had prevented him from operating his system in the usual way. What he did was not gambling. He had sat at the tables for eleven hours at a stretch, and he called that absolute hard work. This last remark prompted laughter.

The Assistant Official Receiver, Mr Pope, appeared to have an abnormal interest in the specifics of Wells' 'system' and began to quiz him about it. 'Could your system be reduced to writing?'

'I think so,' Wells replied.

But then the registrar interjected, 'We cannot very well go into that.'

With an air of disappointment, Pope said, 'I ask, sir, because it might be a valuable asset.' [Laughter.]

When asked about the source of his capital, Wells said that his backer was a Miss Lizzie Ritchie, and that he now owed her some money (although her name does not appear in the list of creditors. We have, however, encountered her before, as she was his co-applicant for the musical skipping rope patent). He told the Official Receiver that Miss Ritchie had married someone – a Polish gentleman, he believed. As far as he was aware she was living in Poland and he was no longer in touch with her.

Next he was questioned about his letter to Jeannette, written from a prison cell in Le Havre. He denied having concealed anything in a secret drawer in his desk. When asked about his relatives, he said he had 'lost sight of' all his family.

The *Yorkshire Evening Post* reported that Monte Carlo Wells 'suffers no harm in temperament from the enforced seclusion of Wormwood Scrubbs … He was most affable to everybody who wanted to know anything. He seemed to comport himself as a man should in whose hands tens of thousands of pounds had been trifles.'

When he was further interrogated about money which seemed to have mysteriously disappeared, he explained that he had entrusted a very substantial sum to a man named Thibaud, whom he met in a French café. He did not know where this individual lived, but perhaps if they were to ask the head waiter of the café he might be able to enlighten them. This explanation met with considerable mirth.

With an air of exasperation, a lawyer representing the trustee in bankruptcy challenged him; 'Do you really mean to say that you trusted a man you did not even know the address of with £30,000?'

'Miss Phillimore never saw me, and she sent me a lot of money,' Wells replied. To quote one of the popular newspapers, 'The laughter which followed was a hearty appreciation of the happy retort'.

'You say that M. Thibaud owes you £30,000, so that if we can get hold of him ...'

'Then we shall be all right,' said Wells cheerily. 'I believe him to be an honest man, although he should have come and helped me when I was in trouble.'

Wells had won this round of the contest and he knew it. Emboldened by the good-natured laughter, he told the enquiry that people had been given the wrong impression. Even Captain Smith who was 'so opposed to him' admitted that Wells was more moderate than himself:

> [Wells said he] ... went about shabbily dressed, and cooked for himself at Great Portland Street. He had worked incessantly at his inventions, and was not what people took him for. He would be successful one day and would pay everybody. He was now doing his best to behave himself well, and although these were not the happiest days he had passed, they were very quiet, and he was well satisfied.

The examination came to an end, and Wells was taken back to his cell. But he still had another trick up his sleeve. At Buckingham Palace, a letter addressed to Her Majesty Queen Victoria was received, requesting a royal pardon for Charles Wells. The letter purported to come from Vienna and was signed Lizzie Ritchie:

July 17th. 1893

To her most gracious Majesty the Queen.

I humbly pray your most gracious Majesty to pardon my writing, as I am one of your most gracious Majesty's faithful subjects in great grief and sorrow ... I am the niece of Mr. Charles Wells, who was sentenced to prison last March. ... I am a poor orphan girl, without sisters, brothers, without any one in the world but my dear uncle, and the sorrow of knowing where he is, is killing me. ... This is my last hope; for the sake of God! help my poor old uncle.

The letter continues in similar fashion for several pages. The queen's private secretary forwarded it to the Home Office, where officials decided that it merited no further action. As mentioned, no credible trace of Lizzie Ritchie has been found and it seems probable that Wells got one of his friends to write this grovelling letter, and arranged for it to be sent from Vienna, where he is known to have had contacts.[*]

During his stay at Wormwood Scrubs, Wells was put to work sewing mailbags, and on Sundays he sang in the prison's Roman Catholic choir. This state of affairs lasted only until October, when the authorities transferred him to Portland Prison in Dorset. Now the hardest part of his jail sentence was about to begin.

---

[*]   The Austrian address on the letter is a genuine one, but – for what it is worth – the document is written on a sheet of paper of a size common in Britain at the time, though not used on the Continent.

11

Hell Upon Earth

The prison at Portland could be seen from afar – a grim, grey building perched high on a clifftop. Even the hardest, toughest criminals flinched at the sight of its stone ramparts. Prisoners were brought to Portland by rail, shackled together to prevent them from escaping. For the last 3 miles of the journey they were carried in a kind of omnibus up the winding road and through the towering gates of the jail into a 'heart-breaking, soul-enslaving, brain destroying, hell upon earth'.

Here they were stripped of every ounce of dignity or privacy. For the first nine months, men were held in solitary confinement. Each had a small cell like a corrugated iron kennel, with a wooden stool, a small table and a hammock. Some wings of the jail were not heated. For the slightest misdemeanour – such as smiling or looking at the sky – they could be rebuked by brutal warders. At night, 'every sound, every groan, every sigh, every prayer' could be heard as clearly as if it came from the prisoner's own lips.

The men were routinely searched up to four times daily. Once a month the cell was subjected to a particularly detailed inspection, in the course of which any letters found were read by the warders. At regular intervals the prisoners were subjected to an undignified strip search. They stood in a row, stark naked. A prison officer would first look inside the man's mouth. Then the inmate had to bend forward so that his fingertips touched the floor, while an officer performed a degrading inspection of the man's rectum. By the end of this process the prisoners were invariably shivering with the cold and trembling with humiliation.

Every morning just after 5.00 a.m., each detainee had to show all of his bedding to a warder, holding up each article in turn while the slops were collected by another prisoner detailed to the duty. Breakfast consisted of 10 ounces of bread and a pint of cocoa. The cell door was locked until 7.00 a.m., when the captives attended a twenty-minute service in the chapel. They then worked until 11.00 a.m. when 'dinner' was served. The least popular meal consisted of 1lb of suet pudding, 1lb of potatoes and 6oz of bread. They worked again from 1.00 p.m. until 4.45 p.m. and supper was served at 5.00, consisting of a pint of gruel and 6oz of bread. At 6.30 slops were again collected and the men were in bed by 8.00 p.m. at the latest.

After nine months the convicts were allowed to 'associate' with the other inmates, though numerous petty restrictions were still enforced. The men were given laborious tasks to perform and, initially, Wells was sent to the quarries to break up stones.

He wrote to his solicitor in August 1894, begging him to track down Monsieur Thibaud, who owed him extremely large sums of money, he said, with which he could settle all of his debts:

My greatest wish is that my creditors should be paid in full as soon as possible and my greatest ambition is that I may some day do so myself, if they are not paid before I get my liberty, and I feel convinced and have not the slightest doubt that I will do so some day, though a thing I could do with rapidity and ease now, or within a short delay, may be much more difficult in years to come. It is already 20 months since my arrest. Time passes!

If you cannot answer me give instructions to Mr. Vergis, who may write to me on the 6th of November, the date when I shall be allowed to receive my next letter. I am quite well and taking care of myself for the sake of my creditors, so as to work for them when my time is up, sooner or later.

Yours truly, CHARLES WELLS.

One of Wells' fellow detainees was Jabez Balfour, a disgraced Member of Parliament and property magnate, who had also been sentenced on charges of fraud. News leaked out of the jail that Balfour had found it difficult to adjust to prison life and had slumped into a depression. It was reported that Wells, on the other hand, had made the most of his time behind bars and was in good spirits. Surprisingly, perhaps, for a man who was generally considered to be a loner, he appears to have experienced a sense of camaraderie in prison that he had never known before. A news report states:

> [His] affable manner speedily installed him in the good graces of the prison officials, while his financial exploits made him a king among convicts. ... The behaviour of Wells in prison was excellent. Only once was he punished, and this was for a generous fault. He gave a ten-ounce loaf of bread to another prisoner, and for this offence suffered two days' solitary confinement. ... He seems to have heaps of friends ...

After Wells had been transferred to less arduous work, a journalist who had been granted access to the prison spotted him at the workbench:

> At one end of the tailor's shop, where rows upon rows of silent workers plied the needle, I saw Mr. Wells, of Monte Carlo, engaged in the peaceful and by no means arduous

pursuit of bookbinding. Although I was present in court when he received his sentence of penal servitude, I altogether failed at first to recognise in the drab form bending over one of the volumes of the convicts' library the man of address and fashion who broke the bank at Monte Carlo. His hands, however, are still as white and delicate as ever.

While Charles Wells quietly served his sentence, the world outside was undergoing rapid change. In London many of the worst Victorian slums were being cleared. Tower Bridge had been opened in 1894 and its appearance transformed the London skyline forever. A handful of motor cars – many imported from France – mingled with the horse-drawn traffic on British roads.* Increased personal wealth enabled people of ordinary means to buy bicycles, and a craze for cycling swept the country. The Lumière brothers had brought their picture show to Britain in 1896.

Inventions of the 1880s and 1890s, such as cameras, telephones and phonographs – all of which had seemed futuristic at the time – were becoming household objects, and these were all developments in which Wells might have played a prominent role, had he chosen a different path in life. As far as technical progress was concerned, he missed a number of epoch-making events while he was in jail. But the occasion that mattered the most was surely his daughter's wedding. On the morning of 8 October 1896 Marie Antoinette de Ville-Wells, now 29 years old, married Joseph Charles Vayre, a 23-year-old Parisian actor.

Vayre came from a highly respectable family, and his father was a government official. In contrast, the occupation and present whereabouts of Charles Wells were a source of

---

*   In July 1895, a French-manufactured Panhard & Levassor automobile driven by the Hon. Evelyn Ellis made what is reputed to have been the first motor car journey in Britain.

embarrassment for Marie Antoinette and her mother, who were naturally reluctant for it to be known that the bride's father was a fraudster currently languishing in Portland Prison. Bending the truth somewhat, they arranged that the marriage register would record him for posterity as 'Louis Charles de Ville-Wells, engineer, residing in London'.

In spite of all Charles' faults, his wife and daughter evidently still deeply cared about him and were concerned about his plight. Some two years after marrying Marie Antoinette, Joseph Vayre wrote to the British Home Secretary pleading for the early release of his father-in-law. In excellent English, he writes that Charles Wells should never have been put on trial in the first place, arguing that there was a fault in the extradition process. But the Home Office rejected his petition.

It would be an exaggeration to say that Charles enjoyed prison life – but he definitely made the best of a bad job. On Sundays he played the organ in the Roman Catholic chapel. When the time for his release was almost due, he rounded off the service by playing *The Man Who Broke the Bank at Monte Carlo*, followed by *Home, Sweet Home*, to the astonishment and delight of the other prisoners. In March 1899, having earned two years' remission from his original eight-year sentence, he left the jail. He returned to London by train, and his journey could only be described as triumphal, 'persons coming forward at each stopping place to shake hands and to congratulate "Monte" on his release from durance'.

In London, Wells held court at a luxurious hotel. He told journalists that he had used his time in jail to devise an infallible 'martingale' – a gambling system which would make winning 'a certainty'. The procedure required £6,000 capital to make it work, but – if the newspaper reports are to be believed – Wells claimed that he still had £20,000 left from past times, which he could access in three months' time. He intended to buy another yacht and make his way to Monte Carlo to try out the new system.

'He is by no means destitute,' it was reported, 'as his residence at a West End hotel clearly indicates.' However, it is more likely that the newspaper had paid for the hotel suite in return for Wells granting an interview:

> He has improved greatly in appearance since his imprisonment. Owing to the rich living in which he indulged immediately after breaking the bank he became very corpulent and unhealthy looking. He was also round shouldered and of ungainly appearance. The physical exercise he was made to undergo while in prison has made him perfectly upright, while the diet has reduced his obesity … and he now looks barely over forty years of age.

He was, in fact, 57 years old. The same report mentions 'a young niece, upon whom he is entirely dependent, and who was very faithful to him during his imprisonment'. When Charles was convicted six years earlier, Jeannette was left to support herself. She took a succession of relatively menial jobs, working for a time as a cook and later as a kennel maid. But she seemed to possess an innate aptitude for sniffing out money and, around 1898, obtained a job as a lady's maid to a beautiful, rich, young socialite – Zalma Bradley Lee – and soon became her confidante and friend.

The exotic sounding Zalma Bradley Lee started out in life as the not so exotic sounding Daisy Pallen. She was born in St Louis, Mississippi, and was roughly the same age as Jeannette. Her father had been an eminent surgeon and university professor, and on his death in 1890 she inherited his fortune.

As a 'tall brunette' with a 'striking figure' and a passion for horses and dogs, she had caught the eye of one of her father's close friends, David Bradley Lee, a wealthy bachelor from New York City who was no less than thirty-seven years older than she was. In 1895, the couple secretly married in London.

She took this opportunity to change her first name as well as her surname, and now styled herself 'Zalma' Bradley Lee. The couple separated after a short time: he went back to New York, while she lived – and partied – in the capitals of Europe. She became front-page news in America when, on hearing that her husband was dying, she refused to leave 'the divertissements of London' to be at his side. By the time she finally did go to New York he had passed away, and his sisters (both of whom had married into extraordinarily rich aristocratic families in Europe) had buried him before she arrived. A legal battle ensued amid sensational headlines such as, 'WIDOW FIGHTS FOR LEE'S BODY'.

While it was too late for Zalma to do anything about her husband's remains, there was still time aplenty to get her hands on his assets. Her sisters-in-law tried everything imaginable to prevent Zalma gaining a share of his estate but Zalma exploited an obscure legal loophole, and was awarded a settlement of $1 million (worth about £25 million today) to add to her already sizeable fortune.

With, perhaps, some financial backing from Zalma, Jeannette next became the owner of the Terminus Tea Gardens – a café-restaurant at the railway station in the rapidly expanding London suburb of Uxbridge – and supported herself until Charles was released from prison (Plate 8).

Almost immediately after gaining his freedom, Charles applied for a discharge from his 1893 bankruptcy. Observers who attended the hearing on 25 April noticed that he had dyed his hair. His face was pale, he wore sombre black, and with his left hand he carefully noted the registrar's comments.* His total debts had amounted to £35,000, while his assets were a mere

---

* This is the only known reference to him being left-handed. It was then widely believed that there was a direct link between left-handedness and criminality. This connection is now discredited.

£88. The *Palais Royal* had been sold, 'after much trouble', for only £4,500 (though Wells had originally valued it at £20,000). He had failed to account satisfactorily for his deficiency; he had given 'undue preference' to a creditor – Aristides Vergis – by paying him in full; and he had raised some – if not all – of the money by false pretences. His application to be released from bankruptcy was therefore refused.

If he really had hoped to borrow £6,000 and return to Monte Carlo, he would have to abandon the plan: all the time he was an undischarged bankrupt it would be impossible for him to raise money, open a bank account or run a business.

After only two-and-a-half weeks at liberty, he left for Paris, and was not heard of again in Britain for several years.

Many people enjoy a brief moment of fame, only to be forgotten soon afterwards. But Charles De Ville Wells was still talked about and remembered long after having broken the bank. If a child asked for some expensive present, the father might say, 'Who do you think I am – the man who broke the bank at Monte Carlo?' A defendant in a court case, on receiving a particularly harsh sentence, was heard to exclaim, 'Great Wells of Monte Carlo!' In Somerset, a farmer with a sense of fun named his pedigree bull, 'Monte Carlo of Wells'. And music hall audiences still hadn't grown tired of that familiar song about him.

For all his fame, Charles Wells did not quite merit a listing of his own in the hallowed pages of the *Encyclopedia Britannica* – but he was included as a sort of footnote to the entry on his semi-famous father, Charles Jeremiah Wells, the poet.

Around the turn of the century, his namesake – the novelist H.G. Wells – moved to Sandgate on the Kent coast, where a splendid mansion had been built for him beside a cliff lift carrying fare-paying holidaymakers up and down the hill. To boost trade, the owners of this mechanical marvel started a rumour that the house belonged to 'Monte Carlo Wells' and that passengers would pass close to the sumptuous home of the bank-breaker, perhaps even catching a glimpse of the man himself. H.G. Wells noted in his autobiography that, as a consequence of this, when he walked around the district every errand boy and street urchin burst into song or whistled 'The Man Who Broke the Bank'.

By coincidence, Fred Gilbert, who had written the song, lay dying only half a mile from H.G. Wells' home. He had contracted tuberculosis in the late 1890s, and, to escape the polluted air of London, moved to Honeysuckle Cottage in Sandgate, where he died in 1903. Though he had been responsible for one of the most popular songs of all time, his worldly wealth at the time of his passing amounted to just £15.

When Charles and Jeannette first arrived back in France, they lived at first in the Paris suburb of Sannois, and then in the Rue Godot de Mauroy, a swanky street near the Opéra Garnier. By 1901 they had moved to Maisons-Laffitte, an expensive suburb 10 miles from central Paris. This area had long been a major equestrian centre, and a world famous racecourse was situated there. Zalma Bradley Lee, Jeannette's former employer, had bought a vast château in the district, with extensive grounds and a stable full of racehorses. Jeannette, Charles and Zalma were on friendly terms and spent an appreciable amount of time together, and Jeannette finally became a governess to Zalma's young daughter, Loyala.

Fin de siècle Paris was a very different city from the one Charles had known when he last lived here in the mid-1880s. The Eiffel Tower, completed in 1889, had already gained symbolic status. And in 1900 another Great Exhibition reflected the very latest technological developments, which could not fail to reawaken Charles Wells' passion for inventions.

Herr Rudolf Diesel exhibited an engine which ran on peanut oil – an example of the recent ascendancy of the internal combustion engine over steam power. Herr Otto (whom Wells had so admired) and Herr Benz were also represented.

Electric lighting was now a practical proposition, not just for royal palaces and the casino, but for well-to-do homes as well. A power station – dubbed the 'Palace of Electricity' – had been specially constructed to serve the exhibition. The current it produced was enough to light a spectacular display of 5,000 electric lamps, while it also provided power to the exposition's numerous art deco buildings. These were exciting times for an engineer such as Charles.

To distance himself from his criminal past, he assumed the name 'Charles Deville' and declared himself to be a 'metallurgical engineer' and inventor. In 1901, he registered French Patent No. 295133 for a method which he claimed could augment electrical currents, thus providing remarkable financial economies (this sounds suspiciously like an electrical version of the energy-saving steam engine). Other discoveries which he claimed to have made included the 'accurate representation of mines' and 'aerial advertising'.

In May 1902, he registered seven separate inventions at the Patent Office in Namur, Belgium. In this instance, the applications were submitted in the name of 'Charles Deville' acting as the agent of 'Jeanne Pairis' of 27 Passage de l'Opéra, Paris – an address in close proximity to his earlier premises in the Avenue de l'Opéra.

Patent No.

163401	A combined walking stick and shopping trolley.
163402	A bottle which cannot be re-filled without leaving traces.
163403	An illuminated light switch.
163404	A speaking clock.
163405	A floating marine anchor, submersible to any required depth.
163406	Envelopes to contain sticking plasters.

163410   Paper with one side for writing on, and blot-
                      ting paper on the reverse.

The patent system in Belgium was evidently less formal than
in Britain: the applications are in Charles' own handwriting, with sketches also penned by him. Overall the effect is
whimsical, as is the quirky nature of some of the inventions
themselves. Here, for example, is part of his description of the
speaking clock:

> The clock rings the hours and then sets in motion the phono-
> graph, which will announce the time, recite some sales-patter,
> or sing a song, etc. ... The phonograph may be located in the
> base or in another part of the clock, and may even be driven
> by the same spring as the clock, or separately by means of
> springs, weights, electricity, etc. But, if the phonograph is
> situated at some distance, or if there are several phonographs
> connected to a single clock, it is necessary to have recourse to
> electricity, compressed air, or some other means of connec-
> tion, for setting them in motion at the required moment in
> their respective locations.

The scheme evokes memories of his patent scam of old. Some
individual – one of his investors, no doubt – took legal action
against him, probably in a civil court. Then the police in
Belgium or France – possibly both – began to take an interest
in his affairs, and opened a dossier on him. However, there is no
record of any criminal proceedings: like the British police ten
years earlier, the authorities seem to have been slow to respond
to complaints.

Before any official action was taken, Charles and Jeannette
left France once more, and settled in the peaceful coastal village
of Ahakista, in the south of Ireland. The setting was idyllic, the
pace of life serene. Perhaps, at last, they had found the tranquil
place of their dreams, a home for the rest of their lives. They

Duplicata

Plan de l'Invention de Mlle

Jeannette Dairis   163401

" Une canne porte-paquets.

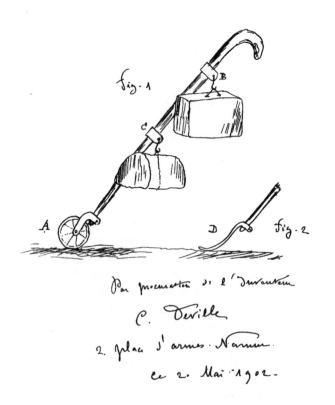

Par procuration de l'Inventeur

C. Deville

2 place d'armes. Namur.

ce 2. Mai 1902.

The patent application for a combined walking stick and shopping
trolley, written and drawn by Charles Wells.

assumed the aliases of 'William and Lily Davenport', and stayed initially with a man named Sullivan, the owner of Sea View Cottage. Charles recruited a local man, Daniel Burke, to help him build a cottage on some land he had acquired – a further sign that he and Jeannette intended to settle here permanently. He also purchased a small yacht and two other boats and, with Burke's assistance, used them for fishing.

In addition he had a motor boat built to his own specification at a shipbuilder's yard in Cork. On one occasion this vessel broke down and Charles, Jeannette and Daniel Burke spent six days and nights at sea, finally limping into port using the boat's sails alone. Shortly before Christmas 1904 one of his boats was badly damaged in a storm, and – if local legend can be believed – he and Jeannette had to swim for their lives for two miles until they reached the shore.

It was not long before Charles grew restless again. He told Burke that he was going to Canada for a few months. But in fact he returned to France instead, and assumed a new identity as 'Louis Servatel', stating that he was born in 1848 at St Pierre in the French colony of Martinique.

He set up a company in November 1903, the Omnium Général de France (General Combine of France), with a nominal capital of 7.5 million francs. It appears that this entity would run subsidiary companies in various engineering and mining sectors. 'Louis Servatel' was at the same time director of the holding company and chairman of the board for the rest of the group. It goes without saying that the whole organisation was just a vast swindle, and many investors lost their money.

'Servatel' vanished as soon as the police started to investigate. When they tried to check his identity they came up against a brick wall, because as recently as 1902 the town of St Pierre, where he claimed to have been born, had been obliterated by a massive volcanic eruption. Virtually the whole population had been killed, and all records of births, deaths and marriages had been destroyed. 'Servatel' had artfully chosen an identity which he knew could not possibly be verified.

In March 1905, he was sentenced in his absence to three years in prison and a fine of 3,000fr. for violations of company law, fraud and misuse of funds. Meanwhile, though, he had reverted to his alter ego of 'William Davenport' and was back in Ireland with Jeannette, enjoying the scenery, the boating and the fishing.

12

A Royal Personage

In 1905, Britain staged a major event to commemorate the 100th anniversary of the Battle of Trafalgar: the Naval, Shipping and Fisheries Exhibition, at Earls Court exhibition hall in London. Visitors flocked to the venue to witness the many treasures on show, which included a model of HMS *Victory*, a quilt which purportedly came from Nelson's bed, some of Captain Cook's navigation instruments and a full-size replica of a naval cruiser. Patrons could enjoy the traditional fairground rides, as well as Hiram Maxim's astonishing new Captive Flying Machine. Adventurous visitors could even take a simulated trip in a submarine.

In a more sedate corner of the exhibition, small booths were laid out in which various businesses demonstrated their wares to prospective customers. One of these was the South and South-West Coast Steam Trawling and Fishing Syndicate, an organisation run by none other than Charles De Ville Wells (masquerading as William Davenport) and the Reverend Vyvyan Henry Moyle, a clergyman whose credentials included a master's degree from Oxford University and a seven-year prison sentence for forgery.

Some forty years previously, Moyle had been appointed vicar of a small country parish near Middlesbrough in Yorkshire. As a young clergyman he did much to benefit the parish and was popular with the locals. However, after some years it was noticed that his standard of living had become unusually lavish for a young priest on a limited stipend. When the Archbishop of York visited Moyle one day, he was astonished to be met at the station by a smart carriage and pair of horses, driven by a liveried footman. Moyle intimated that he had inherited a fortune, and suspicions were temporarily allayed.

But the truth of the matter was that in 1873 he had forged share certificates to the value of £22,000 (approximately £3 million in today's values). When the counterfeit documents were eventually traced to him he was sent to prison. On his release, the bishop forgave him and appointed him to the parish of Ashampstead near Reading. But once there Moyle seems to have spent very little time looking after his parishioners. He conducted services in the local church only three times in six months and appeared to be spending most of his time in London. And when he was not 'on business' in the capital, he immersed himself in his duties as president of the local literary and scientific society, and as secretary of the Berkshire Beekeepers' Association. Finally he was declared bankrupt and jailed again. The prison authorities allowed him out on Sundays to take the service at Ashampstead, where the theme of his sermon, on one occasion, was 'Owe no man any thing'.

When Wells and Moyle met, the plump, red-haired, scurrilous, beekeeping vicar probably reminded Wells of his own father.

At the Naval, Shipping and Fisheries Exhibition, Moyle's role was to show visitors a life-saving machine invented by Wells, which incorporated a novel method of artificial respiration. Wells had set up a demonstration using a Japanese doll in a glass case (to represent the unfortunate victim) together with an assortment of bellows, tubing and other material (the life-saving apparatus). Air was pumped into the tank, and the doll was made to breathe.

1. Charles De Ville Wells, the man who broke the bank at Monte Carlo. (*Daily Mirror*)

2. The docks at La Joliette, Marseille. Charles Wells worked for the Messageries Maritimes, a steamship company based here. (Author's collection)

3. The Avenue de l'Opéra, Paris. The Opéra Garnier can be seen in the distance facing down the avenue. Wells had offices in the second block on the left-hand side. (Author's collection)

4. This portrait of Jeannette Pairis by W. & J. Stuart Photographers of Brompton Road, London, dates from about 1893. It was used by Scotland Yard to confirm her identity. (The National Archives)

5. The only known picture of the *Palais Royal* (depicted here in her earlier incarnation as the *Tycho Brahe*). (Author's collection)

741. - MONTE-CARLO. - Entrée du Casino

6. The casino at Monte Carlo. In 1891 Charles Wells left the building late at night, crossed the square in the foreground, and slept at the adjacent Hôtel de Paris with 1 million francs beneath his pillow. (Author's collection)

7. Interior of the Monte Carlo Casino. The room shown is almost certainly the one where Charles Wells broke the bank. The 'bulls-eye' windows above the doorways provided a secret spy hole for Camille Blanc to watch proceedings. (Author's collection)

8. Jeannette Pairis (centre, front) ran a station buffet at Uxbridge, probably in the late 1890s. (Pairis family collection)

9. Place Boïeldieu, Paris. Wells based his bank here, with a placard on the balustrade where the *A Louer* (To Rent) sign can be seen (right). The building was the birthplace of author Alexandre Dumas (*fils*). (Author's collection)

10. Charles Wells lived at this house in Edith Grove, Chelsea. (Author's collection)

11. Charles De Ville Wells was born at this house on the High Road, Broxbourne, in 1841. The property is now known as Walton House.(Author's collection)

12. Wells had an office here at 5 Avenue de l'Opéra around 1883. (Author's collection)

13. Jeannette Pairis in the 1890s. The nautical theme of her dress suggests that this may have been an outfit to wear on yachting expeditions with Charles. (Pairis family collection)

14. The HQ of the *Sûreté*, 36 Quai des Orfèvres. The manhunt for 'Lucien Rivier' was directed from here. (Author's collection)

15. The yacht *Excelsior* at her moorings just after the arrest of 'Rivier'. A wistful Captain Emery stands on deck – possibly wondering whether his employer will return. (*Daily Mirror*)

16. 39 Oakley Crescent (now Oakley Gardens), Chelsea. The entrance to Jeannette's apartment is beside the tree. (Author's collection)

Davenport a.k.a. Wells had obtained a patent on the life-saving device, No. GB9538 of 1905, 'An artificial breathing appliance'. This was almost certainly the last patent he ever registered. Moyle, in his clerical dress, took charge of the apparatus, and lectured on the merits of the device, which he claimed could restore people who appeared to be dead ... and even people who actually had died!*

A secondary aim of the exhibition stand was to attract investors into a fraudulent investment scheme which Wells and Moyle had dreamed up.

This time Wells stayed away from his former territory around Great Portland Street, and turned instead to the south bank of the Thames. He first went to 156 Stamford Street, not far from Waterloo Station. The owner of the house, a Mrs Ashton, had advertised an office to let. Wells introduced himself as 'William Davenport' and informed her that he was engaged in a fishing business. The landlady said she hoped he would not be bringing any fish back to the premises, and he reassured her, 'Oh no, all our fish goes to Billingsgate market'. He then took a room just down the road at number 147 as his living quarters; at the same time, Moyle moved into lodgings above a nearby coffee house, where he was known as 'Mr Henry'.

The two conspirators then purchased a steamship, the *Shanklin*, a vessel of 61 tons, 99ft in length, built at Cowes on the Isle of Wight. She may have been a magnificent sight when new in 1873, but now, thirty-two years later, her timbers were rotten, her engines rusty and she had been lying at her moorings for the last five years, unloved, unwanted and unusable. No longer fit for the purpose she had been designed for, she was instead a boat for buying, for selling and for pledging as security for loans. In the last seven years, she had changed hands five times, being passed from one owner to the next like a hand grenade with the

---

* Again, we are reminded of Charles Wells' father, who had once claimed the ability to bring people back from the dead.

pin removed. Wells and Moyle then appeared, and made an offer of £140. This was doubtless accepted by her then owner with a combination of relief and incredulity.

As in Wells' previous schemes, advertising played a prominent part. This time, though, he cautiously avoided using Willing's as his advertising agents, knowing that there was a strong possibility that he would be recognised. Instead he went to Charles Pool & Co. of 92 Fleet Street, who arranged for announcements of the following kind to be inserted in newspapers:

> If you don't mind my rather common business, somewhat similar to farming, and can invest £100 on mortgage on short or long notice, you may secure a monthly income of about £20 without liability or partnership. Box 4,970, care of Pool & Co., Fleet Street, E.C.

The announcement was spotted in July by Christopher Walton, a resident of Brixton. Walton went to 156 Stamford Street and met 'Davenport', who told him about the syndicate's 'fleet' and said that the vessels were worth about £3,000 each. On the strength of 'Davenport's' representations Walton decided to invest £100 in the venture.

Another advertisement caught the eye of a convicted fraudster, Alfred Braithwaite Emanuel – a 55-year-old man with a most unsavoury past, whose wife had divorced him some years previously on the grounds of adultery and physical cruelty. He had once masqueraded as a financial journalist, and had even owned a publication for a time, the *Stock Exchange Times*. It was his custom to call on financial firms, such as stockbrokers, asking them to advertise in his newspaper. Should anyone decline to do so, he would threaten to publish highly defamatory statements about their financial standing which were likely to panic their clients and bring about their ruin. This practice resulted in him being convicted for extortion, and he received a two-month prison sentence.

Emanuel later conceived the idea of scouring the small advertisements in newspapers and looking for obvious scams – something his long years of experience made him eminently qualified to do. He would then approach the advertiser and offer to sell him a mailing list of potential clients. He would also write flattering paragraphs about the scheme in newspapers for which, apparently, he was the financial editor.

In the course of this exercise he stumbled on the advertisement for the Fishing and Trawling Syndicate, and recognised an opportunity in the making. When they finally met, it was agreed that Emanuel would supply Wells with 500 names and addresses of potential investors, to whom the promotional brochure and other documents could be sent. Emanuel was to receive 2½ per cent commission on funds received from these new clients. He also agreed that the name and address of his firm, William Freeman & Co., could appear in Wells' literature, and that he would act as a broker.

A glowing report – doubtless written by Emanuel – soon appeared in a journal called *Financial Truth*. It recommended the syndicate as an investment, and informed readers that 'the business was conducted by this company on legal lines, and there appeared to be but little risk, if any'. Similar testimonials appeared, with Emanuel's help, in the *Hackney Mercury* and the *Sussex Advertiser*.

Enquiries from the public flooded in. Wells responded to them by sending out 'voluminous literature, much of it got up in a very expensive style'. The package enticed would-be investors to buy shares in the Fishing and Trawling Syndicate, secured on the 'first-class vessel' *Shanklin* – a description which had not been applied to the leaky old tub for many a year. The prospectus pointed out that fishing was 'one of the best paying lines of business'. In the previous year, it claimed, profits had been no less than £320 per £50 invested (£32,000 per £5,000 invested). Wells enclosed a copy of the catalogue from the Naval Exhibition, and an illustrated pamphlet depicting the syndicate's

vessels. Enclosed, too, was a copy of a letter of recommendation concerning the life-saving apparatus, purportedly signed by
'J. H. Hart, MD, USA, LRCP, LRCS, LFPSG, Edin.'*

Shortly after receiving this package of promotional material, enquirers would receive a separate letter from the Reverend
Moyle – the 'respectable-looking and ostensibly independent
referee who vouches for the bona fides of the party who holds
the cards'. In comparison with the near incomprehensible language that Wells himself would have used, Moyle's letter was a
model of clarity (though he did somehow achieve the remarkable feat of cramming 120 words into a single sentence):

> Dear Sir,
> Happening to call at the office of the S. and S.W.C.F.
> Syndicate this morning, Mr. Davenport, the energetic man-
> ager, showed me your letter and asked me if I would write to
> you thereon, which I do with pleasure, because I am perhaps
> better qualified than many to speak on this matter, as I was
> born near an important marine fishery centre, and so from
> childhood knew the lucrative character of this industry, and
> also after leaving Oxford prior to my ordination as a clergy-
> man of the Church of England used to yacht a good deal off
> the S. West Coast and North Devon Coast and *as an amateur*
> trawled also, so practically and in many ways I understand
> this work. I have also put several old and valued friends into
> it as mortgagees for substantial sums. ... The profits are very
> good, and with good reason, for there is no *rent to pay* for *the
> sea*, and *no stock to buy or feed*. The fish feed themselves and are
> *awaiting capture*. I can strongly recommend this investment.
> Yours sincerely,
> Rev. V. H. Moyle.

---

* It probably goes without saying that no such person has been traced.

The investors came from all walks of life. Some were rich, while others had only meagre savings with which to speculate. John Ord Hume, a man in his early forties from Edinburgh, bought £50 of shares. He was a distinguished musician and bandmaster, who had composed the regimental march of the Green Howards. The wife of Lord Dartmouth, Lady Mary Legge, invested £200.

Many were taken in by Moyle's reassuring patter. John Gilbert, a labourer from Liverpool, put up the whole of his £100 savings on the strength of Moyle's recommendation. Mrs Lucy Carlyle, the wife of a clergyman, had received from Moyle a letter saying that he considered the syndicate to be worthy of full and serious consideration; that he had persuaded some old friends of his to buy shares – a viscount and a city official of high standing, hard-headed men who would not have taken part if they had any doubts about the business. The letter, and the fact that Moyle was a man of the cloth, reassured her enough that she participated to the extent of £25.

Hugh Richard Dawnay (Lord Downe) had retired from the British Army in 1901 with the rank of major general. He was a trusted confidant of King Edward VII: upon the king's accession to the throne, it was Dawnay who was chosen to visit the rulers of Belgium, Italy and the Netherlands to convey in person the news of Queen Victoria's death. He, too, became a shareholder in the syndicate.

The high-ranking official referred to in Moyle's letter was Thomas Bowater – a sheriff of the City of London, and paper-manufacturing magnate. He ventured £50 and was issued with two shares in the vessel. Other investors were much less well known. Amy Elizabeth Elliott, a single woman, lived in a tiny house in Goods Station Road, Tunbridge Wells. She earned a meagre living as a dressmaker and supported her elderly widowed mother. She, too, paid £50 for two shares.

Wells and Moyle pretended that *Shanklin* was worth £1,600, but its true value barely exceeded one-tenth of that figure. And as if that wasn't bad enough, they sold each share several times over and raised £5,333 on a ship worth at most £180.

In addition to the 'puff' paragraphs written by Emanuel, Wells publicised the scheme by approaching a recently launched weekly newspaper, *Farm Life*. Early issues reflect a distinct lack of interesting news, and are full of sleep-inducing articles about muck spreading in Suffolk, goat rearing in Lancashire and the like. Its publishers were clearly overjoyed to have some content which could be considered even remotely interesting, and reproduced a grainy photograph of the *Shanklin* lying on a slipway – presumably at Birkenhead, as she was in no condition to be moved. The caption describes this image as that of the 'underpart of the Stern and Propellor of the First-class Steam Fishing Ship, No. 212, belonging to the South and South-West Coast Steam Trawling and Fishing Syndicate'.

Although he was using the alias of 'Davenport', and was anxious not to disclose his true identity, Wells could not resist harking back to his days as an inventor. He claimed that the vessel incorporated a fuel-saving device of his own invention. 'This curious Patent Propellor of 5-feet diameter, with Gunmetal Bronze Blades has increased the speed of this Ship by one knot without further expense of fuel'. An almost identical photograph and text later appeared in the *Penny Illustrated*, a popular newspaper with a much higher circulation than *Farm Life*. The advertising campaign was further stepped up with semi-display advertisements in national newspapers, including the *Daily Mirror* and *Daily Express*, as well as regional papers, such as the *Manchester Courier*.

While Wells was operating the scheme in London, Jeannette took care of the home front in Ireland. She spent £800 of the proceeds to buy the lease on the Ahakista Hotel, and used her business experience – gained in part from running the station buffet at Uxbridge – to control the finances. All the while she reported to Charles by mail. One of his replies to her reads as follows:

£1 A DAY
and **12** per. cent.
A YEAR **£50**
for each
Withdrawable deposit.
Smaller sums in proportion.
Capital and Interest absolutely secured
By BRITISH MORTGAGE BONDS.
Third year of continually increasing success.
The Bonus for each £50 Mortgage Bond
entitled to monthly interest and Bonus has
been: In 1903, £293 5s. In 1904, £320 5s.
In the first 6 months of 1905, £183 17s. 9d.
Prospectus free. Write Dept C. South Coast
Syndicate, 156 Stamford Street, London, S.E.

Advertisement from the
Daily Mirror, 17 July 1905.

Nest of Love, 17 September, 1905.
In reply to your dear letter, always very dear to me, like mine
to you. ... First, my favourite choice would be to retire from
the world completely, and to live for ourselves alone in a
small house near the sea in the South of France, to live on our
income, to have some fowls for ourselves, and an old, unsuspecting servant. In that manner, my dear, you could rest your
poor head, and rest your weary body. I would like to have
the sum of 50,000 *f.* [£200,000]. ... It would be necessary to
draw from the bank all our money to form the Jap[*] society
which might profit us ... Then comes the hotel, which also
requires thousands.

They are clearly concerned about how much money they can
extract from the Fishing and Trawling swindle before they
are caught.

We must also calculate the two boats, the buying of the
second, the men's wages, the keep of the house, the keep of
the hotel, etc. We would require at least a capital of £3,000

---

[*]   Probably a reference to his invention with the Japanese doll.

to be sure of not getting stranded half-way. ... Destroy this
letter after having well read it, and tell me frankly what you
think of my reply.

He later sent updates by telegram – 'Five hundred mackerel
today. All perfectly well for the moment but I fear your mother
will have to be seen in about a month.' This presumably meant
that £500 in new investments had been received, and the second
part of the message seems to indicate that the deception might
have to be terminated within a month. In subsequent telegrams
Wells says, 'we are catching lots of mackerel' and 'over one
thousand mackerel this week'. Later he reports that he is making
satisfactory progress:

My fairy Rose, with the pretty little round arms,
£50 arrived this morning, £50 are promised for Tuesday ...
the individual has given notice to the Post Office Savings
Bank, and this time is necessary to him ... others hesitat-
ing. Twelve new letters went off yesterday; 11 today, but
the replies are no longer so numerous as at first. Fresh bait is
therefore necessary, for at any price the matter must be carried through now, and, as you see, there is hope. The cash
reserve, however, does not increase very rapidly on account
of the enormous expenses. When amounts of £25 go for the
company, £15 and £20 for advertising, money is indeed necessary. However, quiet progress is made. In any case we are
advancing little by little.

But it was clear that the days of the scheme were numbered:

The newspapers which have inserted my advertisements
begin to ask for information about my business. It is necessary then, at any price, for me to push on before the doors
are closed. Two or three bonds of £150 or £200 and one can
close the bank.

Wells then describes how Moyle had offered to introduce him to a royal personage:

> The 'parson' came to see me this morning ... he wishes to present me — guess to whom! It is not worth while trying. Why, to the King himself!* It is for the 'Jap'. As you will imagine, I do not desire it for the moment, for without doubt all sorts of inquiries are made with reference to the chum who aspires to that honour. I told him that it was too soon, we are not ready, etc. but, as you see, he is going ahead, this Bishop!

Wells ends his letter with a reference to one of his recent inventions, 'Turbril' – a food product using fish as its main ingredient.

> Ah! If the affair of the 'Turbril'** company came off, how contented we would be! A lover alone knows how. However, we will see, but I cannot stop. The fishing business must be carried on even if all that is spent in advertising is lost.
>
> I embrace thee as a lover alone knows how.
>
> Thy Loulou***

If Wells' letters to Jeannette are anything to go by, the Turbril project seems to have been a legitimate attempt to establish a new mass market product. He later writes:

> For the 'Bouillabaisse à Nana' matter. I have seen 'M'. It is an important and old established company and everything seems *bona fide*. ... If it comes off we shall forever be free from worry. ... They offer to form a company, capital £5,000, of which £1,000 in cash will be for me and £1,000

---

* There can be little doubt that Moyle's contact at the Royal Palace, Lord Hugh Dawnay, would have acted as go-between in this matter.

** Possibly a hybrid name derived from turbot and Bovril™.

*** Further evidence that Louis is his pet name. Jeannette is later referred to as 'Nana'.

cash for working expenses ... and my monthly salary of about £20, so that one should be comfortable and without worry. The agent tells me that since they are going to risk one half or more of the expenses it is because they feel certain of being successful.

As Wells had revealed in his letter to Jeannette, newspapers were beginning to ask awkward questions – including some of those which had carried his advertisements. The Reverend Moyle, with his persuasive testimonials, also tended to arouse suspicion as he popped up and urged would-be investors to part with their money. And, at length, it was noted that the address at the top of his letters, a house in St Stephen's Square, was in fact an empty property.

The *Manchester Courier*, which had, until very recently, published advertisements for the syndicate, warned its readers not to have anything to do with the firm. Some anonymous person – probably Wells – replied, 'We are fully prepared to rebut attacks of this kind, and you are doing your paper no good in libellous writing.' But it was too late for bluster of this kind. On the very same day, Henry Labouchère's *Truth* waded in with a scathing double-page spread about the syndicate. Labouchère made reference to the lavish publicity material sent out to prospective investors – 'everything that ingenuity and glowing eloquence can do to convey an impression of the lucrative business of the fishing industry, and the big business that the syndicate is doing'.

Labouchère had still not yet realised, though, that 'Davenport' was Charles Wells – the man he had mercilessly hounded during the patent scam twelve or so years earlier. Instead he concentrated on the chequered career of the Reverend Vyvyan Henry Moyle, who in the past had been no stranger to the pages of *Truth*, and whom he described as 'a scoundrel of the very blackest type'.

It was Labouchère's article that finally spurred the police into action. The next day, Detective Inspector Knell waited outside the office at 156 Stamford Street, saw Moyle coming out and followed him as far as Blackfriars Road. He stopped him and asked for his name.

'What has that got to do with you?' retorted the cleric.

'I shall arrest you for conspiring to obtain money by fraud,' the officer countered. 'I have a warrant for your arrest.'

'I haven't conspired with anyone,' Moyle replied. 'I don't know what Davenport has done. Why don't you arrest him? He is the head of the concern.'

Wells was arrested at the office, where a great number of documents were found, but no account books to suggest that a genuine business was being carried out. Subsequently Emanuel was also interviewed by police. Reading between the lines, it quickly becomes apparent that he offered to testify against Wells and Moyle in exchange for his freedom.

As Wells settled down in a police cell, he must have regretted his decision to keep the fraud going as long as he did. He probably wished, too, that he had not taken on any accomplices. In the past he had always worked alone: on this, the first time he had involved others, both Moyle and Emanuel had betrayed him without a second thought.

The court case began at Tower Bridge Magistrates' Court on 20 November 1905 with a sensational statement by the prosecuting counsel – 'Davenport' was, in fact, Monte Carlo Wells.

What began as an ordinary case of fraud instantly escalated to a major news story. 'MONTE CARLO WELLS – FAME OF YEARS AGO DRAMATICALLY RECALLED', a *Daily Mirror* headline declared. 'Everybody recalled the time when "the Man Who Broke the Bank at Monte Carlo" was a topical figure of such dimensions that his feats were made immortal.'

It was shown that the syndicate's 'fleet' consisted of a pair of ramshackle steamers and an old launch. One of the steamers 'leaked badly and burst her steampipe on a voyage to Cork', and the launch had sunk at her moorings. The firm's total assets were these unseaworthy vessels, some fishing tackle and a Japanese doll in a glass case. Predictably, these statements caused laughter in the courtroom.

Emanuel gave evidence as a prosecution witness, and the precise nature of his connection with the syndicate was deliberately smoothed over by the police. He was introduced as a partner in a respectable stockbroking firm, and no mention was made of his criminal past or that he had turned 'king's evidence'. In the event, however, his testimony was not of much use to the prosecution. He said that he had found 'Davenport' to be a straightforward man with some sound business ideas. He had worked for the syndicate on a commission basis, he added, and the idea to put 'puff' paragraphs in newspapers was not 'Davenport's', but his own. 'Davenport' had told him that money was 'coming in fast, every post almost, today £150, £50, and £25 – in all £225, and the day is not over'. Emanuel claimed that at this point he had become suspicious, and refused to have any more dealings with the business.

A clerk at the Customs House, the aptly named Mr Salmon, confirmed that two small ships, the *Shanklin* and the *Rosenhaugh*, were registered to the syndicate. The prosecution set out before the court a flurry of unconnected bits and pieces of evidence, and this prompted the defence solicitor to make the unintentional pun that they were 'on a fishing expedition'.

When the case was transferred to the Old Bailey, the first witness was Christopher Walton, the Brixton man who had invested £100. He described his meeting with 'Davenport', adding that the picture of *Shanklin* in *Farm Life* had influenced him and reassured him that he was dealing with a solid company.

After several other witnesses had appeared, Amy Elliott of Tunbridge Wells was sworn in. She said that she had been impressed with the information received from the syndicate, and then the letter from Moyle was delivered. 'I had not made up my mind to invest before I received that letter. The letter settled it. I am a member of the Church of England, and the fact that he was a clergyman influenced me a great deal.' She had sent £50 in £5 notes to 'Davenport'. 'They were practically the whole of my savings, but not quite,' she recalled, taking care to tell the whole truth. Her testimony, and her unmistakable sincerity, must have had a visible effect on the jury. Wells and Moyle evidently noticed this, and after a whispered conversation with their defence lawyers they promptly changed their pleas to 'guilty'.

The judge remarked that Wells was 'a man of very considerable ability', and sentenced him to three years' penal servitude. This was, he said, a light sentence imposed in the hope that Wells would reform when he came out of prison. Moyle was thought not to be the originator of the scheme and received an eighteen-month sentence.

13

An Amusing Case

This time Wells was sent to Dartmoor Prison to serve his three-year stretch. He was now 65 years old, and was assigned to relatively light tasks in the tailor's workshop instead of breaking up rocks in a quarry.

Jeannette visited him whenever he was allowed visitors, and when she was able to make the journey. She was now in her mid-to late thirties, and her waistline had expanded considerably since she had first met Charles Wells. But their passion seems to have been undimmed by the passing years, and when Charles was permitted to write to her he told her how much he missed 'the touch of golden tresses flowing through my fingers', and similar endearments. Such outpourings of love would seem perfectly tame today, but in England in the 1900s – despite a general loosening up of attitudes in the Edwardian era – his letters would have been considered distinctly racy. Convicts' mail, both incoming and outgoing, was routinely scrutinised by prison officials, and it so happened that one of Wells' letters to Jeannette was referred to the prison governor himself, Basil Home Thomson.*

---

* By coincidence, Thomson was the son of the Archbishop of York who had 'pardoned' the Reverend Vyvyan Moyle following that individual's conviction for fraud.

Although still in his mid-forties, Thomson had already gained more experience of the world and its inhabitants than most men see in a lifetime. At the age of about 22 he had fallen in love with a young woman, Grace Webber. Her parents agreed that the couple could marry if Thomson were to find suitable, well-paid employment. So he took up a position with the colonial service and was sent to Fiji. Not content with simply having secured this post, he began to acquire a thorough knowledge of the Fijian language. He was then transferred to Tonga – where again he studied the language and customs in depth. Promotion quickly followed for this vigorous young diplomat, and he married Grace in 1889. By the time he was in his early thirties he had become deputy prime minister of Tonga. However, when Grace's health deteriorated, the couple moved back to Britain, and Basil embarked on his prison service career.

When he first encountered Charles Wells in about 1907, Thomson had already been assistant governor of Liverpool Prison and governor at Northampton and Cardiff. Unlike many of his colleagues, Thomson made it his business to get to know all of the prisoners in his care, and not just the troublemakers:

The contented convicts go through their sentences giving as little trouble as possible [he later wrote], never incurring 'reports' and never putting their names down to make an application to the Governor. Wells was one of these. I had made it a practice to find some excuse for sending for these men with a clean sheet in order to give them some reward or encouragement for their consistent good conduct and to get into their confidence. I found that this policy was bread cast upon the waters: it returned to me in the form of a better and more contented tone in the prison generally.

... [Wells' letter] was a most refreshing document. The writer represented himself to be in the best of all possible worlds, where the food was excellent, the warders kind and considerate, the work congenial, and the library full of interesting books.

Wells was summoned to Thomson's office. 'I have been looking at your sheet, Wells,' the governor said. 'I see that you have never been reported and have never made a single application in more than two years.'

'No, sir – the fact is I didn't like to trouble you.'

'You have been a long time in the tailors' party. Would you like a change? You have earned it, you know.'

'No, sir, thank you. I am very happy.'

'Have you all the books you want?'

'The librarian is very kind to me, sir. I never have to wait long for a book. The fact is I am making a study of Dickens. I never had time to read him before. A wonderful author, sir.'

As Thomson himself explains in his memoirs, the library was stocked with 3,000 books, which were regularly changed. The works of Sir Walter Scott and Charles Dickens, which had for a time fallen out of favour with the inmates, were presently regaining their former popularity.

'You will be discharged next year,' said Thomson. 'What are your plans?'

'Ah, sir – there you are asking me a difficult question. My head is full of things – little inventions, little plans.'

'That is what I fear. Your optimism may carry you away again, Wells.'

Thomson – clearly one of the many people over whom Wells had cast a spell – went on to write, 'At intervals of about three months he would appear, and I could not help feeling that the air of that gloomy place was brightened every time he came.'

Wells gained his release from Dartmoor on 7 May 1908. The prison door swung shut behind him and he was a free man once more after two years behind bars. As he stepped outside he breathed the untainted air of freedom again. But at 67 years of age he was no longer young. His faithful Jeannette had stood by him for almost twenty years and, out of necessity, she had supported herself and saved some money of her own. Perhaps she hoped that Charles would keep out of trouble for the next few years and leave it to her to earn enough for them to settle down again beside the sea in Ireland, or in the South of France, to fulfil the promise he had once made to her.

But as Charles had told the prison governor, he had his own plans for the future. At the end of that month he said farewell to Jeannette and made his way to Paris. This may have been part of some carefully thought out plan – but perhaps there had been a disagreement, as subsequent events might suggest.

In Paris, Wells adopted the name 'Ernest Beauparquet'. He came with very little money, and used what he had to buy some reasonable looking second-hand clothes. Two weeks later, he travelled to Lyon, then France's second largest city, some 250 miles to the south-east. He probably chose this location because it was a long way from his old haunts of Paris, Marseille and Nice, and he was not known there.

Once there, he renamed himself 'Ernest Cuvilier' and pretended to be 55 years of age. He took a room at a hotel in the town centre, and then moved into more permanent lodgings at the Quai de la Pêcherie – the quay on the bank of the River Saône where fish were unloaded and sold. He had with him a young woman, 18 years of age, by the name of Myriam d'Etigny. Predictably, he told people that she was his niece and he was acting as her guardian, but it was common knowledge that she was his mistress. She also seems to have gone under the name of 'Marie Chalandre'. (It was never explained why an 18-year-old girl would need an alias or, indeed, why she would consort with a man almost fifty years her senior.)

'Cuvilier' rented a large office on a mezzanine floor at 8–10 Rue de la Charité, and launched a travel company – the *Touriste Universel Centennaire* – which, according to him, had its registered office 'in London'. Since he had reportedly been trawling the flea markets of Paris for presentable clothes only days before, it is a mystery that he was able to finance such sumptuous business premises.

He also produced what was described as a 'long prospectus with an extraordinary phraseology' – a comprehensive forty-page brochure, sent out free of charge to anyone who requested it, containing an abundance of tariffs, charts and explanations. Its contents resembled one of Jules Verne's more fanciful novels. The company offered cruises to various parts of the world for the bargain price of 1½ francs per day, all expenses included. The trips would last from eighteen to twenty-four months. Passengers would be entertained, fed and transported around, whether at sea or on land. The tourists would participate in once-in-a-lifetime mountain climbs; they would hunt and go fishing; they would catch whales, 'each weighing the equivalent of an army of three thousand men', according to the prospectus. There would be priests to take care of marriages and baptisms during the journey, and teachers of both sexes to provide lessons for the children, which even included tuition in horse-riding.

The brochure described the history of the charitable foundation which had made this profoundly generous offer possible. During the Battle of Castelfidardo, Italy, in 1860, the Sardinian Army had defeated troops defending the Papal States. Some of those killed in the action had left their money to loved ones, who set up a society to carry out humanitarian works. The sum involved was 11 million francs, and it was claimed that over the course of half a century this had grown to 88 million. Unusually for a charity, the money accumulated first, before anyone decided what to use it for.

Then, according to 'Cuvilier', a descendant of one of the families was left with a broken heart after a love affair went awry. He became so depressed that his doctor pronounced him incurable. Someone recommended a holiday to take his mind off his grief. He took their advice, went on a world cruise, returned completely cured and lived to the age of 100. The families were so thankful, they decided to benefit humanity by providing subsidised holidays for the public.

To gain public confidence, 'Cuvilier' had created a dazzling panel of administrators, some real, some fictitious. And to advertise the new enterprise he produced a newsletter – the *Revue du T.U.C.* – though only two issues of this were ever published. It was couched in the sort of language we have come to expect from Charles Wells, and was full of awkward circumlocutions and glaringly obvious truths, such as, 'By taking the journey more slowly the traveller will have more time to see the towns and the interesting sights'.

A two-year cruise could be had for 1,000fr., while a week's holiday was only 10fr. To quote a contemporary source, the explanations were 'as numerous as they were incomprehensible', a claim borne out by the following excerpt:

> The work of the Touriste Universel, eminently productive and humanitarian, which resembles the ultimate stage in a long evolution, the roots of which extend back to well before the unfathomable recesses of the human heart, was conceived by people of substantial means, who ... have become compassionate people with results that give the spectacle of grandiose efflorescence to generate substantial and flavoursome fruit for the relief of misery and the salutary regeneration of the human body as a whole.

However impenetrable the language, *some* people were clearly impressed, and the money flowed in. The police in Lyon were far from impressed, however. They finally raided the office, uncovering piles of letters from would-be customers. But most of the envelopes contained only small amounts of money, and the total haul did not amount to much. 'Cuvilier' was arrested at the end of September 1908 and in accordance with newly introduced procedures he was photographed and fingerprinted.

In England, meanwhile, there was a surprising event in Jeannette's life. On 10 December 1908 she married a Dr James Burns at Fulham register office. Two days later, the newly-weds boarded the passenger steamer *Pretorian* at Liverpool, and crossed the Atlantic Ocean in a first-class cabin, bound for Halifax, Nova Scotia. But when the ship docked there, they evidently changed their minds and stayed on board until the vessel reached its final port of call, Philadelphia. Here they disembarked, and told US immigration officials that they were going to Chicago. One explanation for these unexpected events is that Jeannette had somehow heard of Wells' association with the young Myriam d'Etigny and had decided to part company with him. Another possibility is that she married an Englishman in order to gain British citizenship. It is interesting to note that the true identity of Dr Burns has never been established. No person matching the details which he gave on the certificate of marriage can be found in any of the usual records in either Britain or the USA.

'Ernest Cuvilier' was held in detention for eight months awaiting trial, while the police interviewed victims all over France, and searched for the people he had named as members of the governing committee. His case finally came to court in June 1909. It was a sweltering mid-summer's day in Lyon and the heat in the courtroom was oppressive. 'Cuvilier' was brought up from the cells, 'a little old man who claimed to be 56 years old, but looked older'. He wore a frock coat of a good cut – though he spoiled the effect by wearing a soft black cap. His beard and hair had not been cut, giving him a somewhat desperate appearance. With blinking eyes he followed the proceedings attentively, making copious notes on a thick file of papers that he had been provided with.

The judge, Monsieur Deschamps, began by questioning 'Cuvilier' about his identity. He asserted that he was born in Paris on 25 January 1852, and his parents were Charles and

Emélie Cuvilier (Charles and Emily actually *were* his parents' first names). He further said that he had entered into negotiations in London for the purchase of the ships with a Robert Hill. This was the name of his uncle who – if still alive – would have been in his nineties by then.

'I went on a sea voyage when I was seven years old,' he told the judge. 'The ship I was on was wrecked and I landed at New Orleans. Since the accident I have lost my memory.' *Le Matin* – the Paris newspaper –reported on what it called this 'amusing case'. 'As he recites this drivel, Cuvilier maintains a pious, discreet manner.'

'One might assume you wanted to conceal your identity?' the judge said.

'Of course, you can assume anything you wish. I promised to keep a secret and I have a major interest in hiding my identity.'

Monsieur Deschamps went over the story of his arrival in Paris, and then his activities in Lyon. He then told the tale of the charitable fund, expressing disbelief at the claim that 11 million francs had become 88 million.

'That's not much,' 'Cuvilier' retorted. 'With interest mounting up at more than 5 per cent a year it comes to more than 80 million. That's all. It's simple.'

Deschamps moved on to the schedule of fares, wryly observing that it was cheaper to take one of the cruises than to stay at home. He then joked, '*En somme c'était un bateau bien monté* [all in all it was a well-organised boat].' This was rather a clever pun: *bateau* is French for 'boat', but is also used figuratively to denote a 'fib' or an untruth.

Completely missing the point of the judge's little wisecrack, 'Cuvilier' responded with pride, 'Yes I think it was. The proof is that the world at large thought it was, too, and the members of the organising committee believed it more than anyone did.' [Hearty laughter.]

The verbal sparring continued. The whole scheme was fanciful, the judge declared.

'The court cannot say what is fanciful and what is not, because the court doesn't know,' 'Cuvilier' replied. 'I am only the representative of M. Raoul Montpensier, the man to whom I promised to keep a secret.'

'Then tell us where M. Montpensier is.'

'I've made promises and I will keep them – even at the cost of my liberty. You may find me guilty but you'll regret your mistake.'

'Perhaps there are others in it with you. If these people exist, which is doubtful, they are certainly fraudsters for whom you are the representative. Your guilt, therefore, is beyond doubt, whichever way you look at it.'

'Why am I not allowed to believe what other people – such as the members of the committee – believe?'

'Yes, but they could claim it's you who told them this cock-and-bull story.'

'There have been some irregularities in the transfer of assets, that's what I've been given to understand. But there really are 88 millions!'

'Where?'

At this point 'Cuvilier' ran out of answers. In summing up the case, the judge said that the frauds amounted to only 7,000fr. (£280). It was, he remarked, 'a very unremarkable swindle'. No doubt these words wounded Wells' pride more than the two-year jail sentence which he then received.

Wells was taken to Clairvaux Prison, 120 miles east of Paris. It was one of the toughest jails in the country, and a decidedly unpleasant place for a man in his late sixties. Yet Wells seems to have almost enjoyed his day in court: he had lost, but had put up a spirited, though implausible, defence. He had proved how easy it was to make the public believe the unbelievable, and he had shown that he could assume more than one identity without the authorities working out who he really was. The experience as a whole had strengthened his resolve.

There were lessons to be learned, though. In future he would need to be more cautious. His adventure with the Fishing and Trawling Syndicate had taught him that he could only push his luck so far. On that occasion he had kept the deception going for too long and had been captured: and, worse still, he had made little money. But his previous venture, the Omnium Général, had been moderately successful, and he had narrowly escaped being caught.

The challenge now was to invent a scheme where he would make piles of money *and* get away with it. It was a question of finding the perfect balance. And in jail he had plenty of opportunity to set his mind to work on the problem.

Charles Wells was released from prison a year later on 8 June 1910, after being granted several months' remission for the time spent in custody before the hearing. By the end of July he was back in Paris again, 'absolutely penniless'. But in the meantime Jeannette and the mysterious Dr Burns had separated. She returned to France and apparently there was a joyful reunion between her and Charles.

Wells soon returned to the area he was most familiar with – the southern end of the Avenue de l'Opéra. A woman there had two offices to let. He called on her and introduced himself as 'Lucien Rivier'. At first this little old man in worn out trousers, his artful face hidden by a long, greying beard, did not make an especially favourable impression. However, as their conversation progressed, the landlady was won over by his charming manner, and finally came to the conclusion that he was 'a very correct and extremely pleasant gentleman'. He paid six months' rent in advance, and took possession of the suite on 20 August with three employees. He had letterheads printed which showed that he was an 'industrial chemist' with two business addresses: the Head Office was at 11 Avenue de l'Opéra, while the Commercial Services were at 12 Rue d'Argenteuil. However, the latter address was just the back entrance to the same building (see map, p.37).

He informed the landlady that he was from Nice, and that he was perfecting a product called Chocolite* – a new version of chocolate, with seaweed as its principal ingredient instead of cocoa. He confidently predicted that this invention would 'revolutionise the world and put the other manufacturers out of business'. He told the landlady that he was constantly at work at his factory elsewhere in the city, but asked her not to send anyone to him there as it would disturb his experiments.

By early September he was ready to move on to the next stage in his campaign. He placed an advertisement in *Le Matin* on the financial page, next to the share prices, exchange rates and other business news. It offered fantastic returns of 1 per cent daily – 365 per cent annually. In line with methods he had tried and tested in the past, once potential customers had been snared by the advertisement, he sent them a leaflet. In this he explained that he had found a way to bring the Stock Exchange within the grasp of every person, not just professional investors. No specialised knowledge was required whatsoever: the customer needn't do anything.

The leaflet proceeded to answer every imaginable question that a prospective investor might have:

> The profits are unbelievable? Not at all. For example, if a merchant buys something for 100 *f* in the morning and sells it for 102 *f* in the evening, would you call that a miraculous feat? We buy a product for 100 *f*, and – thanks to a method of ours, unwritten but completely proven – this generates two francs, one for us, one for our clients. Where's the miracle in that, if you please?

He goes on to address those still in doubt:

> A few years ago, if someone had claimed to be able to see the inside of a human body they would have been classed as mad.

---

*   There is no connection with any trademarked product available today.

A person who claimed to be able to send a telegraphic message to a ship on the high seas would have been treated as a fool by the great scientists of his era. To predict that manned flight would soon become a possibility would have invited public ridicule. But now these – and many other wonders – seem quite normal and very simple, now that the problem has been solved!* So why doubt the solution of a financial problem?

To those sceptics who still wondered how it was possible to pay a daily interest of 1 per cent, he wrote:

Very small daily increases, repeated constantly, allow us on average to earn a modest 2 per cent per day. It's not a question of earning ten, twenty or a thousand francs from a single 1,000 *f* note, and it's not an instant fortune. It's the work of an ant which, one twig at a time, erects an edifice, fills it with provisions, and lives thereafter sheltered from cold and hunger.

'Rivier' assured prospective investors that his methods were completely proven over thirty-five years, and that his institution had never failed in any of its obligations. 'Naturally you will understand,' he wrote, 'we don't want to reveal any more about our system. Our secret is our fortune.'

The enterprise outgrew its small offices in the Avenue de l'Opéra within a few weeks. 'Rivier' received so many replies that he had to engage extra staff to deal with them all. In October, he relocated to much larger premises at 1 Place Boïeldieu in the financial district of Paris, near the Stock Exchange (Plate 9). He amended his advertisements to take advantage of this happy coincidence, artfully adding the phrase 'Stock Exchange' to enhance the impression that his was a solid

---

*   Wells had drawn on several recent developments in creating his prospectus. Röntgen had discovered X-rays in 1895; Guglielmo Marconi had recently won the Nobel Prize for Physics on account of his work with wireless telegraphy; the Wright Brothers had made the first powered manned flight in 1903; and Blériot had flown across the Channel in 1909.

and reputable financial institution. For emphasis, he repeats the words a little further down, and then again at the end, as if they were part of the address:

1% Guaranteed every day: STOCK EXCHANGE
The only establishment guaranteeing profits: 15% paid twice a month.

The least initiated person in the affairs of the Stock Exchange can profit from our systems with ease. Do not judge without seeing the proof, but study the explanatory leaflet which will be sent free of charge.

Minimum accepted: 25 *f*; Maximum: 100,000 *f*. The RENTE BI-MENSUELLE [fortnightly dividend], 1, Place Boïeldieu, 2nd. *arrondissement*, Stock Exchange, PARIS.

The imposing building in which the bank was situated occupied the whole of the northern side of the square, opposite the Opéra Comique.* 'Rivier' moved into offices on the third floor at a rent of 6,500fr., and paid for six months in advance. Inside he spent 10,000fr. decorating the rooms to a sumptuous standard, with lavish furnishings, wallpaper, curtains and carpets. He also fixed to the balustrade a sign advertising his bank. 'The wonderful promises and the beautiful surroundings inspired confidence', as one observer later wrote. 'Rivier' recruited a team of twenty employees, headed by his chief clerks, Monsieur Armand Coste, a former lawyer from the Auvergne, and Monsieur Gente. 'Rivier' would strut around the offices, keeping a watchful eye on the proceedings, a respectable-looking man of 'about 60' wearing a wig most of the time and always dressed in a frock coat.

He lived in the same building, but the contrast between his private quarters and the bank's offices could not have been more striking. He occupied just one small room furnished with a table,

---

*   Not to be confused with the Opéra Garnier in the Avenue de l'Opéra.

a chair and a little iron bedstead with a mattress that was stuffed with seaweed – perhaps a leftover from the Chocolite escapade. As in the past, he prepared his own meals of boiled eggs and tea over a spirit lamp.

To attract customers he flooded Paris and the provinces with tens of thousands of leaflets, and the money came pouring in by every post. At first clients invested small sums, often 25fr., the minimum allowed. But when, after three months, they got back twice the sum they had ventured, they were ecstatic. The 25fr. clients became 4,000fr. or 5,000fr. clients. One man, with tears in his eyes, begged 'Rivier' to waive the rules and let him invest more than the 100,000fr. maximum. But 'Rivier' was intransigent. With dignity but firmness he declined to accept more than the upper limit.

'Rivier's' concierge handed over his own little inheritance. The postmen who delivered the sacks of applications deposited their money. His employees entrusted their savings to the bank and encouraged their friends and acquaintances to do the same. The general public came in a continuous stream to open accounts, and the twenty employees could hardly cope, while 'Rivier's' deputies, Coste and Gente, worked incessantly from morning till night just to keep on top of things.

Among the most assiduous clients were priests. 'Rivier' had particularly directed his publicity towards the clergy. And despite the seeming improbability of the scheme, he did regularly send the promised payments to his clients, and as he did so, the word got around. Daily receipts soared: 2,000–4,000–16,000 francs. Every delivery of mail brought more money orders from subscribers. And every day the bank paid out up to 20,000fr. in interest – sometimes more. One man invested almost 14,000fr. and doubled his money in 100 days. Around the beginning of March 1911, an investor placed a 500fr. note in an envelope and sent it to 'Rivier's' bank. Such was his haste to avoid missing out on any interest, he forgot to include a letter with his name and address. One of the bank's cashiers conscientiously pinned a slip of paper to the banknote to say that it was from an unknown investor, and put it to one side until such time as the sender realised his mistake and claimed it.

Jeannette, meanwhile, was hardly ever seen at the bank. She spent her time in London, where she had been taking care of business for the past few months. She lived in a modest house, 22 Micklethwaite Road, Fulham, the same address she had given at the time of her marriage to Dr Burns.

Once a week, Charles would make the trip from Paris to London with another suitcase stuffed full of cash. While they were together during these brief visits, he and Jeannette carefully pondered over how best to invest these funds. In March 1911 they formed a company, the Excelsior Yachting and Trading Club Ltd, with a registered office at 235 High Holborn, the premises of Wells' accountant, Walter Bonavier. The company's shareholders were listed as 'Charles de Ville' (merchant), and 'Janet de Ville' (married woman), both of 28 Essex Street.*

Charles and Jeannette opened a company account at the London, County & Westminster Bank in Earls Court. Jeannette also had a private account in the name of Joséphine Binet, as well as a box at the Chancery Lane Safe Deposit. (Incidentally, it is not difficult to guess how Jeannette thought of the name Binet as an alias: a shop almost next door to the safe deposit was owned by one Roland Binet.)

As the weeks went by the bank balance and the cash in the safe deposit reached stupendous proportions. Beginning in late March, Jeannette began – with the assistance of their solicitor and accountant – to acquire assets with these funds. When she had run the Terminus Tea Gardens at Uxbridge in the late

---

*   A narrow road off the Strand, near the Central Law Courts, with many offices populated by lawyers, architects and accountants. At number 28, a Marion White was the resident caretaker. Marion and her sister, Catherine, had been the witnesses at Jeannette's marriage to Dr Burns in 1908.

1890s, she could not fail to have noticed the rapid expansion of London's suburbs, and her business sense would have told her that a fortune was to be made in districts like this. She and Charles had decided to lend a large proportion of their money in the form of mortgages to property investors: they chose areas close to Uxbridge for these speculations – especially Southall, where the population had doubled in ten years.* Eventually the loans reached a total value of £8,000, secured on about forty-five separate properties. They included a row of three shops in the Railway Approach at Southall (reminiscent of Jeannette's station buffet of former times); a boot shop and a draper's store in Elmfield Parade; several small terraces of houses and a few individual shops and dwellings.**

Later that year they purchased £17,000 worth of annuities on Charles' life (over £1.5 million), and these produced a sizeable yearly income of about £2,200 (over £200,000).

In Paris, daily receipts of the Rente Bi-mensuelle topped 25,000fr., and continued to grow at a runaway pace. The bank's early clients continued to receive their 1 per cent daily interest – being paid, of course, out of the ever increasing deposits from new investors. It was, to quote *Le Matin*, 'a splendid affair – splendid up to the point where it became suspect'.

At 36 Quai des Orfèvres, the French equivalent of Scotland Yard, Octave Hamard – 'a blustering man with an ample waist and a more than ample temper' – had only recently been appointed to the top position in the *Sûreté*. Faint rumours about the bank had already reached his ears, but he had refrained from taking any

---

*   The population of Southall was 13,200 in 1901, and 26,323 in 1911.
     (Grundy, p.9.)

**   The real estate on which the mortgages were secured has soared in
     value, as property values have risen at a faster rate than other measures.
     Forty-five similar properties in the same area would be worth about
     £12 million today.

action since there was no evidence that any crime had been committed. And then the would-be investor who had absentmindedly sent in a 500fr. note without a covering letter lodged a complaint saying that he had not had a receipt for his money.

Hamard sent one of his best detectives to investigate. *Sous Brigadier* (Detective Inspector) Jean Roux, a thickset man with a moustache, belonged to an elite squad of only thirty-nine detectives whose job it was to investigate the most serious of crimes – assassinations, murders and important thefts. They travelled far and wide, both in France and abroad, to catch the criminals they were seeking, sometimes disguising themselves so as to infiltrate criminal circles. Only recently, one had gone undercover as a priest to help bring a gang of crooks to justice. It could be dangerous work. While dealing with a political disturbance in Paris a couple of years previously, Roux and two other police officers had been attacked and suffered head injuries.

On Tuesday, 18 April 1911, Roux presented himself at Place Boïeldieu, and was politely received by the dapper 'Lucien Rivier'. Roux questioned him at length about the bank's operations. 'Rivier' gave reasonably satisfactory answers, but Roux's instinct, sharpened by years as a detective, told him that something was amiss. He reported his suspicions to Hamard, who summoned the banker to attend his office on the next day.

That evening, at about 8.30, 'Rivier' left the apartment. 'I'm going out, Paul,' he said to the office boy who doubled as his personal valet. 'I'm sure to be out until very late. If you hear a noise in the night, don't be concerned.'

14

A Business Genius

The morning of 19 April dawned, and the city of Paris awoke. At the Place Boïeldieu all was quiet as street sweepers brushed away the cigar butts and ticket stubs discarded outside the *Opéra Comique* by the previous night's audience. At exactly 7.40 a.m. an office boy named Zinkernagel arrived at the bank opposite the opera house to take over from his colleague. The first office boy, Paul, was bemused. 'It's strange,' he said, 'when the boss went out during the night he forgot to lock the door.'

And 'Rivier' had not yet returned. At opening time there was still no sign of him. The usual stream of customers came and went, depositing and withdrawing their money. Within an hour the cashiers were running out of ready cash. In their chief's absence, his two deputies decided to open his private safe. Inside all they found was a note, which read, 'I have been summoned by the police. My state of health and advanced age prevent me from resisting this harassment. I have been grossly insulted. I therefore tender my resignation. I am handing over the cash in my possession to my successor, who will arrive at mid-day.'

The deputies went back to the bank's offices, white-faced and stunned. 'Don't accept any more applications,' they told the staff. 'As of this minute, suspend all operations.' Anxiously they

The only known photograph of
Inspector Jean Roux.

clung to the hope that 'Rivier's' successor would indeed be there at noon. But when no one showed up they contacted the police.

As he made his way to England, Charles Wells could finally take stock of the past twenty-four hours. The interview with Inspector Roux had shaken him more than he cared to admit. There had been no previous inkling that the police were interested in his affairs, and he had expected to squeeze a few more drops out of the scheme before having to leave France. Yet he had handled the interrogation well: he had kept his cool when the stakes were high, just as he had at the tables of Monte Carlo, twenty years ago. The inspector had gone back to report to his superiors, and he, Wells, was still at liberty with the 1.2 million francs (£4.5 million) he had embezzled. And he had learned his lesson well. This time, unlike the Fishing and Trawling scam, and the Touriste Universel debacle, he had got away before he was caught.

During the past six months he had made this journey from France to England at least twenty times. And on each occasion he carried more cash and more gold. Today was no exception. But this would be a one-way trip – the last. The police would soon start looking for him. In fact they had probably already started. Had he left any clue to his identity? No – the *Sûreté* would ask around, and look into his affairs, but it would be too late. They would blunder around Paris, picking up local crooks at random and putting the screws on them, as likely as not. But 'Rivier' had no accomplices – only the one person in the world he trusted and relied on – Jeannette. And she was in England. Anything the police might find would only lead them back to 'Lucien Rivier' – and 'Rivier' existed no more. When the investigators realised that they had run up against a dead end they would just have to give up.

Wells had pulled off the perfect crime, just as he had once found a way to win at Monte Carlo. Perhaps now, while in a more reflective mood, he cast his mind back to the time he had spent in prison; the hours spent reading the works of Charles Dickens, and the idea that had probably come to him while reading Martin Chuzzlewit – an idea about an institution whose offices are 'newly plastered, newly papered ... newly fitted up in every way,' with a gleaming brass plate on the door. Its director publishes circulars aimed at the public and:

> fully proves to you that any connection on your part with that establishment must result in a perpetual Christmas Box and constantly increasing Bonus to yourself, and that nobody can run any risk by the transaction ...

He, Charles De Ville Wells, had done just that. This time he really had broken the bank. But it was time now to look to the future, not the past. Tomorrow he would begin a new life. It was, on reflection, a most appropriate time for new beginnings. The next day would be his seventieth birthday.

Next morning the collapse of the Rente Bi-mensuelle, and the flight of its director, were splashed across the front pages of the daily newspapers. But by the time they appeared, the headlines were already old hat. News of the bank's collapse had rapidly spread by word of mouth across Paris, and far beyond:

FINANCIER FLEES LEAVING 3m LIABILITIES
365 PER CENT … HOW COULD RIVIER
GUARANTEE SUCH
A PROFIT?

When crowds gathered in the Place Boïeldieu, it was usually to queue for the *Opéra Comique*: this time, however, everyone's attention was focused on the building opposite, where the Rente Bi-mensuelle was based. The day was chilly and overcast. Grey, rain-laden skies reflected the sombre mood of the crowds of people, who gathered in anxious little huddles:

> For the whole of yesterday a veritable procession of distraught people came to the place Boïeldieu: small pensioners, employees of limited means, workmen, priests, all of whom had entrusted their savings to the fraudster. Some came to collect their interest and, learning of the bank's collapse, cursed the dishonest banker … An air of despondency hung over this great crowd of people, who were more heartbroken than angry.

The litany of complaints and grumbles was broken every so often by a burst of laughter when some unsuspecting dupe who had not read the newspapers came to invest his money, and thought – to everyone's amusement – that they were all here to deposit their savings, too.

'That bandit!' said a big man with a flushed face, and a red rose in his buttonhole. He had the look of a retired military man. 'If I get my hands on him I'll shoot him with the six bullets from my revolver – one bullet for every 1,000 *f* he owes me.'

An elderly woman said:

> I shouldn't have been so trusting – they were far too polite to be honest in that establishment. As soon as you set foot in there, a member of staff would leap out and offer you a comfortable seat in an armchair and enquire about your health.

And once the transaction was done he'd accompany you to the door with a great deal of bowing and scraping.

The victims came from all corners of the country: Brittany, Auvergne, Picardie and the Midi. Many of the people in the crowd were unwilling to accept that 'Rivier' had done anything wrong:

> The big banks stifled it because they couldn't compete – in six months they wouldn't have been in existence with him around. This one did the same as the big banks but instead of two or three per cent he gave a large slice of his profits. He's an honest man.

'He'll be back,' another man said confidently. 'He's put our money somewhere safe and he'll pay us back.' Others insisted that they had always been well paid: some had tripled their initial capital. 'He was such a good man,' they said, 'so simple, so paternal.' Another claimed that if 'Rivier' came back tomorrow he would trust him with all his savings again.

Shysters and conmen mingled with the crowds, approaching individuals and persuading them to invest whatever money they had left in their own preposterous schemes. A man named Poteau placed an advertisement in *Le Temps*, headed 'Stock Exchange Disputes'. He gave the impression that it was an official notice, and urged victims to contact him urgently. Those who did so were persuaded by Poteau to invest in his personal adaptation of the Rente Bi-mensuelle. 'It's a really admirable system,' he enthused. 'You could make a bank of this kind work perfectly honestly, and that's why I intend to pick up where Rivier left off, but only with his concept – not his method of implementing it.' He, too, came under the scrutiny of the *Sûreté*.

The story of the disappearing banker kept the newspapers busy for days, as new information came to light, a piece at a time. Immediately after the story broke, *Le Matin* interviewed

'Rivier's' employee, Monsieur Coste, who was adamant that up to now he had never suspected anything was amiss:

> He's a clever scoundrel. Just think, I'm in it for quite a hefty sum – several thousand francs. I met Rivier in September and straight away he made me part of his scheme. The interest rate sounded very high, but Rivier assured me he had teams of experts on the European markets, and there was nothing to worry about. As I earned the money, little by little I made several investments with him, including two lots of 2,000 f, as my wife and I had just received an inheritance. Everything was going well and then – my God! – only yesterday I returned from a trip back home and deposited another 1,000 f, and he gave me a receipt. What a crook!

The cashier, Monsieur Bardin, gave his own version of the story:

> We all had absolute confidence in Monsieur Rivier. All of us are his victims. None of the employees, however junior, failed to place their savings with the Director. A new employee who started yesterday brought in 200 f after the lunch-break.

Newspaper reporters jostled to interview 'Rivier's' former landlady at the Avenue de l'Opéra, who told them, 'He had loads of people come to see him – all kinds of people, especially from the rural areas. One was a man from the North who wanted to invest 10,000 f. It was all the rage and everyone wanted to be part of it.' Even in the early days of the business, before 'Rivier' moved to a larger building, the landlady remembered huge amounts of mail being delivered. 'Perhaps he would have liked to have me as a client,' she added. 'Some time ago I met him in the street and he told me how splendidly his business was going. That it was marvellous that one of his clients was about to sell a property for 100,000 f and invest the proceeds in his fund.' When the reporter told her that 'Rivier' had absconded, she said, 'My instincts haven't let me down, then.'

The *Petit Parisien* described how a woman waved one of 'Rivier's' leaflets in the air. 'How could you not be taken in by a circular like this?' she cried. She handed the document to the reporter.

'It's a veritable work of art,' he agreed. 'The man who produced it must have been a business genius.'

When they had run out of people to interview, the newspapers resorted to pure speculation as a source of material. The biggest puzzle of all was 'Rivier's' true identity. Little was known of his past, but he had told people that he was born in St Pierre, Martinique. (This, of course, was the same ploy that he used in his 'Louis Servatel' persona.) It was rumoured that he was really an eminent London jeweller in disguise. Some people believed that he was Belgian; others said he was a *parfumeur* from Nice with a shady past. One thing was already clear – he had 'a passion for "little ladies"', and already police were trying to locate a Mademoiselle Clérico, said to have been his mistress in Paris up until the time he skipped the country. Even his longest-serving employees had no real idea who he was. Monsieur Coste told a correspondent:

> The man was a mystery. He never spoke to anyone. ...He opened all his mail himself, and kept any money he received to one side. He was out all day – I don't know where. After signing the mail of an evening he'd have a boiled egg in his quarters and then we wouldn't see him again till the mail was delivered in the morning. Every Friday evening he went away and regularly returned the next Wednesday. In a very vague sort of way he hinted that he'd been to London. Sometimes he wore a wig, sometimes he didn't.

Surely Monsieur Coste was suspicious? 'No, the money kept rolling in from all corners, there were many customers, and none of them ever complained.'

There followed waves of analysis, recrimination and speculation. *Le Radical*, a socialist journal, felt that the so-called victims were partly responsible for their own fate: '[Rivier's] dupes virtually blame the police for forcing him to flee. They don't want to view such a generous man as a swindler.'

Another newspaper, *La Croix*, adopted a 'told-you-so' stance:

> On many occasions we have warned readers against financiers offering miraculous returns in order to attract a lump sum which is never seen again. In spite of all our advice about taking basic precautions we have also had to say that priests, officers, teachers and widows are often victims of this kind of crash ... to seek abnormal rates of interest – quite apart from the moral standpoint – is to expose oneself to almost certain loss.

Interestingly, the *Journal des Finances* printed a piece comparing the Rente Bi-mensuelle with a casino – a rather apt comparison, as it happens, and one that Wells would later make himself. The only dupes were the latecomers, this article pointed out. Those who complained were simply peeved because the bank collapsed when it did.

And so it went on, the endless finger pointing and apportioning of blame. (Long afterwards, when the British newspapers finally became aware of the case, they used it to mock the 'gullible French'. 'Rivier' had 'paid a large rent for his premises and decked the place with red carpets and hangings, which are more regarded in Paris as a sign of financial stability than they would be in London'.)

Everyone looked to the press, hoping for at least some good news, but there was none. 'Rivier' had vanished without leaving a trace, it seemed. However, not long after his disappearance, *Le Matin* made an important discovery. The paper claimed that 'Rivier' had often visited a 'sister-in-law' named Madame Burns, who lived for a time at 1 Rue Cherubini. She was said to be 'of

Belgian origin', and seldom went out. She had reportedly said that she was homesick for Belgium and was going back there, and had not been seen since. Though it was a rather garbled version of the facts, this would prove to be a more important clue than anyone realised at the time. In fact, the house in the Rue Cherubini was the home of Jeannette's elder sister, Léonie. Jeannette and Charles had stayed there for a time when he was starting the bank.

As soon as the police became aware of 'Rivier's' disappearance, they had immediately telegraphed his description to all points of the compass. Every frontier station received details of the arrest warrant against him. But it was too late. He had already left the country.

On reaching the bank's headquarters on the evening of 19 April, the *juge d'instruction**, Monsieur Bourdeaux, and the chief of the CID (Criminal Investigation Department), together with their subordinates, had searched the premises. Had 'Rivier' left at a time of his own choosing, he would no doubt have removed all of his documents from the bank. But in the event, he had fled in haste and had left behind a good deal of paperwork. Bourdeaux and his team collected together numerous documents, including seventy newly arrived applications for accounts with the bank. This material would take them some considerable time to go through.

The investigators faced another urgent task – to contact all of the victims of the fraud. Worried, exhausted investors were arriving at the bank in a constant stream, and a police inspector was duly stationed behind a little desk at the foot of the stairs. 'With a grave air he writes on a never-ending list the numbers

---

*   The role of the *juge d'instruction* is to co-ordinate all investigations
      leading up to the arrest and prosecution of an offender, and to prepare
      the indictment prior to the trial, which is presided over by a separate
      judge, referred to (below) as the 'trial judge'.

and amounts that these latecomers entrusted to the crooked financier.' Bourdeaux himself received many letters from depositors, anxiously enquiring whether their money orders had been cashed before 'Rivier's' disappearance. He also met a luckless wine merchant who had been completely ruined by the bank's collapse. This individual had invested the whole of his savings, 100,000fr., in the fund, in the belief that he would live like a millionaire for the rest of his life. Instead, he had finished up penniless.

A forensic accountant, Monsieur Alphonse Louis Malétras, was brought in to examine the financial affairs of the bank and return the newly received deposits to the senders. He temporarily based himself at the bank's headquarters and quickly established that 'Rivier's' daily receipts had reached at least 60,000fr. Indeed, money orders to that value were still arriving in every day's mail. 'Rivier' had been paying out up to 30,000fr. each day in interest. The rest went into his pocket.

As Bourdeaux sifted through the mass of documents he had seized at the bank, he very likely experienced a fleeting sense of satisfaction. He had felt all along that there was something suspicious about 'Rivier' and the Rente Bi-mensuelle, and his hunch had been proved absolutely right. But this flicker of self-congratulation quickly passed when he realised the immensity of the task ahead. Although every border crossing and every port had been alerted, not a single sighting of 'Rivier' had been reported. Rumours about his identity swirled around like leaves in the wind: many of them were plain nonsense while the rest contradicted one another. The only thing that most people agreed on was that 'Lucien Rivier' was not the banker's real name.

The accountant, Malétras, announced that the missing sum of money could be substantially more than previously thought. French citizens had been defrauded of up to 2 million francs (about £7 million), he asserted. The newspapers were pressing for answers, and everyone looked to the justice system to locate the fugitive banker, punish him for his offence and restore the funds to their rightful owners.

Recent techniques such as fingerprints, photography and an elaborate system for recording information on individual criminals had made life much easier for the police. But the case of the missing banker was clearly going to be a tough nut to crack. Bourdeaux began by sending for the files on any offender with the name 'Lucien Rivier'. There were none, he was told. 'Rivier' was not a very common surname, and the only record of anyone with that name referred not to a perpetrator, but to the *victim* of a crime committed almost a decade earlier. 'Let me see it anyway,' he grunted.

The individual in question was a merchant living on the Rue Oberkampf in Paris. What Bourdeaux read next was an eye-opener. The man had put funds into a company, the Omnium Général de France. He had lost the whole of his investment when its director, 'Louis Servatel', had absconded. Letters from 'Servatel' to Rivier had been preserved in the folder. Bourdeaux now turned to the many documents he had removed from the offices of the Rente Bi-mensuelle, and found a sample of 'Lucien Rivier's' handwriting. It didn't need an expert to see that the writing was identical. 'Rivier' and 'Servatel' were obviously one and the same person. Somehow 'Rivier' must have inadvertently taken on the name of one of his former victims of long ago.*

When Bourdeaux read further into the dossier, his excitement quickly evaporated. The papers recorded that 'Servatel' had disappeared then, just as 'Rivier' had vanished now. It was beginning to seem as if the case defied any solution, when

---

* In his interview with Dr Francesca Denman, the author asked whether it was possible that Charles Wells might have had some subconscious wish to be caught, causing him to give out a clue to his identity. Dr Denman felt that this sort of thing normally only happens in works of fiction: in reality, it was more probable that he had needed to think of a name, and 'Rivier' simply sprang to mind.

Bourdeaux received a letter from a judge in Lyon, who had read about 'Rivier's' disappearance. The case had jogged his memory and reminded him of 'Cuvilier' and the *Touriste Universel*.

'Send me a picture of this Rivier,' the judge in Lyon wrote, 'so I can compare it with one of Cuvilier.'

Bourdeaux quickly replied that he had no photograph whatsoever of 'Rivier'. 'Instead, *you* send *me* the picture of your Cuvilier!' The image was sent post-haste. Bourdeaux showed it to Inspector Roux. 'There's no doubt about it,' said Roux, remembering the recent meeting at the bank. 'It's Rivier.'

Perhaps the case was not unsolvable after all. By now, police had also traced 'Rivier's' young 'niece' in Paris, Mademoiselle Louise Clérico, who had known him since 1903. Bourdeaux showed her the photograph of 'Cuvilier'. Same result. It was her lover, the man she knew as Louis Servatel.

'Rivier', 'Servatel' and 'Cuvilier' were one and the same. So far, so good. But it was obvious that all of these identities were bogus. Who *was* this man? Perhaps 'Rivier's' safe deposit box at the Crédit Lyonnais would yield some clue. Bourdeaux ordered it to be opened. But it was empty.

In early May, almost three weeks after 'Rivier's' disappearance, a large number of leaflets were printed, showing a set of his fingerprints and photos of him – with and without wig – from his earlier arrest as 'Cuvilier'. A full description followed, including a reference to his unusual gait, described as more of a trot than a walk. The document gave his approximate age as 60 (whereas it was actually 70) adding that he had the appearance of 'an old pensioner'. His previous aliases, 'Servatel' and 'Cuvilier' were mentioned, as were a number of names he almost certainly had *not* used: Méjean, Coraly, Levallois, Saguenet-Ripensier. Intriguingly, the police stated as a fact that he was born in Martinique. They evidently had not yet put two and two together and realised that 'Rivier' had deliberately chosen

Saint-Pierre as his alleged birthplace because the records there had been destroyed.

The leaflet goes on to say:

> This fraudster, whose identity it has not been possible to establish, usually has with him a young woman whom he passes off as his niece and to whom he has promised his fortune, which, he claims, is substantial. ... Recently, at 100 Rue Lazare, Paris, and later at 1 Rue Cherubini, he was accompanied by Joséphine-Jeannette Burns, who claims Belgian origins.

These circulars were sent far and wide, and the description and photos of 'Rivier' were extensively reproduced in the French press. For some reason which remains unclear, aside from 'Rivier's' rumoured visits to England, a copy was sent to the police in Liverpool. As the constabulary in that city knew nothing whatsoever about 'Rivier', his aliases or his associates, the paper was forwarded to Scotland Yard after a short delay. The Metropolitan Police clearly did not consider the enquiry to be very important, and only perfunctory efforts were made to find the fugitive. They eventually replied to Monsieur Hamard at the *Sûreté*, saying, 'enquiries have been made at hotels, restaurants and other likely places, but no traces of the accused have been found. Informants have been seen and a description of the accused circulated in our printed Information, but no information obtained.'

Towards the end of May, 'Lucien Rivier', trading as the Rente Bi-mensuelle, was adjudged bankrupt in his absence by a tribunal in Paris. It was a small step in the right direction for the French justice system, but brought little comfort to the thousands of victims. In all other respects, the authorities were making painfully slow progress in his case, and by now more than a month had elapsed since 'Rivier' had vanished. Disappointingly, the British police had been no help at all.

By early June, however, the *Sûreté* had some possible leads to follow up. Thanks to information from Mademoiselle Clérico, they had connected 'Rivier' with the 'Charles Deville' who, in 1901–02, had registered patents in France and Belgium, including the shopping trolley and the speaking clock. A note in the files stated that he had been investigated at the time, though no prosecution had followed. However, the *Sûreté* was still under the false impression that he was a Frenchman, and incorrectly identified him as a Charles Deville who was born in Paris in 1842. This mistake was subsequently corrected when detectives went even further back and found records of Charles Wells' arrest at Le Havre in 1892.

This was a crucial watershed for the enquiry, as the police now had a definite suspect for the first time. Hamard sent a letter dated 3 June 1911 to his British counterpart, Assistant Commissioner Macnaghten, containing several facts which the British ought to have known, and which they should have communicated to him much earlier: 'Rivier, alias Well [*sic*], is apparently none other than the individual referred to in London in about 1890 as having 'broken the bank' at Monte Carlo. He and his so-called niece were the subject of a music-hall song.' Hamard's letter goes on to say that 'Rivier' is the father of a young woman who is an artist. He encloses a sample of Rivier's handwriting on a small scrap of paper left at the offices of the Rente Bi-mensuelle. Hamard's letter also asserts that Wells was thought to have connections with various London criminals including a man known as 'the Italian' – a snippet of information hardly likely to be of much use to Scotland Yard.

Over three weeks pass before Macnaghten replies. Again, the Metropolitan Police have enquired at 'hotels, cafés, and other likely places, but no trace of the accused has been found' (this seems to have been a stock answer). 'So far there is no indication that he is in the country.' But they have checked the set of 'Rivier's' fingerprints on the original leaflet – something they presumably could have done some six weeks previously, if they had felt disposed to do so. The prints matched those taken from Wells (masquerading as 'Davenport') on his arrest after the Fishing and Trawling scam. No information whatsoever was available about 'Rivier's' alleged associates, but if the Paris Police would care to send photographs the Metropolitan Police would see if they could be identified. Inspectors Knell and Pike, who had worked on the Fishing and Trawling case, had been consulted: Wells had once indicated to them that his intention, ultimately, was to settle down in Canada or Argentina with 'his paramour'. This last piece of news was, of course, not quite what Hamard had hoped for.

Hamard replied two weeks later, enclosing photographs of two murderous looking denizens of the demi-monde, one of whom apparently was 'the Italian'. He sends a description of Jeannette Burns (who is, according to the *Sûreté*, also known as 'Jeanne Paris [*sic*] or Périsse'). In particular, Hamard asks for a photograph of Wells (a request Scotland Yard could not comply with, as they did not seem to have one) plus 'all information in your possession on his past, his marital status, his family, his associates, and his activities – especially in 1893 and 1906 …'

On receiving Hamard's letter, senior Scotland Yard officers seem to have realised at last that the French police had no intention of letting this matter drop. It was clear that the Metropolitan Police would be involved if Wells really was in Britain, and Superintendent Frank Froest, the CID chief, decided to put one of his top investigators in charge of the operation. Because of the international dimension to the case, one man was the obvious choice: Detective Sergeant George Nicholls, one of the new generation of officers who were changing the public's perception of the police. The force had moved on since the days of Jack the Ripper and, like their French counterparts, had adopted new, scientific ways to solve crimes. Only recently, for example, they had used forensic science to prove guilt on the part of Dr Crippen, whose subsequent capture was also aided by an up-to-the-minute invention – wireless. Naturally the use of these sophisticated methods required men of education and intellect.

George Robert Nicholls was born in 1877, the son of a nightwatchman. At school he was an outstanding pupil. By the time he left at the age of 14, he had gained a fluent command of French and German. His first job was as a barrister's clerk, but he yearned to join the police, and he enlisted as a constable with the Metropolitan Police as soon as he had reached the minimum age of 21.

His superiors were so impressed by his intelligence and his linguistic skills that after only two years he was taken off the beat and transferred to the CID. Described as 'tall and unassuming', and 'a man of splendid physique', he became Scotland Yard's expert on the many foreign criminals who made their way to London in the 1900s. By the time the 'Rivier' case came up he had already collaborated with police in France as well as Germany on several occasions.

He began his new assignment by assembling a detailed biography of Charles Wells, beginning with the patent fraud of the 1890s and the ensuing prosecution. He mentions the appearance at Wells' Old Bailey trial of Wells' brother-in-law, Henry Jartoux, who testified that Wells had lived in Marseille until 1879. The résumé continues with an account of the Fishing and Trawling Syndicate, which had much in common with the Rente Bi-mensuelle – 'Substantial sums out of capital were paid as interest, the investors being induced in this way to sink further and larger sums. The fraud was assuming vast proportions when Wells and Moyle were arrested ...'

Nicholls goes on to say, 'Wells was an exceptionally reserved man, frugal and simple in his habits. He appeared to have no friends or relatives.' But, as his letter reveals, the British authorities knew no more about Wells' origins than did the French. 'To the prison authorities he gave London and Oxford as his birthplace and the years 1833 and 1835 as the date of his birth. He has at times described himself as a French Canadian.'*

Nicholls had gone back to Inspector Pike and had shown him the photographs of 'the Italian' and another alleged associate, but Pike recognised neither of them. Besides, Nicholls added, Wells was never believed to have had any accomplices apart from Moyle. The British police had nothing whatsoever on file concerning his daughter. However, on a slightly more hopeful note – at least as far as the French police were concerned – Nicholls mentioned letters sent by Wells to Jeannette in 1905, in which 'he stated he was looking forward to the time when he would have gained sufficient money to settle down with her at some quiet spot in the South of France. There was also found in his possession a book on extradition law.'

Hamard and his colleagues digested this new information. For all the considerable detail it contained, it was hard to see how it could bring them closer to finding the fugitive 'Rivier'/Wells. But the reference to Henry Jartoux held out some hope. Hamard's next move would undoubtedly have been to contact the register office in Marseille, where he could expect to find a record of Wells' marriage. Perhaps that would yield some further lead. Since every other clue had led them nowhere, it had to be worth a try.

Out of Marseille's population of around 200,000, more than 1,000 marriages took place annually. The details, including full particulars of the bride and groom, their signatures and those of the witnesses, are recorded in numerous weighty registers. Every ten years an alphabetical index – the *Table Décennale* – is compiled by a team of clerks. This index shows which volume and page to consult for any individual's record.

---

* As mentioned above, the correct information had been published in the newspapers in 1893, shortly after his trial. Evidently, the police had not taken note of these revelations. (*Lichfield Mercury*, 28 April 1893)

But the entry for Wells' marriage to Marie Thérèse Jartoux is unaccountably missing.* It seems that Hamard and his team concluded that the marriage had not taken place in Marseille after all, and abandoned that line of enquiry.**

---

*   Author's note: I suspect that the usual confusion between the letters 'W' and 'V' may have been partly to blame for this. Some of the 'W's are shown in a separate section (they are very few in number) but most are lumped in with the 'V's. Conveniently for Charles Wells, his entry seems to have been omitted from *both* groups.

**   Birth, marriage and death records in France are archived locally. There is no central register, as in Britain, for example. Having failed to locate entries in Marseille, the police would have faced the almost impossible task of searching in every single *commune* in France.

15

The French Captain

On the night of 21–22 August 1911 – almost exactly four months after 'Rivier' had fled the country – an event took place which shook France to the core. A thief removed Leonardo da Vinci's painting, the *Mona Lisa*, from the Louvre. The painting was a cherished part of the national heritage and there was hardly a Frenchman or woman who did not feel that they had personally been a victim of the crime. Octave Hamard, as head of the *Sûreté*, took immediate control of the situation. He had the Louvre closed to visitors for a week; each and every employee there was subjected to a harsh and unrelenting interrogation. Yet the police failed to discover any hint as to the fate of the portrait.

As crime of the century, the Rente Bi-mensuelle affair had been overtaken by this new outrage. It is not known for certain whether Detective Inspector Roux was temporarily reassigned to the *Mona Lisa* investigation, or whether he was left to continue the hunt for 'Rivier' with a greatly reduced staff. Either way, precious resources, which would otherwise have been used to track down the missing banker, were withdrawn and deployed elsewhere. But the disappearance of the painting proved to be an insoluble puzzle. Hamard searched every corner of the gallery, including the rooms where the guards left their civilian clothes and where the cleaning equipment was kept. Monsieur Bertillon – an early pioneer of forensic science – visited the scene in person and took photographs and fingerprints. Every day new and increasingly pessimistic reports appeared, one of which said, 'Twelve days have elapsed since *La Joconde* disappeared, and every effort has ended in the same failure. At this moment we know nothing. Every day that passes the mystery deepens.' A few days later, *Le Figaro* mournfully declared, 'We have to accept the bad news – the *Mona Lisa* is lost.'

The police were criticised for their inability to reclaim the nation's best-loved work of art, and it was clear that Hamard would need to produce results quickly or face the prospect of being removed from office. (In the end, the *Mona Lisa* case never was solved by the police. The painting only reappeared when the thief voluntarily returned it two years later.)

Attention shifted back to the Rente Bi-mensuelle. Hamard couldn't find the painting but he redoubled the effort to find Wells, aka 'Rivier'. The search for details of Wells' marriage was begun afresh. This involved a mind-numbing trawl through thousands of pages of the marriage registers in Marseille, and possibly many other towns and cities, too.

At length, researchers stumbled upon the entry which had been omitted from the indexes – the 1866 record of Charles Wells' marriage to Marie Thérèse Jartoux. Further investigation revealed the marriage of Wells' daughter to Joseph Charles Vayre. The former actor was now a novelist. It was discovered that the couple lived at 267 Rue St-Honoré, Paris, a prestigious address adjoining the Ministry of Finance, close to Charles Wells' old territory around the Avenue de l'Opéra. The Rue St-Honoré was popular with artists, writers and other creative people, and the house itself had once been the home of minor royalty. Wells' estranged wife, Madame de Ville-Wells, resided here sometimes with her daughter and son-in-law; for the rest of the time her home was at Saint Tronc, the Marseille suburb where she had previously lived with Wells.

This new information revived Hamard's hope that the case could be solved. There was every possibility that Madame de Ville-Wells or her daughter knew the whereabouts of Charles: but there also remained a distinct possibility that, if questioned by the police, they might alert him, and he would take flight again. Acting with great caution, Hamard ordered his men to keep both addresses under discreet surveillance and even arranged for the mail to be covertly scrutinised before it was delivered. In mid-September his persistence was rewarded with a positive clue when a registered letter was delivered to Madame de Ville-Wells. Its origin was the post office at Earls Court, London. Charles was almost certainly sending money to his wife and daughter.

The police could not very well open a registered letter: indeed, if they had failed to deliver it unopened, the sender – Wells – would eventually have realised, which was the last thing they wanted. Instead they wrote to Scotland Yard, asking the Metropolitan Police to confirm the originator of the letter. They also asked whether Macnaghten and his team could determine whether Charles Wells or Jeannette Pairis had placed large sums of money in British banks – an enquiry which would have been overwhelming, given the number of banks in London alone.

In Paris the police kept searching for Jeannette's sister, Léonie, but she had moved away from her home in the Rue Cherubini – probably to escape unwanted attention from the media and the authorities. The *Sûreté* finally caught up with her at her new address, 1 Rue de la Collégiale, and began to keep her under close observation, too.

The *Sûreté* had discovered that Wells once lived with his wife and daughter in Plymouth, and suggested that enquiries might be made there. Their letter to Scotland Yard also claims (incorrectly) that in 1893 Charles Wells and Jeannette Pairis had lived in London at 'Raydnor Street, Bermontsey [*sic*]'. Finally, among 'Rivier's' papers at the bank, they had evidently discovered an old photograph of Jeannette, probably dating from the 1890s, when she first knew him. A copy of this photo was made, and was sent to the Metropolitan Police (Plate 4).

In reply, Sergeant George Nicholls said that he had inter-viewed the post office employee who had dealt with the letter to Madame de Ville-Wells, but the clerk could not remember who had posted it. The name of the sender of a registered letter was never recorded, apparently. He adroitly sidestepped the request to determine whether Wells had been depositing large sums of money in banks, with a vague assurance that the matter would be looked in to. The Plymouth Police had told him that Wells had not been seen there since 1892, when he had 'a large steam yacht anchored in Plymouth Sound'. They had also given the routine answer that 'enquiry has been made at all principal hotels, and other likely places in this town, but without success'.

As far as 'Raydnor Street, Bermontsey' was concerned, Sergeant Nicholls said that no such street, or street with a similar name, existed in Bermondsey, and he pointed out that at the time in question, 1893, Wells was in prison. (The correct reference is probably to *Radnor* Street in Chelsea, where it is said that Charles and Jeannette first met in 1890. Radnor Street adjoins Redesdale Street, where the skipper of the *Palais Royal*, Captain Smith, and the estranged wife of Aristides Vergis used to live. Possibly, Jeannette lived there later while Wells was in jail.) Nicholls also paid a visit to the photographers who had taken the picture of Jeannette, the firm of W. & J. Stuart of 47–49 Brompton Road. He was told that the order could no longer be traced in their books, but if he could obtain the reference number on the back of the original, there was a possibility of identifying the original customer. This suggestion was not, it seems, followed up.

'Rivier' had disappeared from France in April. It was now November, and although some progress was being made there was still no certainty that he would ever be caught.

Shortly after his escape from France to Britain, Charles Wells bought a smart 60ft steam yacht with two masts, a black hull and white funnel, from a broker in Southampton (Plate 15). The yacht's official name was *Harbinger*, but Wells renamed her *Excelsior*, to mirror the name of his company, Excelsior Yachting and Trading – though he neglected to register this change officially. He engaged two local sailors as crew: Ernest Emery was appointed skipper, and Henry Knight became engineer. Together they sailed 200 nautical miles westwards, along the south coast, to Falmouth in Cornwall, where Charles and Jeannette had decided to settle.

In 1912, Falmouth was still a port of considerable significance to the British economy. Many ships stopped here as their last port of call before they set out across the Atlantic, or their first as they returned. The town benefited from 'one of the finest and most capacious harbours in the country' in the broad estuary of the River Fal. During the winter storms as many as 350 ships could find shelter here. Falmouth had foundries, engineering works, shipyards, tug services 'and all other conveniences for repairing ships and taking in and discharging cargoes'. Yet its population was only 11,000, and it retained more of the atmosphere of a large village than that of a small town.[*]

Wells arranged to rent a mooring from a local firm, Cox & Co., shipbuilders and engineers. With more than 600 staff, they were the biggest employers in town. The company was run by Herbert Henry Cox, a man in his early forties. As well as his business interests, Cox was well known for his civic duties. He served as a local magistrate, an honorary position open to men of good character who wanted to help the community. From time to time he also chaired a committee of enquiry into shipwrecks.

Wells set about making improvements to his yacht. He spared no expense and the local shipbuilders and engineers received many profitable orders from him. Cox & Co. were no doubt

---

[*]   Falmouth's port has significantly declined since then in commercial terms. The emphasis now is on boating for pleasure.

contracted to carry out much of this work, and in return they allowed him to have mail sent to him at the company's office, to be collected at his convenience.

With the boat safely at anchor off Custom House Quay, 'Charles Deville', as he now called himself, engaged two Falmouth men as extra crew members: William McClusky was given the job of steward, and Cecil Kiddell was taken on as deckhand. From the outset, the yacht and its unusual owners attracted much local curiosity. 'Mr Deville' acquired a reputation in the town as a 'kind old gent'. As he spoke English with a slight foreign accent and almost invariably wore a yachting cap, the locals nicknamed him 'the French Captain'. He gave the impression of being 'a typical millionaire yacht owner with a fastidious taste for ease and luxury and enjoyment'.

The couple seldom came ashore, but sometimes a small boat would bring them to the quayside, and they would visit the local shops. 'Mr Deville' was a good customer and spent money on a lavish scale. One tradesman told him he could open an account and settle at the end of the quarter, but he replied, 'I have plenty of money. Why should I not pay when I buy?' When repairs and alterations were carried out on the *Excelsior*, 'Deville' 'almost wanted to pay before the work was done'.

The elegant 'Madame Deville' – 'quite thirty years his junior' – was 'thoroughly Parisian in her tastes and loved to come ashore in fashionable gowns and hats'. On the rare occasions when they ventured into town in the evening it was usually to attend a play or concert at the Star Theatre, or the Drill Hall. Sometimes they would visit one of the travelling booths in the marketplace to watch the new and increasingly popular moving pictures.

In fine weather they spent most of the time fishing and shooting. Wells constructed a little cabin at the aft end of the vessel from which Jeannette could 'lie down unobserved and shoot wild fowl with a double barrelled gun while the yacht was anchored in one of the numerous small inlets on the Cornish coast'. He also designed and commissioned a machine to assist her when she was fishing:

> The lines were paid out from a couple of reels fixed in the interior of the shooting-box, and outside was a small engine, also designed by him, which rapidly wound up the line when the bait was taken. By means of this mechanical arrangement Mademoiselle [sic] was able to land her own fish without the risk of cutting her fingers with the line.

Charles never tired of altering and improving the yacht to make it as comfortable as possible for Jeannette, and was once overheard by a crew member to say that all he wanted was 'to make his little doll happy'. He had the entire vessel rigged up with electric lighting, including a new searchlight on deck. '[Jeannette's] boudoir on the yacht was a model of exquisite ease, being supplied with luxurious settees and easy chairs. The sleeping cabins, too, were on the same scale of elegance and comfort.'

It can justly be said that the *Excelsior* was the fulfilment of Charles' dreams – a smaller version of the *Palais Royal*. Twenty years earlier, Charles had promised Jeannette a floating palace, but events had conspired against him. Now his plans had succeeded at last, and he could fulfil his pledge.

The four crewmen came to form an affectionate bond with their new employers, though they suspected that some mystery surrounded the couple. 'Mr and Mrs Deville' were evidently extremely wealthy, but the source of their wealth was something the crew were unable to establish. Aside from a faint rumour that Madame had inherited a fortune of £45,000, nothing further was known. But the men did notice that at intervals of roughly three months the couple went to London, returning a few days later.

Unknown to the crew, these trips to the capital were for Charles and Jeannette to confer with their accountant and lawyer about their investments. Occasionally Charles went on his own, and wrote to Jeannette, telling her about the business he had conducted. One of his letters reads as follows:

30 June 1911

Adored love, more than you believe it.

I have just handed to the solicitor £1,800 to add to your little fortune. Tomorrow I think of adding some more money for the one I love so much. I am now going to the bank to arrange matters there as well ... When I have finished your business today I shall look after you, for you are before everything in my body, heart and my soul. I love you so much, so much, so much. Tomorrow I shall have copies of all your mortgages which at the moment amount to £6,000 – 150,000 *f* for my Nana. I hope you will love me not for 150,000 *f* but for millions ... I am waiting to squeeze you tightly in my devoted arms. Sweetheart, I embrace you, your Loulou.

Jeannette, meanwhile, was in regular contact with her sister, Léonie, in Paris. She wrote that Charles was planning to obtain boats in connection with a fishing business, and expressed the hope that they would always remain together near the sea. Charles also corresponded with Léonie, whom he had come to regard as an unofficial sister-in-law. To avoid detection, they always arranged for these letters to be posted from London, probably by Jeannette's close friend, Marion White, so that the London postmark disguised their true place of origin. Similarly, Léonie had been instructed to reply *poste-restante* at the Earls Court Post Office.

Charles sent a letter to Léonie at the beginning of December, and was rather concerned when no reply came. He wrote again a few days later, 'Not having had any news from you, I wait for your reply before writing at length. I will just say that we are well and we hope your letter will bring us good news about all the family.' A few days later no reply has been received to either letter and he is becoming anxious. 'If you do not reply straight away we will have been without any news from you these last three months, because we are leaving on Sunday [17 December]. Jeannette is anxious to know how you all are, especially her uncle, and her brother Léon.'

It was time for Charles and Jeannette to make their regular three-monthly trip to London to consult their accountant and lawyer. They returned to Falmouth on Christmas Eve and surprised their crew members by giving each man a week's wages as a present.

The *Sûreté*'s painstaking surveillance of Léonie was about to repay the effort. Having noticed that she used a particular mail box to post her outgoing correspondence, they surreptitiously went through its contents for envelopes in her handwriting. She had sent letters to Charles in London, some addressed to him in his full name, others using just his initials, C.W. These were opened and scrutinised by the police.

They also intercepted any correspondence sent by Charles or Jeannette to Léonie. But the letters were written on plain paper, with no address shown. Apart from the obvious fact that they had been posted in London, they gave no clue whatsoever to Wells' whereabouts.

Forensic science was still in its infancy. Subjecting the envelopes to a minute examination might seem an obvious step today, but in 1911 it was a giant leap. It gave the detectives their first big break in the case. Under the gummed strip along the edge of the flap, the name of the maker of the envelope was embossed. An urgent letter was sent to Scotland Yard:

20 December 1911

Further to my earlier communications concerning Charles Wells, also known as 'Rivier' ... I have the honour of enclosing these letters sent by him to the sister of his mistress ... One of these letters bears the stamp of the Earls Court Post Office; the paper seems to originate from Cosby

Broom Ltd., 3 Station Buildings, Earls Court, whose mark it bears ...

It was not until 12 January that Sergeant Nicholls replied, but his letter was well worth the wait:

I have ... through Messrs Cosby Broom, the manufacturers of one of the two envelopes which were forwarded by Paris Police, ascertained that Wells is interested in a company formed here in London, and I believe that further enquiry will locate him.

It was the first time in the entire investigation that anything as hopeful as this had been heard. Hamard was so encouraged by the news that he immediately dispatched Inspector Jean Roux to London.

In mid-January, it was reported that Henry Labouchère had died at the age of 81.* Wells would doubtless have received the news dispassionately, neither rejoicing in the passing of his nemesis, nor mourning the loss. In fact, with the exception of Jeannette, people did not mean very much to him. But, if only from a logical viewpoint, he felt that the world of Charles Wells was a much safer place without Labouchère.

Two or three days later, Nicholls called at the offices of Wells' company at 235 High Holborn, where he was informed that Wells had not been seen for some time. Nicholls sent a memo to his chief on 19 January:

Further enquiries show that Wells has had letters or parcels addressed to him recently in the name of C. de Ville, c/o

---

*   Remarkably, in his latter years Labouchère had himself been accused of questionable financial dealings, having published defamatory articles in his publication, *Truth*, with a view to lowering certain share prices. He was said to have bought the shares at an artificially low price and had profited when they later returned to their normal level.

Messrs Cox & Co., Engineers, Falmouth. It seems therefore quite possible that Wells and the woman Pairis are on board the yacht which may be at Falmouth, or if not that he is living at Falmouth. At any rate discreet enquiry of Messrs. Cox, may lead to the discovery of Wells. ... Detective Inspector Roux of the Paris Police has been here several days making enquiries, and he was also in charge of this matter in Paris, so that he is acquainted with all the details. He also can identify Wells.

Inspector Roux had no official powers to act as a police officer in Britain, though there was nothing to prevent him from asking questions. As he spoke practically no English, he was undoubtedly accompanied on these missions by Sergeant Nicholls. Nicholls wrote:

He is proceeding tonight to Falmouth and I respectfully beg to suggest that a copy of this report together with the [arrest] warrant be forwarded to the Falmouth Police with a request that they make enquiry and arrest Rivier and the woman Pairis if found and telegraph to this office, also that their property be seized.

Roux boarded the midnight train from Paddington to the West Country with arrest warrants for 'Rivier' aka Wells and for Jeannette Pairis aka 'Mrs Burns'. The journey would be long and tiring but the inspector felt sure that it would be worthwhile, and that his search for the missing banker was almost over. Today was 19 January, which meant that it was precisely nine months since 'Rivier' had vanished.

Just over ten hours later Roux arrived at Falmouth, tired, bone-shaken and dishevelled. A welcome sight greeted him among the milling crowds of passengers and those waiting to meet them – a British bobby in full uniform, sent specially to look out for the important detective from far-away Paris. Out of Falmouth's ten-man police force, 31-year-old PC Herbert

John Crocker was the one best qualified for this assignment. To Inspector Roux's delight, the young constable spoke excellent French, and had been detailed to act as his interpreter and guide.

A little later, the two men – already firm friends and conversing animatedly – went for a stroll through the town. It was Saturday morning. Ignoring the overcast sky and freezing temperature, the hardy citizens of Falmouth flocked into the narrow main street, busy with their weekend shopping. The sight of Constable Crocker (now in plain clothes) in the company of a burly foreigner did not go unnoticed and sparked a great deal of gossip and speculation among the townspeople. While Crocker was showing the French inspector around, and helping him to familiarise himself with the surroundings, Charles and Jeannette were strolling about the town at the same time. During their jaunt, Charles reserved two seats at a performance of the melodrama *No Mother to Guide Her*, which was being staged at the Drill Hall on the following Wednesday. The booking clerk asked for his name. 'Wells,' he replied, absent-mindedly. Then he quickly corrected himself, 'Deville'.

Falmouth is a long, narrow town, stretching for nearly a mile along the edge of the vast harbour, from the docks in the south-east to the yachting club in the north-west. The main street, where most of the shops are to be found, runs roughly parallel to the shoreline. Roux scrutinised the face of every passer-by, trying to recognise the man he had questioned in the Place Boïeldieu nine months earlier. But the fugitive was nowhere to be seen. The two parties must have been wandering around different parts of the town.

Charles and Jeannette returned to their yacht in the harbour. Their appetites sharpened by the fresh sea air, they started eating lunch at about one o'clock. At roughly the same time two policemen approached the quay. The tide was exceptionally low, and festoons of slippery brown-green seaweed hung down from the high watermark, like curtains on a pole. The sea rippled with the sluggish movement of water near the point of freezing. The two men, Falmouth's superintendent of police and his sergeant, cautiously made their way down the slippery, grey, granite steps, lowered themselves into a borrowed dinghy, rowed across to the steam yacht *Excelsior*, and went on board.

Charles and Jeannette, though taken by surprise, quickly recovered their composure. The superintendent asked them whether they had any objection to a French detective coming on board, and Charles consented. Roux, who had been waiting impatiently on the quay, was then rowed out to the *Excelsior*. However unperturbed he may have seemed, Charles must have experienced the shock of his life when he recognised the portly inspector who had quizzed him so thoroughly the previous April.

Both Charles and Jeannette were arrested. 'Time was given Mlle Jeanne Pairis to complete her shore-going toilette,' it was reported, and she appeared on deck a little later, exquisitely dressed and wearing 'a large quantity of beautiful jewellery'. Charles, with his 'well-brushed, pointed, iron-grey beard and moustache, and grey hair', looked 'dapper and distinguished' in a blue serge suit, heavy blue coat and the perennial yachting cap. Keen observers noticed that his trousers were fashionably pressed in the latest style, with creases* fore and aft.

Escorted by the two British police officers and by Roux, they boarded the *Excelsior*'s motor launch. As the boat started for the shore Wells looked despondent, but Jeannette seemed quite unconcerned. 'Keep the yacht clean,' she called to the captain, 'we'll be back in a day or two.' The party landed at the Prince of Wales Pier, and made their way up the steps and along the jetty. They then cut across the Market Square, where only recently

---

* The late King Edward VII had created a fashion for creases in trousers – but at the sides. Creases at front and back became the norm, however.

Charles and Jeannette had enjoyed the moving pictures. At the police station in Berkeley Vale they were both searched, and their belongings listed.

Jeannette had a veritable treasure trove on her person:

> One £20 Bank of England note; 12s. 3d. in coin; 7 gold bangles; 2 gold watches (1 set with diamonds); 2 gold chains; 1 gold safety pin; 1 gold necklet; 4 gold rings (3 set with diamonds, 1 set with red stone); 2 pairs ear-rings set diamonds; 1 gold brooch; 1 gold bracelet; 1 diamond star brooch; a leather handbag; a leather bag purse.

Considering the weight of all these trappings, it seems a miracle that she was able to stand upright. The contents of Wells' pockets were more modest: a gold watch and chain, a sovereign purse and £4 10s 2½d in cash.

An ecstatic Inspector Roux sent two telegrams, one to Scotland Yard, the other to the *Sûreté*, bearing the news that Wells and Pairis had been captured. For the French detective this moment marked the end of an exhausting and seemingly endless pursuit. But he could have had no idea of the obstacles that would still have to be overcome.

'The accused had their meals at the police station together, and chatted freely with the police officials in whose charge they were,' a local paper recorded. One officer showed Wells a photograph in a newspaper, supposedly of him. Wells laughed heartily and joked that if that picture had been all the police had to go on, they would never have found him. 'The parties were allowed to have some meals from one of the principal hotels of the town' (probably the King's Hotel, near the police station). 'They have had their meals together in a private room at the police station, and have been allowed to sit on a plain wooden form in front of a fire, thus being able to converse pleasantly together – always in French.'

News of the arrest spread quickly. The *New York Times* was first off the mark (thanks to the time difference of a few hours), and carried a report on the actual day of the arrest. Later, the *Yorkshire Evening Post* regaled its readers with:

ANOTHER EPISODE IN A REMARKABLE CAREER
The 'Man who broke the Bank at Monte Carlo,' the hero of the song which all London whistled and sang in the nineties, has been arrested in Falmouth Harbour on his own yacht under circumstances as dramatic as Scotland Yard has ever known.

In France, where thousands of investors had been anxiously waiting for news of their money for the past nine months, reports of the arrest of 'Rivier' were seized upon avidly. The French newspaper *Gil Blas* reminded its readers that nothing definite had been heard of 'Rivier' since his disappearance until very recently:

The *Sûreté* put one its finest bloodhounds, Inspector Roux, on to the search for Rivier. It has turned out brilliantly. Yesterday he announced the arrest of Rivier (a.k.a. Wells) and of his mistress, Jeanne Pairis, on a yacht ... for which he had paid 250,000 francs, and that [Rivier] had in his possession at the moment of his arrest, a large sum of around one million [francs].

The piece must have raised the hopes of many a French victim – quite unrealistically, as it would turn out. A more subdued account appeared in the Paris journal *L'Aurore*, which stated that Monsieur Bourdeaux would be seeking 'Rivier's' extradition, though it was unlikely that this would be granted by the British.

Some newspapers said Rivier had forty-three aliases, while others claimed that he had fifty.* And just as he changed his name whenever it suited him, he also claimed different nationalities at will. *Le Figaro* reminded its readers that no one knew for certain whether he was British or French, though his country of birth would undoubtedly be a crucial factor in deciding whether extradition could take place. He spoke fluent French, English and Italian, the report added, and would undoubtedly make life difficult for the justice system.

---

*   The presumed number of Wells' aliases seems to have crept up day by day in the press. The actual number – excluding variant spellings – was about ten.

16

A Vast Roulette

At Falmouth Police Station on the day after the arrests, Jeannette enjoyed a breakfast consisting of two raw eggs, a cup of tea and a cigarette. 'Pairis is a great lover of cigarette smoking and was allowed to freely indulge in the habit when in custody.' Wells spent the morning with a solicitor, Edward E. Armitage, who was also the local town clerk.

At about noon, George Nicholls arrived at the police station from London, accompanied by his wife, Alice, who had been enlisted as an escort for Jeannette. An urgent telegram from Scotland Yard was waiting for them. Inspector Pike had suddenly remembered that 'when Wells last arrested his woman had bank notes sewn in [her] corsets'. Pike recommended that she should be searched – just the sort of task that Mrs Nicholls had been brought along for.

Wells looked up at Nicholls, who towered above him. Nicholls began the process of formally identifying both prisoners. 'Is your name Lucien Rivier?'

'My name is Charles Wells.'

'You have passed under the name of Lucien Rivier in Paris.'

'If they like to call me Rivier, very well; yes, it's me.'

'Is your name Jeanne Pairis?'

'Yes, that's my name. I have nothing to conceal.'

'I hold a warrant for the arrest of you both for fraud and participating in fraud committed within the jurisdiction of the French government.' Nicholls started to read the warrant aloud to both of them, but Wells immediately pointed to Jeannette. 'It is absolutely false as to her. She has done nothing.'

Nicholls produced one of the printed leaflets from the French police and showed it to Wells: then he showed the small photograph of Jeannette to her. 'These are the photographs of you?'

Both said yes. Nicholls then informed them that he would seize all of the property on the boat, and Wells replied, 'Very well, you'll find everything open on board.'

Because the warrant had been issued in a different county, certain legal niceties had to be observed when the prisoners were formally charged. A local magistrate had to be present, and Arthur William Chard, JP, was asked to attend. As a marine engineer and surveyor, Chard was an acquaintance and near contemporary of Herbert Cox, the shipbuilder who had done work for Wells, and on at least one occasion the two men had jointly presided over the committee which investigated wrecked and missing ships. Chard had no doubt heard all about the 'French captain' and his pretty wife: gossip about them had been circulating in the town for months. And he had almost certainly learned still more about the yacht and the couple's lavish lifestyle from his friend and colleague, Mr Cox.

In happier circumstances, with their shared interest in engineering, boats and the sea, Chard, Wells and Cox would have got along famously together. But today Chard was there to deal with more serious matters. He turned to Wells, and asked him whether he disputed the allegation that he was the man named on the warrant.

'Not at all,' Wells said. 'I can't deny my name. I'm the man you used to sing about. I'm Wells, the man who broke the bank at Monte Carlo.'

There. He had said it. After all the months of secrecy, pretence and deceit he had revealed his true identity. In many ways it must have been a relief not to have to dissemble any longer.

At the harbour, meanwhile, police officers had carried out a thorough search of the *Excelsior*, and had listed the property on board – an exercise which bore a close resemblance to the annual stocktake at a major department store. Jeannette's wardrobe included a lavish assortment of high-quality clothing, including coats, jackets, a nightgown, silk blouses, '6 pairs knickers' and '3 shemise [*sic*]'. Wells' wardrobe, on the other hand, seems to have comprised: one white jersey; two pairs of pants; two singlets; one cardigan jacket; three shirts. The vessel was made secure and Captain Emery was retained to stay and look after it. A police officer stood guard around the clock.

The arrest of the 'French captain' and his alluring companion was the talk of Falmouth. The townspeople could scarcely remember another story of such proportions. A rumour circulated that the prisoners would be taken to London by train on the Sunday, and around five o'clock in the afternoon, large crowds gathered at the station, in the belief that the accused would leave on the 5.20 to Paddington. But Nicholls was still sifting through huge quantities of evidence, and their departure was postponed. In a telegram to Scotland Yard, Nicholls advised Superintendent Froest that he had found receipts and chequebooks relating to the couple's bank accounts and to Wells' safe deposit box. In addition, the Excelsior Company held an account at Barclays, Fleet Street. Nicholls urged his CID colleague, Sergeant Crutchett, to visit all of these places without delay, in case Wells' solicitor tried to remove any of the assets or other evidence. His telegram ends with a warning, 'Have information heavy cheques likely to be presented tomorrow morning. Nicholls.'

Detective Sergeant Alfred Crutchett was five years older than Nicholls. Although he had a head start on his friend and colleague, his rise through the ranks of the Metropolitan Police had taken longer because of the old-fashioned practices of the time. 'I was a uniformed constable for six and a half years, and in those days one had to show some special aptitude for detective work before one could become a plain-clothes man down in the East End, acting as a patrol to assist the recognised detectives,' he later said.

In 1905, while still a lowly constable, he had assisted in the investigation of a murder in Deptford, south London. An elderly couple were beaten to death during the course of a robbery by two brothers, Albert and Alfred Stratton, who forced open a cash box, which they left on the floor, and escaped with £12. Crutchett was one of the first officers on the scene. Realising that the cash box might furnish important clues, he carefully picked it up using pieces of paper to avoid contaminating the evidence with his own fingerprints. The offenders' prints were later discovered on the box, and the men were subsequently found guilty and hanged. This was a landmark case in Britain – the first conviction for murder to rely on fingerprint evidence. And without Crutchett's presence of mind it undoubtedly would have failed.

Soon afterwards Crutchett was promoted to detective, and eventually he worked on several cases of fraud. 'At that time Chancery Lane and the Strand were full of bogus firms,' he recalled, 'and most of my work for a time lay in tracing out the long firm frauds and dealing with bogus concerns.'

When Crutchett visited the banks where Charles and Jeannette had placed their money, he thus found himself in familiar territory. At Barclays in Fleet Street he discovered a balance of £1,200 and £60 was found in the London County and Westminster Bank in the name of 'J. Binet'. Although he had no official power to take control of these funds, police records show that he 'induced' the managers of the banks to hold the money. He then went to the safe deposit office in Chancery Lane, and found that Charles and Jeannette had a box there, as Nicholls had said.

Next day – a Monday – crowds gathered at Falmouth Station yet again before the 1.30 p.m. and 5.20 p.m. departures. But each time, they were disappointed. Nicholls had returned to the yacht, and was still sifting through masses of material.

Yet the people waited patiently. A crowd of 150 locals huddled in the falling temperatures and drenching rain to catch a glimpse of Charles and Jeannette. They were finally rewarded for their patience when, at about nine o'clock in the evening, two cabs appeared. Charles Wells, Jeannette Pairis, Detective Sergeant Nicholls, Mrs Nicholls and Inspector Roux got out. They were accompanied by the local police superintendent and his sergeant. Pandemonium followed, as the mass of people surged forward to see the man who broke the bank, and his mistress. The excited crowd spontaneously burst into song:

> You can hear them sigh and wish to die,
> You can see them wink the other eye
> At the man who broke the bank at Monte Carlo.

As the little procession entered the booking hall, the throng parted to allow them on to the platform. Charles and Jeannette spoke with the well-wishers, and shook their hands, like members of the royal family at a society ball. An onlooker shouted, 'Goodbye, good luck!' and Jeannette replied, 'Thank you'. Two crewmen from the *Excelsior* greeted them warmly. Charles and Jeannette asked them to pass on the 'compliments of the master and mistress' to the other two.

Reporters scribbled furiously, noting every detail of the couple's appearance. Wells was described as wearing his familiar yachting cap and a dark overcoat. He carried an umbrella. Jeannette – 'short in stature, but of good figure' and 'distinctly of French appearance' – wore a black outfit with black feather boa and a light, mauve veil which only partly obscured her face. As press photographers jostled for a better picture, a flashlight went off immediately in front of her and she gave a little scream.

'I can hardly see,' she exclaimed. Mrs Nicholls took her arm and led her on to the train where a third-class smoking compartment had been reserved for them.

'Wells seemed to be much interested and amused at the attention which was being paid him, and would have liked to remain on the platform for a while, but Detective Sergeant Nicholls would not allow this, and he entered the carriage to occupy the seat opposite his companion.' Edward Armitage, the solicitor, stepped on to the train for a few moments to bid Charles and Jeannette farewell, and the superintendent of Falmouth Police and his assistant said their goodbyes. The couple thanked them for the kind and considerate treatment they had received while in custody.

> Close to the door stood the *Excelsior* sailors, and from time to time the accused would turn to them, and, smiling, wave their hands to them – Wells rather wistfully, but Pairis cheerfully. The blinds of the compartment were then drawn, and the crowd were unable to see them again. An ubiquitous photographer, however, got around to the other side of the carriage and again 'snapped' the occupants.

Wells sat in one corner of the compartment, and appeared to be 'as comfortable and unconcerned as an ordinary traveller'. Next to him was Sergeant Nicholls. Roux occupied the seat immediately opposite Wells. Next to the inspector sat Jeannette, and beside her Mrs Nicholls. 'All five were obviously interested in the conversation, in which the French detective appeared to be a vivacious leader.'

The train rattled and wheezed its way up the steep branch line to Truro, where the party had to change for the London express. A few onlookers had gathered here, too, along with more reporters and photographers. Shortly before midnight the train halted at Plymouth's Millbay Station, and was delayed there for half an hour. As they waited for their journey to resume, Wells must inevitably have been reminded of times gone by, for they were close to Walker Terrace, and to the dock where the refit of the *Palais Royal* had been completed a few years after.

On the following morning, as they pulled into Paddington Station an hour late, they were tired and irritable, their muscles cramped from the long night in the confined, smoky compartment. Here, too, a small crowd had gathered despite the early hour. 'Those who saw a short, slight, grey-bearded, rather benevolent-looking man step from the milk train at Paddington in the gloom of the early morning were rather surprised at his appearance.'

As the little group made its way along the platform, Wells was tetchy when photographers tried to take pictures of him. He opened his umbrella and hid his face. 'His companion ... looked very much frightened. ... The pair looked very tired and care-worn as they were driven off to Bow Street in the company of officers from Scotland Yard.' A taxi-cab full of papers and other evidence from the yacht accompanied them.

Charles Wells stood in the dock at Bow Street Magistrates' Court, where he had appeared exactly nineteen years previously. But this time Jeannette was at his side. Her presence added considerably to what was already intense public excitement:

> The unusual interest created throughout the country by the news of the arrest, was reflected in the appearance of the Court. Before the ordinary business was commenced persons interested arrived in order to make sure of securing admission and by the time the magistrate took his seat the Court was fairly full. It became crowded long before the prisoners made their appearance in the dock. Both are smartly dressed, the woman particularly so.

Jeannette was described as 'short, plump, and vivacious' with 'clean-cut features and long eyelashes'. She looked much younger than her 42 years. Wells was said to have 'little trace of the "independent air" mentioned in the song'. Instead spectators saw 'a man whom age has withered'.

This time the purpose of the hearing was to hear evidence of the crimes, and for the magistrate, Sir Albert de Rutzen, to judge whether the French government's claim for extradition should be granted. If he was not satisfied that Wells and Jeannette had committed the crimes, or if he considered that for any reason extradition should not take place, he could refuse France's request, and the couple would walk free. 'Rivier is sure to use the argument which succeeded at the time for Guérin, the Devil's Island escaper,' claimed a French newspaper, the *Petit Parisien*. Guérin had committed a particularly violent bank robbery in Paris in 1901 and had been sent to Devil's Island, French Guyana, to serve a life sentence. After four years he escaped and made his way to Britain. When France requested his extradition he proved that he was a British national and extradition was consequently refused. The *Petit Parisien* concluded that 'Rivier will plead that he is [also] a British citizen and will rely on a certificate which proves that he was born in 1841 at Broxbourne as Charles Wells. Besides, the [extradition] warrant describes both prisoners as British subjects.' (Jeannette had gained British nationality upon marrying Dr. Burns who was, ostensibly, a British national).

It was far too early for the court to consider these matters in detail: the police investigations were still continuing, and it was anyone's guess as to how long it would take for all the evidence to be processed. For now, Detective Sergeant George Nicholls gave formal testimony that he had identified, arrested and charged the prisoners. He read out the list of property found in their possession, and when he came to the long list of Jeannette's jewellery, she was seen to smile broadly. Otherwise she seemed to take no notice of the proceedings. Wells, on the other hand, listened intently to the evidence and once or twice whispered to Jeannette.

Their solicitor, Mr Clarke Hall, said the prisoners had a complete answer to all the charges. They had considerable property, which had unfortunately been seized. Wells had £1,200 in Barclays, but two cheques he had drawn for his defence had been stopped by the police. They could not access any funds – not even for their immediate requirements, such as 'food and sleeping accommodation in prison'. He urged the magistrate to allow a trifling sum such as £5 to be made available.

'We have heard of large means, and we have also heard of large frauds,' the magistrate replied. 'They sometimes mean one another.'

'I entirely appreciate that,' Clarke Hall said. But his next statement came as a surprise. 'I do not think those who are acquainted with him will ever seriously suggest that Mr Wells has not a considerable amount derived from other sources.' This assertion contradicts all of the evidence we have seen up to now, which tends to suggest that Wells had failed to hold on to any of the vast sums which had passed through his hands long ago. However, the solicitor would later attempt to show that the funds now in Wells' possession were not the proceeds of recent frauds in France but money that he had retained since his casino wins of the 1890s. For this gambit to succeed, he needed to plant the germ of the idea at this early stage. Clarke Hall's statement fuelled persistent rumours that Wells had stashed away a secret fortune from his patent activities or his Monte Carlo profits (or both). It is unlikely, though, that these stories had any foundation: if Wells had been in possession of a fortune he surely would not have mortgaged the *Palais Royal*, for example.

The magistrate, in the event, would not release even the smallest sum, and to make things worse, he also refused them bail. Looking 'downcast' they were led down to the cells to await their next court hearing. Prison was nothing new for Charles, who had spent several years in captivity and was inured to life in a cell, but for Jeannette the abrupt change from her life of luxury on the yacht to an existence behind bars must have been a brutal shock.

Wells surreptitiously passed an envelope to Sergeant Nicholls. Inside was a scrap of paper bearing a hastily written note in pencil. He asked to be allowed a private interview with Inspector Roux: 'It is for the very great benefit of creditors that I wish to give him most important information ... out of hearing of any witnesses.' He ended with a postscript in which he thanked the British officers for their 'great kindness'. His exact intention remains a mystery, but it seems likely that he wanted to negotiate an arrangement with the French detective, under which he would return all the money to his French victims in exchange for being allowed to remain in Britain as a free man. However, Nicholls decided not to pass the note on to Roux.*

Now that Charles and Jeannette were under lock and key, Nicholls and Crutchett set about tying up the loose ends of the investigation. Nicholls wrote a full report on the arrest, and itemised the documents found on board the yacht. While he was in Falmouth, he had discovered that Wells had also left several very large locked trunks and some fishing tackle in the custody of Williams & Co., a local firm of ship's chandlers.

Soon afterwards, strongbox number 340 at the Chancery Lane Safe Deposit was opened. Inside were Consols, cash, War Bonds, Australian bonds to the value of £2,500, and other securities. There were receipts and letters in the name of Joséphine Binet addressed to her at 28 Essex Street and at 22 Micklethwaite Road. A copy of the marriage certificate for James Burns and Jeanne Pairis was also found. Finally, statements were taken from witnesses, including Jeannette's friend, Marion White, and a number of individuals living in the vicinity of Micklethwaite Road.

---

*   The note remains in Wells' police file at the National Archives to this day.

Charles and Jeannette made a further court appearance on 8 March 1912. George Nicholls – who had meanwhile been promoted to the rank of detective inspector – read out some of Wells' intimate letters to Jeannette which had been found during the police searches. Coming from the lips of the lofty, urbane detective, phrases such as 'you are before everything in my body, heart and my soul' and 'waiting to squeeze you tightly in my devoted arms' must have sounded awkward, perhaps even comical.

The lawyer representing the French government claimed that more than £40,000 had been brought to this country from France, and that the defendants had made wills in each other's favour. In one of many appearances in court Wells made a spirited appeal to the magistrate, asking to be set free immediately. He held up a copy of the extradition treaty recently signed by Britain and France. Wells pointed out that the wording of this document suggested that it was the British Foreign Office who ought to have made an application for their extradition, and they had not done so. (It would, of course, have been nonsensical for the British government to have to apply to itself, but this was how Wells interpreted the phrasing of the document, and his advocate backed him up.)

'We have been here three times in 14 days,' Wells said. 'This lady is an English lady, having married Dr. Burns, and I am an Englishman. The law is that an application must be made by the diplomatic agent of [the accused person's] country.' The magistrate replied that the point must be further argued. Perhaps the Home Office would release Wells, but he was certainly not going to do so.

'And I can't take a cab and go to see the Home Secretary?' Wells asked.

'I must remand you.'

Leaving aside such legal hair-splitting, his lawyer argued that up to the point where Wells had left Paris, no one had lost any money, everyone had been paid their interest and some had doubled their initial capital in 100 days – just as Wells had promised.

Wells had never undertaken to invest their money in stocks and shares, or in any other investment for that matter. 'The money was not handed to him for any specific purpose. He might, if he chose, use it at Monte Carlo, a place with which he was not unfamiliar. His clients did not mind where the interest came from so long as they got it.'

And, he contended, some of the so-called evidence from France was only hearsay, and not admissible in a British court. One witness, for example, was supposed to have heard a man say, 'Don't trust him. He looks like an old swindler.' (At this remark, both Charles and Jeannette laughed heartily.) 'Many well-known banks in this country would find themselves in a curious position if they were called upon to meet all their obligations at once without the assistance of new business,' the barrister asserted.

But these arguments did not persuade the magistrate. He declared that the case was 'eminently one for extradition' and ordered that Wells and Pairis be sent to France to stand trial, along with all the documents and property which had been seized by the police.

At a subsequent hearing it was explained that Jeannette had been married in 1908, had gone under various names, and was with Wells when they were recently arrested. Clearly there were doubts about her marriage to the mysterious Mr. Burns. The judge asked, 'Is she a widow?'.

Her counsel chose his words carefully: 'She says she has not seen her husband for some time.'

There was, at the end of this legal labyrinth, an appeal by Wells before the Lord Chief Justice. The Solicitor General, however, pointed out that since the extradition treaty had been amended three years earlier, it had become *optional* for either state to hand over its own citizens if it chose. The book on extradition law that Wells had been relying on was out of date.

Wells made a final, desperate attempt to halt the process. He wrote a long, rambling letter to a Major General Geoffrey Barton – a retired officer with a distinguished service record.

Wells begins his letter with a jaunty introduction:

I am C. Wells, 'the man that broke the Bank at Monte Carlo'. I have just heard of your return and venture to write to you on the following matter. I am to be extradited to France, with Mrs. Burns née 'Jeannette Pairis' who, some 8 or 10 years back was minding a baby for Mrs Zalma Bradley [*sic*] in Maisons Laffitte, and in other places.

He asks General Barton to put in a good word for him at the Home Office. But there is a hint of blackmail. He implies that Barton had been on intimate terms with Zalma, and that if this were made public there would be a 'great society scandal'. Barton wrote to the Home Office, saying, 'I do not know the writer, nor any of the people he refers to … I have no wish to be troubled with any more of his effusions'. In fact, Wells had written to the wrong man. It was not General Barton but a General Sir Charles *Barter* who had been involved in some way with Zalma Bradley Lee. Wells' last-ditch attempt to halt the extradition had failed.

On 29 May – over four months after their arrest – Charles and Jeannette were extradited to France. Detective Inspector Nicholls and Sergeant Crutchett escorted them to Boulogne on the steamer *Invicta*, and handed them over to Inspector Roux. The *Sûreté* was taking no chances – Roux was accompanied by no fewer than five other officers.

A French newspaper report welcomed the fact that they would face justice in a Paris courtroom, but it ended with a dig at the British: 'The sum of one million [francs] seized on board his yacht did not accompany them, as the Treaty intends.'

Charles Wells arrives
at Boulogne on board
the cross-Channel
ferry *Invicta*, following
extradition from Britain

RIVIER DEBARQUE A BOULOGNE

This large sum of money would become the subject of a bitter
wrangle between the French and British governments over the
coming months, and it threatened to drive a wedge between the
two nations at a time when the alliance between them would be
crucial to their survival.

That night, as soon as the train had come to a standstill at the Gare
du Nord in Paris, Inspector Roux and his agents took Charles
and Jeannette straight to the Dépôt, an austere, foul-smelling,
overcrowded cell block attached to the Palais de Justice, a stone's
throw from the Quai des Orfèvres. Later, Charles was sent to
La Santé, a jail on the outskirts of Paris where the only event to
break up the tedium of life behind bars was the occasional exe-
cution by guillotine. Jeannette was transferred to Saint-Lazare

Prison – a grim institution dating from the Reign of Terror in 1793. For the last century it had housed female convicts. Saint-Lazare was, according to an official report of 1912, 'totally incapable of achieving the object for which it was designed, and equally incapable of improvement'. Many inmates were prostitutes, or unmarried mothers, or both.

From prison Wells wrote to his lawyer, Monsieur Caen, explaining that he was 71 years old and was suffering from the harsh conditions. Food was inadequate. 'I am very low-spirited, and that again compromises my health.' As for the outcome of the impending trial, he feared that he might be found guilty: 'I will not survive such a calamity – simply hearing the sentence is quite enough to kill me immediately'. He pointed out that it was in the interests of his creditors for him to survive. 'It is urgent to prolong as much as possible the life of a man worth £2,182. 10. 10. per annum' (the income from the annuities).

A British Board of Trade memo written a few days later states:

> … it would appear prima facie desirable if possible to preserve the health and life of the bankrupt, whose annuities form a considerable portion of the assets.'

The same memo states that if Wells was found guilty of the crime of fraudulent bankruptcy he could be given a life sentence, 'that is to say he would be placed in solitary confinement for the rest of his life, communication with others being forbidden, and he would wear a special garment including something in the nature of a mask.'

As Charles and Jeannette languished in their respective cells, the prosecutors built up their case – an unenviable task as many of the relevant documents were still in England. Following a preliminary hearing in June, a process known as the 'open questioning' began on 14 September and was conducted by Monsieur Bourdeaux, the *juge d'instruction*. The forensic accountant, Malétras, said that more than 6,000 victims had lost a total of almost 1.5 million francs. It was plain that the Rente Bi-mensuelle would have collapsed before long: he had calculated that in another few months the scheme would have required over 21 million francs just to keep going. He revealed, too, that at the time of their arrest Charles Wells and Jeannette were in possession of about 850,000fr. in annuities, bonds, sums lent on mortgage and cash. As things stood, all of these assets were being retained in England for the creditors of his 1893 bankruptcy.

Wells was then called on to give evidence. He denied having committed a fraud, saying, 'I have an extraordinary martingale which gives me a daily return of 2 per cent. I give half to my clients and keep the other half. Nothing could be fairer.' Monsieur Bourdeaux was unconvinced. On seeing this, Wells offered to write down the secret, put it in an envelope and give it to Bourdeaux so he could try it for himself. Wells added that he did not take the investors' complaints seriously. 'They are gamblers and like all gamblers they should be prepared to lose as well as win,' he said.

Bourdeaux interrupted him, saying that the only reason they had lost was that Wells had run away with their money.

'But I am quite willing,' Wells continued, 'to give up the £34,000 seized by the police at the time of my arrest to the so-called victims.'

'That's an easy offer for you to make,' the judge said, 'because you know very well that England will never let this money go. The authorities there intend to apply this money to debts incurred by you at the time of your bankruptcy twenty years ago.'

'You can be a bankrupt and still be an honest man,' Wells replied.

Bourdeaux turned his attention to Jeannette Pairis. In his opinion, she could not have been unaware of her lover's crimes, as she had lived with him for about twenty years. Once before, in 1892, she had been arrested with Wells when both of them were wanted by the British police. On that occasion the case against her had been dismissed but Wells was sentenced. Jeannette answered that she had believed her companion was gaining large profits on the Stock Exchange. Wells, too, was insistent that she knew nothing of his business activities.

The full criminal trial began on 14 November, before the trial judge, Monsieur Schlumberger. Every newspaper of any consequence had a reporter in attendance. The courtroom was packed solid with pressmen and curious members of the public, anxious to see for themselves 'the King of Fraudsters', as one journal called him. An American commentator hinted that under French law Wells could expect a sentence of at least fifteen years. Yet, according to another source, he seemed almost amused at the prospect of another long spell in prison. Certainly there was a wealth of material to entertain the assembled crowds: the whole of the first sitting was taken up by a long recitation of his extraordinary life story. In the next day's edition of *Le Matin* the trial was front-page news:

> If daring bankers were to elect a prince they would indisputably choose Wells.
>
> No-one is certain that Wells really is his name. He is an Englishman. His wife, disapproving of the life he led, still lives in the Marseille suburb where she went when she left him. De Ville Wells is a little old man with a polite demeanour and wily features.

He was from an honourable family, it was explained, the son of a noted *romancier anglais*. The article made reference to his linguistic and musical skills – and his powers of persuasion:

> He speaks with great abundance. 'To promise a return of one per cent, *monsieur le président*, is not an enormous promise. In business if one were to earn one franc on a capital of 100 francs it would hardly be worth mentioning. If what I

promised was impossible to achieve, how is it that people start off with nothing, and then become millionaires?'

One observer dubbed him:

> ... a strange character, this little old seventy-one-year old man, with his bald head, his white beard, and his blue over-coat, which is too big for him. One would think he was a dutiful little clerk of respectable behaviour.

> He answers questions with ease: he knows just how to wriggle around M. Schlumberger's questions. His voice is quiet, but he knows how to raise it at the required moment ... Around 1890 he found the company that suited him, Jeanne Burns, now forty-two years of age. She is of simple character, devoted, and docile in his hands. She adapted wonderfully to the life-style of her lover.

Those who knew Jeannette better may have found words such as 'simple' and 'docile' ill-suited to her. It could be argued with some justification that she had encouraged Wells in his life of crime. Since he lived so frugally himself, it is plausible that at least some of the motive behind his crimes came from a desire to – in his own words – 'make his little doll happy'.

Reports of Jeannette in the French press were, overall, less complimentary than they had been in Britain, with comments such as, 'Mlle Pairis ... [has] the look of a little housemaid who has hit the big-time. She loudly protests her innocence.'

As the trial continued, the forensic accountant was called as a witness. 'M. Malétras explained the system without accounting for how anyone could have believed Rivier's crazy promises.' The prosecution case hinged on the fact that 'Rivier'/Wells must have known that it was impossible to invest his clients' money in a way which would produce a return of 365 per cent per annum.

But Wells had a ready answer. 'You forget, *monsieur*, that I'm the man who broke the bank at Monte Carlo,' was the essence of his reply. The capital provided by investors allowed him to carry out transactions on the stock market using an infallible martingale, which had once helped him to win 'two million francs' in one night at the casino. The Stock Exchange, he added by way of explanation, was nothing more than 'a vast roulette, after all'.

By now Wells was getting into his stride. 'A professor once told me, "a martingale doesn't work". So I thought, there's only one thing to do to improve it. *Make* it work!' He described his 'system' just as he had described it to journalists twenty years ago, 'wait for the "series" – when you see the same colour eight or ten times. Play intermittently during the series'. (As *Le Figaro* commented, there was no answer to his argument.)

The judge asked whether he really had broken the bank.

'Yes, not once but ten times,' he answered with pride. 'I won altogether in 1889 £80,000 [£8 million], and in August 1910, during the existence of the Rente Bi-mensuelle, I won at Monte Carlo £2,480 [£235,000] using my system.* If I took flight, it's the fault of the police. There was talk of arresting me and searching my premises. My credibility would have been ruined. If you search any banker's property, his credit will collapse immediately. I preferred to flee. In any case, I haven't spent the money that I took with me because they found a million [francs]

---

* He evidently means 1891, not 1889. The amounts he claimed were surely an exaggeration. And no independent evidence has been found to support his claim of a more recent visit to Monte Carlo in 1910. As a rule, the casino did not allow convicted criminals to enter the premises. Some of the current employees had been there when Wells had his major wins twenty years earlier, and would assuredly have recognised him. One member of staff in particular is said to have had an exceptional memory for faces and once spotted a customer who reappeared after an absence of forty years. The man had left owing money to the casino, and was taken aback when he was asked to pay up after such a long time. (Smith, A., pp.342–43.)

in my possession, which the English authorities "forgot" to return when France obtained my extradition.'

Jeannette continued to deny all personal involvement in the plot, and claimed to have no knowledge whatsoever of her lover's activities. She said she was not at all surprised that he was poor in 1910 and a millionaire in 1911.

Their defence lawyer said that at least some of the investors were fully aware of the risk they were taking. A photographer had sent in 100fr. In his covering letter the man had written, 'I know it must be a fraud, but I do not care as long as it lasts long enough to enable me to make money. I do not object to making money out of other people in any way.' As for the others, the lawyer asserted that it was a case of 'buyer beware'. The law was not intended to protect 'either idiots or knaves'.

The prosecution, however, urged the judge to award the severest sentence possible. Wells was found guilty of fraud and misuse of funds, and was, indeed, given the maximum penalty – a prison sentence of just five years and a 3,000fr. fine. Jeannette was found guilty of complicity, given a thirteen-month jail sentence and fined 1,000fr. The judge implied that he would have imposed much stiffer sentences if the law had allowed him to do so.

A tongue-in-cheek editorial in one of the Parisian papers reminded its readers that Wells was not entirely to blame for what had happened. It was the victims who were really at fault:

> The promise of one per cent daily interest – an insult to the intelligence? Apparently not, because a considerable number of honest citizens rushed to hand over their bundles of cash. But all the same, there are several hundred rogues who profited to a great extent from Rivier's fraud. These are the first clients who lent him their money. They *did* receive the fantastic interest that was advertised. Why not arrest them? Why not arrest the three thousand plaintiffs … Why not

arrest the fools who expected to get 365 per cent return on
their money?

But the investors were not the only ones to be made to look
foolish. France itself, with its almost non-existent supervi-
sion of financial institutions, had also been shamed. As a direct
consequence of the Rente Bi-mensuelle scandal, the government introduced a new police department – the Special Eighth
Section – with the aim of preventing further embarrassments of
this kind. 'Close enquiry will in future be made into the antecedents and financial resources of all financiers who describe
themselves as "bankers".'

The court which had tried Wells and Jeannette appointed
Monsieur Joseph Albert Desbleumortier, in his capacity as
administrator,* to set up a scheme for reimbursing the investors
in France who had lost their savings. But the judge neglected to
explain how this was to be done, as the money was still in Britain
– and the British were not prepared to let it out of their hands.
As a matter of fact, the Official Receiver in London was already
working on an identical scheme to use precisely the same funds
to recompense the creditors of Wells' 1893 bankruptcy.

One of those creditors was the Hon. William Cosby Trench.
At his castle in County Limerick, that avid disciple of *The Times*
was studying the latest news from London when one article in
particular attracted his attention. He was a middle-aged man
now, not only older but considerably wiser than he had been in
the early 1890s, when he had entrusted the equivalent of more
than £1 million to the care of Charles Wells. In all the time since
Wells had been declared bankrupt, the creditors – Trench among
them – had received not a penny of the money that he owed
them. There had been few worthwhile assets to seize, and the
Official Receiver could do no more than keep the file open in

---

*   The French term used is '*Administrateur Judiciaire*': there is no exact
     English equivalent.

case this situation ever changed. Now, if the press reports were to be believed, it *had* changed.

Wells' debts in 1893 had added up to £32,000. By chance, the assets seized from the yacht and from Wells' various investments came to the same amount, give or take a couple of thousand pounds. After twenty long years, incredibly, there seemed to be a distinct possibility that his victims would be repaid. Unfortunately, this development came far too late for the elderly Caroline Davison, who had died in 1897, a few years after handing over her savings to Wells, or for Dr White who had passed away in 1909.

But Trench, Miss Phillimore, the Reverend Blake and several of the other victims were still alive and well. And as most of them had long since given up all hope of getting their money back, this fresh news was all the more welcome.

The French government, however, had very different ideas. '*Au contraire*,' they said, the money must be restored to the French citizens to whom it belongs. Britain and France prepared to do battle. Many hearings subsequently took place in the British courts; legal arguments of unfathomable complexity were bandied about. Months went by, and it seemed as if the matter would never be resolved.

Finally the case went before Judge Bucknill, whose unenviable task it was to give a ruling on this judicial muddle. He emphasised from the start that he was most anxious to avoid a falling out with the French, with whom Britain had signed a pact of friendship – the *Entente cordiale* – in 1904 when the prospect of a war with Germany first loomed on the horizon. In the intervening eight years, the threat had by no means gone away, and it was clear that Britain and France badly needed each other as allies. His Lordship said:

> I have come to this conclusion. The French Government has through its agents asserted that it thinks the English Government has not treated it properly under this Treaty and

that is a feeling which must be allayed if possible … I will not
do anything … to give the French Government an opportunity of thinking that we are trying to get out of our proper
Treaty obligations.

However, he did not specify what action was to be taken, and
merely urged the two parties to reach an amicable agreement
between themselves. So, for the time being, the battle continued: the British Official Receiver said he was ready to distribute
the property among the creditors of the first bankruptcy, but
the French government continued to argue that, 'as an honest
man', the Receiver had no right to dispose of funds which had
been illegally acquired from French citizens.

Jeannette was out of prison by April 1913. Having already been
in custody for a long while before the trial, she had served
only another four months or so behind bars. She turned up in
London in an almost destitute state, and approached Detective
Inspector Nicholls at Scotland Yard. He wrote to the Falmouth
Police asking for her belongings, which had been in store there,
to be sent to London, adding that 'The carriage would not cost
much, and Mrs. Burns might be disposed to pay it'. Thanks to
his kindly intervention a quantity of clothing was duly sent to
Jeannette in London.

It was not until late June 1913 – over two years since the collapse of the Rente Bi-mensuelle – that Britain and France agreed
to divide the assets on a fifty–fifty basis: half would be distributed among the creditors of Wells' earlier bankruptcy, and the
other half would be shared out among the victims in France.
The income from the annuities, paid annually, would likewise be
split in two and paid in equal measure to the British and French
victims during the years to come. The Official Receiver was to
retain the annuities and Monsieur Desbleumortier undertook to
certify, at regular intervals, that Wells was still alive, as proof to
the insurance companies which provided the annuities.

A relieved Judge Bucknill expressed his delight at this compromise. 'This has been a case of such difficulty, and has involved such important points of law that I should have found extreme difficulty in deciding it, and the case might have gone to the House of Lords.'[*]

As a side issue, Jeannette was allowed to keep a sum of £835 (£80,000), which she had always insisted was her own money and nothing to do with Wells. Judge Bucknill seemed genuinely glad to learn that she was to receive this sum, along with her gun and fishing rods, which had been impounded.

Wells served his prison sentence in France at the Maison Cellulaire de Fresnes – an institution to the south of Paris which had once been intended as a model prison, though in practice it fell far short of this ideal. When he was released this time, there was no triumphal journey with people waiting to shake his hand or congratulate him. No journalists clamoured for interviews. He was quietly reunited with Jeannette.

The outbreak of the First World War in 1914 had pushed memories of *la Belle Epoque* to the back of people's minds, along with Wells and his exploits, and almost everything else that had gone before. Charles Wells, no longer headline news, slowly but inexorably faded into that part of the public memory that is reserved for people who 'used to be someone'. Even while he had been busy setting up the Rente Bi-mensuelle in Paris, another Englishman had grabbed the headlines by breaking the bank at Monte Carlo.

---

[*]   In the event, it had not been necessary for Charles Wells' case to be referred to the House of Lords, which is the highest court in the land; but a few weeks previously he had been 'honoured' with a brief mention in the House of Commons, during a debate on the costs of certain trials. The Financial Secretary to the Treasury referred to a 'very expensive case in the London Extradition Court, which obtained considerable notoriety in the public Press – the case concerning a gentleman named Wells – Monte Carlo Wells'. (Hansard (Commons), 10 February 1913.)

Arthur Bower was the name of this 'young pretender',*
though he liked to introduce himself as 'Captain Arthur de
Courcy-Bower'. He claimed that he had once been given a high-
ranking position in the army of a South American dictatorship,
though this is extremely doubtful.

Aside from a shared tendency to use adopted names, he had
several other things in common with Charles Wells, including a
criminal record for fraud and a bankruptcy of several years previously from which he had not been discharged. He had even
patented several inventions, though not nearly as many as Wells.
And he was unquestionably a gambler, too.

At Monte Carlo, Bower won the maximum pay-out eighteen times in a row and broke the bank on five separate occasions.
And whereas the title of 'the man who broke the bank' had previously been associated with Charles Wells alone, now it was
Bower's name that came to mind. He was even linked – quite
erroneously – to the famous song.**

As the bitter war against Germany continued, the British
public became fearful that foreign spies might enter their
country and attack them from within. In March 1915 the
authorities announced that, to reduce the risks, a single route
would be kept open for all non-military passenger traffic
between Britain and the Continent. Steamers would operate
a special wartime service between Dieppe and Folkestone, and
the government promised that heightened security measures
would be put in place:

---

*   He was seventeen years younger than Wells.
**   A number of publications, including *Lost Chords* and *The Great Song
Thesaurus*, state that he was the original inspiration for Fred Gilbert's
opus. However, this is impossible as the composition dates from 1891
and Bower did not achieve Monte Carlo fame until twenty years later.
(Gilbert, p.237; Lax and Smith.)

There is a double check here, for all passengers are examined, first by the authorities controlling the movements of aliens, and afterwards by Scotland Yard officials, working in conjunction with the local police ... The work is done by specially trained men, who have had years of experience in dealing with aliens both in London and at the south coast ports.

The new precautions proved their worth at the beginning of December, when the spy Mata Hari arrived at Folkestone on her way to France and was recognised by Detective Sergeant Warrell, a Scotland Yard officer temporarily assigned to the port. She was interrogated and searched. Although nothing incriminating was found, she was noted as a person of interest to the police and security forces.

Warrell was praised by his superiors for his quick-witted actions and, with his sights set on early promotion, he redoubled his efforts to spot other suspicious individuals. His vigilance was rewarded just over two weeks later when one evening he recognised an elderly gentleman disembarking from the Dieppe ferry. Charles De Ville Wells, now almost 75 years of age, was not on any wanted list in Britain at the time, but Warrell still questioned him in some detail.* Afterwards, Wells boarded the boat train to London around 9.00 p.m. The ever vigilant Sergeant Warrell phoned Scotland Yard, where a constable took the message and noted it down:

Charles de Ville Wells, known as the man that broke the bank at Monte Carlo, arrived here from Dieppe this evening and left by boat train arriving at Victoria at 10.45 p.m.

Carriage No. 986. 2nd Class. Second compartment from end of train. Gave as his address for tonight the Wilton Hotel, Victoria. States that he is going to London to see his Solicitor

---

*   Warrell was promoted to inspector soon afterwards. (*Folkestone Herald*, 23 September 1916.)

Mr. Hoddinott, Finsbury Circus. Please direct an officer to meet the train and obtain particulars.

A constable was sent to Victoria Station, where the train arrived later than scheduled:

CHARLES DE VILLE WELLS

I beg to report [he wrote] that I proceeded to Victoria on the evening of the 20th. inst., and was present on the arrival of the Boat Train from Folkestone which arrived at Victoria at 11.05 p.m., but no person alighted from the carriage named whom I thought answered the description of the above man.

From discreet enquiries, I ascertained that no person of the above name had arrived at the Wilton Hotel that evening, or booked rooms there.

Hubert Morse, P.C.

Once again, Wells had cocked a snook at the authorities. There is no further entry in his file and, as far as the police were concerned, that was the end of their long professional association with Wells.

The thousands of pounds that Charles and Jeannette had invested in securities or deposited in banks, together with the proceeds from the sale of the yacht *Excelsior*, were shared among their victims on both sides of the Channel.

Once the tortuous financial arrangements had been settled, the creditors from Wells' British bankruptcy of over twenty years ago received an initial dividend of 2s 6d for every pound they were owed – exactly one-eighth of the total debt. The ongoing income from the annuities was distributed annually, and took the form of a smaller payment, which varied from year to year between about 2 and 4 per cent of the original sum. And since the assets and income were shared on a 50–50 basis with France, corresponding sums were apportioned among the French creditors (who were, of course, far more numerous).

It was not until after the war that Wells was heard from again in Britain. The conflict had had serious repercussions as far as the French economy was concerned. Between 1914 and 1919 food prices had trebled in some cases. Wells got in touch with the administrators of his finances to say that he was living in impoverished circumstances, and could no longer afford to feed himself because the cost of living was so high. Following his release from prison he had been allowed a tiny income out of his annuities. Now he needed more.

He insisted on – and was granted – a hearing in a French court to argue his case. 'Give me some money to live on, or I'll kill myself, and you won't get a penny more,' was his plea. Since the annuity income would have ceased if he died, the French and British creditors promptly granted him an annual 'pension' of about £260 – the equivalent of a skilled worker's pay. Wells was able, once more, to live in relative comfort, and his creditors continued to receive a modest annual dividend.

By 1920, his health had deteriorated and he was given a further £100 a year from the British fund. A government memo states, 'It is in the interest of all parties that the life of the bankrupt, who is now aged 75, should be prolonged'. The creditors agreed to pay him an additional £4 per month and the French authorities were asked to contribute as well.

It was late July 1922 when the *Daily Telegraph* announced:

MONTE CARLO WELLS – FAMOUS ADVENTURER'S DEATH

News has been received in London of the death, in Paris, at the age of 81, of Charles de Ville Wells, known to fame as 'the man who broke the bank at Monte Carlo.'

Readers were reminded of his long career, not only as a gambler, but also as a fraudster extraordinaire, who had obtained many thousands of pounds from his victims. 'Nobody will be more sorry to hear of his death than his numerous creditors,' one columnist declared. Harry Wilson, a solicitor who had acted in the Rente Bi-mensuelle affair, told a *Daily Chronicle* reporter that the British creditors had been refunded with nearly all the money they were owed. This was an exaggeration, but they *had* received almost half – a lot more than creditors in a bankruptcy usually get. On the other hand, they had suffered a very long wait – over thirty years – for their money. And, as a government memo reveals, many of the smaller creditors had died or moved house during that time. As they could not be traced by the authorities they did not receive their share of the funds.

The news of Wells' death spread far and wide, and as it passed from one person to another it was considerably embellished and sensationalised in the retelling:

HE BROKE MONTE CARLO BANK AND DIED BROKE

Charles De Ville Wells, the 'man who broke the bank at Monte Carlo' … died in Paris recently in such abject poverty that his death passed unnoticed until more than a month afterward. He was eighty-one years old.

Readers relying on this article could have been forgiven for picturing a dusty garret in some dilapidated Paris tenement. An old man has breathed his last – he has died alone, unloved and unnoticed – only after several weeks is his body discovered.

But the truth was very different. In death, as in life, nothing about Charles Wells was straightforward. To begin with, he did not die in poverty. He may not have been especially well off, but the yearly income he had been awarded from the annuities was quite adequate for a man with his unpretentious lifestyle. And he most certainly did not die in Paris, as most accounts claim. By the time of his death, he and Jeannette had returned to London. Charles occupied lodgings at 1 Edith Grove, Chelsea (Plate 10) and Jeannette had an apartment not far away, at 39 Oakley Crescent[*] (Plate 16) (a few yards from Captain Smith's former home in Redesdale Street). Chelsea was then, and still is, a relatively prosperous district.[**]

Wells' landlady – a woman named Emily Angier – told a reporter that, although he was such an old man, he was 'quite sprightly until last winter when he began to suffer from his heart. Previous to that he would move about as actively as a man half his age.' She had never had the slightest inkling that he was the man who inspired the song she used to sing as a young girl. 'I knew him as "Mr. Charles", which, of course, was his Christian name,' she explained. For breakfast he always had tea and dry bread. Mrs. Angier had tried to persuade him to have porridge or bacon but he always replied that on his income he could not afford such 'luxuries'. After breakfast he used to return to a little back room which served as his bedroom and a workshop. He was always working on inventions. He often wore shabby clothing. His landlady gave him all her husband's cast-offs and he gratefully accepted them.

Jeannette had a young maid-servant named Mildred who used to collect him from his lodgings each day and take him to Jeannette's flat, about a mile away, where they had lunch together. Despite his illness during the cold British winter, it was now mid-summer, and he seemed to be in reasonable health. 'The end came unexpectedly, death overtaking him with little warning or none at all, as he rested in an armchair.' The

---

[*]   Since renamed Oakley Gardens.

[**]   The Booth Maps of 1898–99 show both streets to be 'reasonably well-to-do'. The 1910 Inland Revenue Valuation Survey shows that at that time the house in Edith Grove had been occupied by a clergyman, the Reverend Buchanan, his wife and their two servants. There is nothing to suggest that this was anything other than a respectable, gentrified area.

unimaginable fortunes that had once passed through his hands were long gone, and he died owing two weeks' rent.

Charles De Ville Wells, the man who broke the bank at Monte Carlo, was laid to rest in North Sheen Cemetery, in an unmarked grave. As he had no known relatives, Jeannette signed the documents in connection with his burial. It is believed that she could not afford a headstone.

Not long afterwards, Sir Basil Thomson – the governor of Dartmoor Prison when Charles was a prisoner there – wrote:

Monte Carlo Wells is dead. A man with such a temperament ought to have been immortal: he ought not even to have grown old. I am quite sure that it was his bodily machine that wore out and that his spirit was invested with perennial youth …

17

How the Bank was Broken

In an earlier chapter we learned that Charles Wells had won
£60,000 (£6 million) at Monte Carlo and I promised that we
would look more closely into how he might possibly have
achieved such spectacular gains.

First, though, we should step back and view his accomplish-
ment in perspective. He was by no means the only individual
to break the bank – or even the first. As we have already seen,
Prince Lucien Bonaparte and Tomás Garcia had in the past
enjoyed huge successes at François Blanc's first casino in Bad
Homburg. In later years others did the same at Monte Carlo.
Over time the casino was significantly extended and the number
of people attending increased dramatically. By the late 1890s,
the bank was being broken perhaps as often as every two weeks*
– not because it was any easier to accomplish, but simply because
the casino had been expanded and there were far more people
placing bets. In fact, by the 1910s, the ritual of placing a black

---

* To put this in perspective, it has been calculated that even in such a short
period as two weeks, approximately a quarter of a million spins of the
roulette wheel would have taken place in the casino as a whole.

cloth on the table had to be abandoned because it had become too disruptive.

By that time, though, Wells had already earned his place in history. In folklore and in song his reputation has survived for more than a century, not so much by his winning a fortune, as by his seeming ability to repeat the trick – apparently at will – a total of ten or more times in a short space of time. Yes, the bank had been broken before, and would be broken again afterwards. But generally the winner was a different person on every occasion, and we can only guess at the large amounts these 'big winners' might have lost before luck came their way. Similarly, we can never be sure how many of them subsequently lost part, or all, of their winnings back to the casino.

Taken as a whole, Wells' successes were against all odds, and his feat was possibly a one-in-a-million occurrence. While it is true that some people do have extraordinary luck, we can virtually rule out 'good fortune' as a possible explanation, simply because the likelihood of such an event is so small. Furthermore, the evidence presented below will demonstrate that Charles Wells went to Monte Carlo with a purpose. Everything we know about his personality suggests that he carefully weighed up his chances of success before commencing any new undertaking, and that he would never have placed his faith in luck alone. We are left, therefore, with four other possible scenarios, all of which have been put forward – or at least hinted at – over the years:

- He used his engineering expertise to help him win;
- He had developed an infallible system of play;
- He found a way to defraud the casino;
- He colluded with the casino.

Let us look, then, at each of these possibilities in turn.

ENGINEERING EXPERTISE

Could Wells have applied his engineering experience to the problem of beating the bank at Monte Carlo? Historically, there may be some justification for believing that he might have done so.

A man named Joseph Jagger, an engineer from a Yorkshire textile mill, had gone to Monte Carlo in the 1870s or early 1880s. He had theorised that roulette wheels might have mechanical flaws, and that these could result in certain numbers coming up more often than others. He is said to have recruited one or more helpers, who wrote down the numbers at every table over a period of time. Analysing the results he found that one wheel, in particular, produced some numbers more frequently than chance would dictate. He backed the 'good' numbers, and it is claimed that he won £120,000 [£12 million].

It appears that casino staff finally realised what was happening and exchanged the faulty wheel for a good one. In fact, after Jagger had broken the bank, the casino introduced stringent daily checks to ensure that all of the wheels were true. This would have made it difficult, if not impossible, for Charles Wells to use a similar method ten years later. Furthermore, if the wheel had been faulty, between the seven croupiers at the table at least one of them would surely have spotted the inconsistency before Wells did.

THE 'INFALLIBLE SYSTEM'

A man who had spent 30 years as a croupier was once asked about 'systems'. 'If there were any possible means of winning there,' he replied, 'do you think I should have been contented to remain all these years a croupier?'

If there was such a thing as an infallible system, logic dictates that the world's casinos would have gone out of business many years ago. On the other hand, some of the gamblers had to win some of the time, otherwise no sensible person would bet at all.

In his testimony before the Paris court in 1912 Wells said, 'A professor once told me, "a martingale [system] doesn't work", so I thought, there's only one thing to do to improve it. Make it work!' However, he needed an explanation for his huge winnings without revealing the true facts, and the "infallible system" could have served as a smoke-screen. If he was to persuade backers to finance him to the tune of thousands of pounds he had to make it appear that he had perfected a winning strategy, otherwise it would have seemed that he was simply taking their money and hoping for the best. And if he really had developed an infallible system, surely he would have continued to exploit it and carry on winning until he had solved all of his financial problems.

Significantly, François Blanc, founder of the casino, had made no secret of his own opinion that there was no such thing as an infallible system, and was so sure of this that he offered a prize of a million francs if anyone could demonstrate one. This promise was continued under Camille Blanc's directorship, yet the prize was never won. If Wells really had perfected such a system he could have simply claimed the million francs without having to spend long hours at the casino, and without any financial risk whatsoever.

Having said this, he may have optimised his chances of winning by a combination of the following: playing for long periods at each sitting; having a large amount of capital at his fingertips; and keeping his head even when the stakes were high. He gained a further advantage by sending each day's winnings home to England so as not to risk losing them.[*]

DEFRAUDING THE CASINO

Considering Wells' record, we must consider the possibility that he somehow swindled the casino. However, this would have been an immensely difficult feat to pull off, even for a man of his ability and experience as a fraudster. The casino had been in existence for a long time and its owners were familiar with all of the tricks. They would have ejected him from the premises instantly if they were in the least suspicious. And he undoubtedly would have needed inside help from a number of the employees. All of these matters would have been hard to arrange, and there was a real risk that the plot would be discovered before it produced any returns.

Admittedly, schemes of this kind have been attempted over the years and have sometimes succeeded ... up to a point. In much more recent times fifty staff and gamblers at a casino in San Remo, Italy, were arrested after 'croupiers and some supervisory staff saw to it that selected regular customers made large winnings and then shared the proceeds,' depriving the casino of between £4 million and £8 million.

At Monte Carlo, however, the supervisors were extremely vigilant and the croupiers were randomly moved from one table to another during the course of a day's work. This would have made it almost impossible for them to help a player to win.

---

[*] Some commentators have also pointed out that most of the money he staked belonged to other people whom he had swindled. Therefore he may have played more recklessly than the average gambler, who risks his own capital. But I disagree with this view. He badly needed to win in order to cover his enormous debts and to complete the purchase and renovation of his yacht. Even though he had obtained the funds fraudulently I believe he would have treated the cash as carefully as if it was his own

Moreover, Wells was a loner, and for him to recruit and orchestrate a sizeable team of accomplices from among the casino staff seems completely out of character.

COLLUSION WITH THE CASINO

This author believes collusion to be by far the most plausible scenario, and as such it will be examined in detail. But why on earth would a casino collude with a gambler to help him win?

It is late 1890 and the future of the casino is uncertain. As mentioned above, Prince Albert had recently married Alice Heine, the daughter of a wealthy American industrialist. With access to her family's millions Albert is no longer dependent on the large annual sums that his father had received from the casino. Camille Blanc realises that his business may not survive for much longer: and to make things worse, there are rumours that a rival casino is being built at nearby Cannes.

Camille Blanc has approached the rulers of both Andorra and Liechtenstein for permission to open a casino in their respective territories, but he has so far received no response. All he can do in the meantime is to squeeze as much money as possible out of the existing business while it lasts. His cost-cutting measures have already blighted the new gaming hall, the Salle Touzet. Although the room was designed to match or even to surpass the opulence of the existing ones, it opened in January 1890 with none of the lavish ornamentation specified by its designer. After all, it would have been pointless to carry out such expensive works while the very future of the casino hung in the balance.

At about the same time, Charles Wells has problems of his own. The patent scam is losing momentum, and some of his victims are pressing for their money back. With every day that passes the risk is that he will be sued by a 'client' or even arrested by the police. In the first few months of 1891, he has half-heartedly registered just five new patents, none of which are completed. Instead he switches his attention to finding another way to finance the purchase of his Palais Royal as well as the luxuries that he wants to bestow upon Jeannette.

Perhaps he recalls the time he spent in Nice several years earlier. Nice is not far from Monaco and Wells could easily have heard gossip about gamblers winning large sums. Indeed, he may even have visited the casino to see for himself.

The sequence of events begins on 13 December 1890. Like most entrepreneurs starting a business, Wells opens a new bank account. Accompanied by his friend, Aristides Vergis, he visits the London & South-Western Bank in Sloane Square. Vergis is an existing customer at that branch and his office is just three doors from the bank. Later records will prove that the account Wells opened that day is indeed the one through which most of his Monte Carlo winnings will be channelled in the months to come.

In early 1891 he travels to Monaco.* Wells always plans his campaigns with great precision, and he probably uses this visit to reconnoitre the casino as an initial step in his campaign, as well as to meet Camille Blanc.

Gaining entry to the casino as such is a relatively easy matter. One only has to arrive looking reasonably presentable to be allowed in. Gaining the ear of Camille Blanc, however, is a much more difficult task. As a member of society's upper echelons and boss of a huge enterprise, Blanc is not in the habit of receiving strangers without some good reason. A judicious spot of name-dropping often works wonders, however, and Wells knows that in Monte Carlo there is no better name to drop than that of Count Branicki.

---

*   Casino entry cards for January were found among his effects when
      Inspector Richards later searched the offices at 154 Great Portland Street

As we have seen, Wells had once been engaged to work on the Branicki family's sugar refinery in the Ukraine. Count Branicki – described in the press as 'a millionaire sixty times over' – had been a regular casino client who used to lose 'hundreds of thousands of francs a year' without a care – a trait which no doubt endeared him to François Blanc. Gambling had run in Branicki's family for many years, beginning at Bad Homburg, where his aunt, the Countess Kisselev, had been such a profitable customer that the street where the casino stood was named Kisseleffstraße in her honour – a label it still bears to this day. The Countess bought shares in the Bad Homburg casino from François Blanc and the income from them helped to offset her prodigious losses at the tables. It is probable that she also had a stake in the Monte Carlo casino when it opened several years later, and equally likely that her nephew, Count Branicki, was a shareholder too.[*] The ties between the Blanc and Branicki families had grown stronger than ever when Count Branicki was an honoured guest at the wedding of Camille Blanc's sister, Louise, to Prince Constantine Radziwill in 1876.[**]

Capitalising on his own connection with the Branickis, Wells has an excellent entrée to Camille Blanc, and almost certainly receives a cordial welcome from the casino boss. He regales Blanc with a description of his role in setting up the sugar factory and his 'success in other matters' – indeed, an echo of this self-promotion can be seen in the letter to Miss Phillimore just a

---

[*] An anecdote from the early days of the casino at Monte Carlo states that on a visit there the Countess had a purse containing £1,000 in banknotes stolen by a pickpocket. François Blanc happily reimbursed her out of his own pocket for the lost money

[**] Camille Blanc and Count Branicki also shared a passion for horse racing. In 1889 Blanc had been declared France's most successful owner of steeplechase horses, with 57 mounts at various levels of training in his stables at Saint-Germain. For their part, the Branicki family kept a stable of no fewer than 170 racehorses on their Bila Tserkva estate in Ukraine – the site of the sugar refinery which Wells had helped to set up

few months later (see page 96). At the same time Wells will have kept his previous fraud conviction in Paris and other less savoury aspects of his past firmly under wraps.

Having met, weighed each other up, and discussed their respective situations, Blanc and Wells prepare a plan. Wells will attend the casino and Blanc will arrange for him to win – or appear to win – headline-grabbing sums of money. From Camille Blanc's perspective, Wells seems a promising partner – an Englishman whose successes are likely to be widely reported in Britain, home of many potential visitors to the casino. Yet, at the same time, Wells' mannerisms and his perfect command of the French language make him seem just like a fellow Frenchman. More importantly, Blanc realises that the resulting publicity – while it may not save the casino from ultimate closure – can at least help to maximise the takings in the short term.

The two conspirators, Wells and Blanc, focus on the details of the plot. To achieve its purpose, there must be a convincing demonstration that Wells has broken the bank. Not just once, for that might be a mere lucky fluke. To boost the publicity impact, Wells must win time after time and in a spectacular fashion. In fact, the whole affair must be presented as a kind of new world record.

They turn to financial matters, in particular the amount that Wells is to carry away from the gaming tables. The evidence suggests that Blanc drives a hard bargain. Wells must bring a certain sum of stake money and will be allowed to keep a substantial portion of the winnings, probably one-third.* He will hand the rest back to Camille Blanc, who can then return these funds to

---

*   Most reports agree that Wells 'won' £60,000 (equivalent to £6 million today). Wells himself stated that he retained one-third of this amount – £20,000 (or £2 million in today's values). The remaining £40,000 (£4 million) went to his un-named 'backer' who – in the opinion of this writer – was no doubt Camille Blanc

the casino's coffers – though, as we shall see, Blanc almost certainly decides to pocket the money for himself.

Blanc imposes a condition: Wells must never, under any circumstances, reveal Blanc's involvement in the affair. If asked, Wells will claim that he had invented an infallible system and had an anonymous sponsor. For his part, Blanc will prepare the way by assembling a small team of hand-picked croupiers who can be trusted with a secret. Timing will be of the essence. This team has to be fully-briefed and in position at the table where Wells is to play, and of course it is vital for Wells himself to be in attendance on the days in question.

In the event, Wells was evidently under some pressure to be in Monte Carlo at the agreed time with the required capital. In the last few days of July 1891, immediately before he was due to begin his trip, he advertised in *The Times* for a loan.

SEVENTY-FIVE POUNDS LOAN REQUIRED
Immediately, for a short period. Full security and 15 per cent interest given. Safe investment. Only private investors treated with. Write Security, May's, 162, Piccadilly.

Most reports agree that he arrived in Monte Carlo with stake money of £4,000 (exactly 100,000 francs). Therefore it was puzzling at first to learn that immediately before leaving London he seemed desperate to borrow the comparatively trivial sum of £75. A credible explanation is that Blanc had stipulated that Wells was to bring *no less than* £4,000 stake money with him, and there might have been a last-minute scrabble for extra cash. (If this explanation is correct it would strongly support the view that the two men *did* have an agreement.)

Part of the plan was that Wells would arrive in Monte Carlo during the quietest period of the entire year – the last week of July and first week of August. The timing is significant. Both Wells and Blanc were well aware that the summer temperatures would be at their sizzling peak, and that sensible visitors stayed away at that time of year. Just in case there were any potential onlookers, Wells made sure he arrived at noon, the least busy time of day at the casino, and stayed until closing time.

Wells takes a seat at one of the tables, as planned, and begins to play, more or less unobserved. But, as the day wears on, onlookers gather around his table. By this time he already has piles of gold coins and bundles of banknotes before him. It is of no consequence whether he has actually won this money, or whether it has been surreptitiously placed there for effect. The illusion is of a gambler on a winning streak to surpass all that have ever gone before. And when still more people join in later, many of them placing their bets on the same numbers that Wells had chosen, the noise and confusion simply enhance the impression.

There is evidence from a reliable source showing that the casino did sometimes make it appear that large sums had been won. Earlier that year a young British aristocrat, Lord Rosslyn, had had a lucky break. Following his win, the customary ritual was performed: a croupier announced that the bank had been broken, and a black cloth was solemnly laid upon the gaming table. The croupiers removed the cash-boxes – ostensibly to be re-filled from the casino's vaults. The famous inventor, Hiram Maxim, was a witness to these events. He later wrote:

> I did not believe for a moment that the bank had actually been broken. ... I therefore remained to see the money taken from the table, when I found it was exactly as I had expected; there was at least a peck of large bank notes. It had not been necessary for the bank to send for money at all; this had been done for effect. ... True, the bank had lost money, but they turned it into a valuable advertisement.

It is likely that some of Wells' wins were faked like this to attract publicity. And Maxim's account shows that there must have been some casino employees who were in on the secret and on whom Blanc could have depended to help create the illusion of a highly-successful gambler on a winning streak.

Of course, Wells must have had at least some genuine wins for the display to be convincing. But with substantial stake-money to tide him over any run of bad luck; a cool head; and his extraordinary ability to keep playing hour after hour, he perhaps needed little more than a small extra nudge to beat the bank. Camille Blanc might even have provided this by arranging for him to sit at a table where the wheel was known to be biased toward certain numbers. (As mentioned above, a faulty wheel was normally removed immediately and replaced with a good one. But on this occasion one of the defective wheels could have been deliberately put back in place, and the 'lucky' numbers communicated to Wells in advance). And at trente-et-quarante it was even easier to 'fix' the game, since with a little sleight of hand the management could arrange for the cards to come out in any desired order – in fact, there are documented cases where croupiers had used this method to help their friends to win.

With the odds stacked in Wells' favour, a tipping-point is reached, after which it is difficult for him *not* to break the bank. It may be recalled that a casino employee, Bertollini, described the *mêlée* at Wells' table,:

'… six or seven deep with people attempting to play with him, and the croupiers were overwhelmed with men and women crying in French, German, English and Italian, in Hindu and Urdu and every known language for their stakes to be placed on the same number Wells backed'.

Wells places his bet on a particular number and several other play-ers, having witnessed his success, follow his lead and stake their money on the same numbers. Wells wins – and so do all the others. In this situation it is highly likely that the table would run out of cash. In other words, the bank would have been broken, though Wells had not necessarily achieved this feat single-handedly.

Furthermore, Wells' habit of playing at the tables from opening time to closing time made it even easier to create the desired illusion. Virtually no-one except Wells would have spent the whole eleven hours in the gaming halls. Any visitor who heard of his winning huge sums, but did not actually see it happen, would simply assume that Wells had won before they had arrived or after they had left the casino.

18

The Power of the Press

Charles Wells and Camille Blanc both used the press as a tool to secure their own fortunes. Each had his own speciality: Blanc had an annual budget of £20,000 which he used to bribe editors to keep adverse publicity out of the public eye. Wells used newspaper advertising to persuade readers to send huge amounts of money to him.

Between them they knew exactly how to create a myth and persuade the world that it was true. Making Wells a household name was a relatively simple matter of drip-feeding information to the newspapers.

A man named John Waller was nominally the Riviera correspondent for *The Times*. In the summer months, however, he served as the newspaper's representative in Switzerland, returning to the south of France in late autumn in time for the busy winter season. Camille Blanc would have been well aware of this. In mid-summer, with Waller safely out of the way for a few months, Wells' wins would be reported instead by the local representative of Reuters news agency, who in matters involving the casino seems to have been considerably less discerning than his *Times* counterpart. Another advantage was that Reuter's dispatches were certain to be widely disseminated throughout the British press generally. In fact, even *The Times* itself relied on Reuters reports in the summer, when its own reporter was elsewhere.

In late July and early August, after Wells had won some £20,000 in the space of a few days, the affable Reuters correspondent sent his bulletins to London and they were widely quoted in newspapers all over Britain and beyond. There is little to suggest that the Reuters man witnessed Charles Wells and his good fortune at the tables. Instead he almost certainly received a press briefing from the casino, took it on trust, and forwarded it to London with no questions asked. Moreover, Wells' wins could not be independently scrutinised since he was already on his way back to London by the time the later, more detailed reports had appeared in print. Phase One of the plot had gone exactly as planned.

Reports in the British press were extensive and – broadly speaking – positive. But one or two newspaper editors were doubtful from the start. As early as 3 August 1891, as Wells was ending his first stint at Monte Carlo, the editor of *The Globe* (a popular evening newspaper) poured scorn on the ecstatic articles about him in certain other publications.

> It is easy to understand how these stories are started; they have their origin in the fertile brains of the [casino] 'administration' ... There is no reason to impugn the good faith of the correspondent who telegraphs them ; but either he must be very easily deceived, or the 'administration' must employ an extraordinarily clever intermediary to get these figments of the imagination accepted as good sober truth.

When Wells returned at the beginning of November, things were arranged very differently. In contrast to his summer visit, news of his arrival was telegraphed to London straight away, before he began to play, not afterwards. And it is probably no coincidence that, once again, it was the Reuters correspondent who filed the initial report.

On 8 November, just before Wells concluded his campaign, reporters from *The Times* and *The Daily Telegraph* had a chance to interview him in person. This time they could watch him for themselves and hear his story at first hand, and both newspapers carried detailed accounts of the meeting, quoting Wells' comments at some length. The publicity clearly had the desired effect: soon gamblers flocked to Monte Carlo in droves, hoping to emulate Wells' extraordinary good fortune themselves.

As mentioned in an earlier chapter, Prince Albert of Monaco and François Blanc had finally come to an agreement allowing the casino to continue as before with no further threat of closure. A flurry of activity followed. Projects which had once been put on hold could now go ahead. Work recommenced on the new gaming room, the *Salle Touzet*, and by late October the builders were working at a frantic pace, ready for a mid-November opening – just a few days after Wells' visit. The plan hatched by Blanc and Wells had already produced impressive results for both men, and although the casino's future was now assured they had no reason to abandon their original agreement. The profitable winter season was just beginning, and there seemed to be ample scope for attracting many more punters over the coming months.

However, their carefully contrived scheme was about to come to an abrupt and unexpected end. Until now Camille Blanc may have known little or nothing about Wells' criminal past, whether it was his conviction for fraud in Paris several years earlier, or – more recently – the phony patents scam. But the truth was about to be revealed. Several newspapers reported that Wells had arrived back in Monte Carlo on Monday, 2 November. Just three days later *Truth* magazine referred to him as 'Charles Wells, C.E.' and posed the question, 'why is this Wells left free to defraud the public year after year?' (He had previously been referred to in *Truth* as 'C. Wells'. This was the first appearance of his full name – Charles Wells).

It is very likely that this article came to the attention of Camille Blanc soon afterwards. It is known that Blanc used a press-cutting agency to monitor any reports about the casino, and – to quote one source – 'not a leader or paragraph concerning them in any newspaper of note is not cut out and duly dispatched to their offices at Monte Carlo'. Blanc might even have received a clipping of the *Truth* article while Wells was still in Monte Carlo and quickly put two and two together. On 8 November, Wells complained to a newspaperman about the casino's 'detectives', stating that he 'was followed about by these men in their endeavour to find out who he was, where he came from, and who were his friends …'. Over the next few days journalists were hinting at an arrangement between Wells and Blanc:

'MR WELLS' AND MONTE CARLO

A strange rumour is going the rounds, says a London correspondent, touching the extraordinary run of luck which 'Mr Wells' is reported to have had at the Monte Carlo gambling tables. It is whispered pretty freely that a mystery attaches to the personality of Mr Wells, which suggests that his phenomenal success is only part of a carefully arranged plan to boom the place, with the view of attracting wealthy English visitors. It is no secret that £20,000 a year is devoted by the proprietors of the tables for advertising purposes, and what is more likely, it is asked, than that they should engage someone to 'break the bank,' in order just to show how easily the thing could be done. The real truth of Mr Wells' connection has yet to be told.

(*Dundee Evening Telegraph*, 18 November 1891)

Finally, on 19 November, the *London Evening News* confirmed that 'Monte Carlo Wells' and 'Wells, the engineer of Great

Portland Street' were indeed the self same individual. Now the connection had finally appeared in print; Monte Carlo Wells was the very man who had been described in *Truth* just two weeks earlier as a law-breaker whose intent had been to 'defraud the public'.

For Camille Blanc this must have been a heart-stopping moment. Wells and his achievements were earning many column-inches in the press, and interest in the casino was growing. But if people realised that Wells was not the man he appeared to be, all the publicity that had been generated up to now would be discredited. Worse still, if the public were to find out that Camille was in league with a common fraudster, his own career – and perhaps the future of the casino itself – might come to an ignominious end. Acting with uncharacteristic speed, Camille severed all ties with his accomplice. Wells suddenly found to his dismay that he was losing instead of winning at every spin of the wheel and, on 8 November, he had acknowledged defeat and left for England.

Just days after his departure, the newly-completed gaming hall, the Salle Touzet, opened for the season. The original plan may conceivably have been for the celebrated Mr. Wells to be present at the opening ceremony. The timing certainly tends to suggest this, but now it was impossible. It may be recalled that Wells turned up again in January. Camille Blanc himself is reported to have acted as chef de partie at his table. Maybe this was a gesture to let Wells know that Blanc was keeping an eye on him – or was it more of an attempt to browbeat Wells, and put him off his game? Certainly, Wells' lucky streak was over, and he ended this particular stay with a net loss of about £3,000.

Even so, when Wells was quizzed under oath at his bankruptcy hearing some two years later, he did not name Blanc as his 'backer'. First he alluded to 'an American gentleman'; then to 'Lizzie Ritchie'; finally he intimated that his backer was the

'Monsieur Thibaud' mentioned earlier – the man he had met in a French café and whose address he did not know. It is clear from the Official Receiver's comments that none of these explanations was believed.

Interestingly, at the same hearing, while Wells refused to implicate Camille Blanc, he did let slip a clue. Wells told the inquiry that the mystery financier was watching him all the time he was gambling. In the ordinary way, of course, this could refer to anyone. But his comment ties in neatly with a story that Blanc was in the habit of spying upon everything that took place on the casino floor. 'The bull's-eye windows all around the room served as observation points over the gaming area. Camille Blanc used to hide there for hours to watch the players and his staff.' This last piece of evidence is especially credible as it comes from the casino itself. (The bull's eye windows referred to can be clearly seen above the doors in plate No. 7.)

In 1891, when Wells broke the bank, he had already been found guilty of fraud in France, and we now know that he went on to commit further deceptions. He would have had no qualms about misleading the public in connection with the casino. But what of Camille Blanc's inner thoughts? On the surface, he appeared to be a respectable member of society. Would he really have risked his reputation by joining forces with Charles Wells?

I searched many books and newspapers from the 1890s to find out more about Camille Blanc's character. It soon became obvious that he did not court publicity, and on the few occasions when his name did appear in the press it was virtually always when one of his thoroughbred horses won a race – and almost never in connection with the casino. Widening my search, I turned to reports from the early twentieth century onwards. A glimpse of Camille's true personality begins to emerge when in 1904 he became the founding mayor of Beausoleil, a small French town on the border with Monaco. He held this office for the next twenty years, but his tenure was always beset by controversy. He was suspected of election rigging, and was accused of arranging for casino employees to vote for him. But it was some years before the full extent and nature of Blanc's dishonesty came to light. Prince Albert had died in 1923 and was succeeded by his son, Louis – an astute man who regarded Camille Blanc with suspicion. Louis ordered an investigation of the casino's finances and this revealed that Camille had seemingly added hundreds of staff to the payroll. Closer scrutiny showed, however, that most of these employees existed only on paper. The inquiry concluded that Camille was pocketing their salaries to fund his personal extravagances.

A further scandal centred on Camille's personal life. He was a married man, but his true love was his mistress, a woman known as Madame Chinon, a former circus artiste whose equestrian act had once been the talk of France. Camille was in the habit of 'lending' her large sums of money from the casino's coffers with which to gamble. It was impossible for her to lose because when she was successful she was allowed to keep all of her winnings; and when she lost Camille simply wrote off the debt.[*] Eventually Prince Louis ordered Blanc to come to the royal palace. Their meeting was reported in the influential American magazine, *Time*:

> Camille Blanc, director of the Casino for 30 years, was summoned to the palace and there informed that he was relieved of his functions. Blanc fainted when the order was read to him and again on reaching his residence; he is now suffering from a paralytic stroke. His dismissal follows the exile from the municipality of Mme. Chinon, famous adventuress, 'Madame Pompadour of Monaco'. It is the outcome of some remarkable revelations of graft unearthed by special

---

[*]   Perhaps Camille could have used a similar ploy to make it appear that Wells had achieved even larger wins at the tables than was actually the case.

auditors appointed by the Prince. Recently Prince Louis discovered that the Principality had been defrauded of more than $1,000,000 [about £350 million today].

Camille was expelled from Monaco, never to return. The fact that he had embezzled millions of francs by 1923 suggests that that his fraudulent behaviour probably began much earlier. He not only had motive, means and opportunity, but also – like Wells – a tendency to resort to dishonest methods when it suited him.

Did the conspiracy between Blanc and Wells achieve its aims? Without doubt, it enabled Wells to replenish his coffers. He gained at least £20,000 [£2 million], sufficient to cover most of the alterations to the Palais Royal, though not enough to pay off all of his massive debts as well. His exploits at the casino had earned him a place in history, and for the rest of his life he took great pride in being 'The Man who Broke the Bank at Monte Carlo'.

From what we now know of Camille Blanc, it seems almost certain that he pocketed the £40,000 that formed his share of the proceeds, instead of returning it to the bank's coffers. Despite this, the casino still profited to an enormous extent from the two men's little intrigue. Stanley Jackson, author of Inside Monte Carlo, describes Wells' achievement as an 'astonishing gambling coup [which] cost the casino a substantial sum but would be worth countless millions in free publicity.' The press coverage which followed Wells' triumphs at the gaming tables attracted many more hopeful players. As the *London Evening Standard* put it:

One result of the great coups at Monte Carlo, of which so much has been recently heard, is that enormous crowds of 'punters' have been besieging the Casino.

And according to the *Manchester Times*:

> Players ... stand five deep round the tables, and are ready to pay two or three louis to anybody who is willing to vacate his seat. It is further stated that nine-tenths of these people are English.

Casino profits soared and the share price rose by almost one-third. Quite apart from the short-term profits they banked, the Blanc family's shareholdings increased in value by the equivalent of more than £120 million in today's values. Camille Blanc's personal share holding rose by some 2.2 million francs – worth about £9 million in today's value.

Writing in 1927, long after Wells' coup, a journalist claimed, '1891 marked the turning point of the Casino. From then on, Camille Blanc feared nothing ... he was beyond any possibility of failure' ... for another few years, that is.

19

A High-Class Crook

Charles De Ville Wells never became another Thomas Edison, a Blériot or a Brunel. As his defence attorney, Edward Abinger, rightly said, Wells was born too late to make any fundamental contribution to the technology of steam engines or electrical devices.

On the other hand, some of his inventions were years ahead of their time. It was in 1889 that he persuaded Miss Budd to invest in the small 'motor for domestic and general use' to drive coffee grinders, boot polishers and knife cleaners. Nowadays we take for granted motorised gadgets of the kind that Wells foresaw: toothbrushes, blenders, fans, hedge-cutters, to name just a few.

The musical skipping rope, for which he sold the patent for £50, proved to be a popular toy. It was mass produced and has sold in substantial numbers around the world for many decades. Versions of it are still available today.

His idea of packaging mustard in tubes took almost fifty years to become a reality. It finally appeared in Britain in 1934, when Colman's Mustard™ introduced it as 'Pic-Nic Mustard'. And every time we open a packet by pulling a little tab and tearing the wrapper along the dotted line, we are using another Charles Wells invention of the mid-1880s. Our modern armies rely heavily on technology to watch the enemy's movements – Wells'

1885 patent for 'Obtaining Photographic Birds-eye Views' used kites or rockets to do the job that is now performed by spy satellites and drones.

It has to be said, though, that his most effective invention by far was the process he developed in Paris for separating people from their money. Almost a decade later, a near identical scheme in America offered 50 per cent interest every forty-five days. The promoter was one Charles Ponzi, whose name is synonymous with get rich quick schemes of this sort – an honour which Charles Wells no doubt felt he deserved himself.

None of Wells' inventions can be said to have made the world a better place, but I for one would love to have witnessed the talking clock, the life-saving torpedo or the combined chandelier and fire extinguishing grenade! I wonder what Charles Wells would be doing if he were alive today. Would he be selling investors a quarter-share in an energy efficient motor car? Or operating some complicated internet scam? Or would he have chosen a career in the financial sector, promoting dodgy insurance plans, rigging the exchange rate, or selling worthless bonds? We can but guess …

Without doubt, Wells left a lasting impression on everyone he met. Members of the police force who came into contact with him often found that the association started them on the road to future success. Walter Dinnie was promoted to detective chief inspector within two years of arresting Wells at Le Havre, and in 1901 he was the driving force behind the new fingerprint department at Scotland Yard. Two years later he became Commissioner of Police in New Zealand, where at first his career flourished. But with his hatred of everything connected with gambling, he vigorously clamped down on even the most harmless games of chance. He voiced the opinion that gamblers, many of whom were arrested during his tenure, should not even be entitled to a trial by jury. As a consequence, he was publicly reviled and was finally dismissed under a cloud.

Detective-Inspector Charles Richards, who had searched Wells' Great Portland Street premises, later found fame as the arresting officer in the Oscar Wilde case in 1895.

Alfred Crutchett, who had helped to bring Wells to book in 1912, eventually became head of CID at Scotland Yard. He retired just as news of Wells' death was announced, and although the timing was coincidental, to many it seemed as if Crutchett could at last relax in the knowledge that Monte Carlo Wells no longer posed a threat to the public. The Wells case cropped up in an interview when Crutchett looked back on his thirty-year career. 'Wells was a really wonderful man, possessed of many gifts,' he reminisced, adding that Wells would undoubtedly have succeeded in life if he had stayed on the right side of the law.

Crutchett's place as head of CID was taken by none other than his colleague, George Nicholls. Both men had built enormously successful careers in the police force, particularly after their work on the Wells case. Nicholls was made a Member of the British Empire in 1932 and was appointed chief constable of Scotland Yard's CID later that year. He retired in 1934.

Wells' fame rubbed off on to other people who had only the slightest acquaintance with him. In 1923 Cecil Kiddell, a 36-year-old tugboat skipper, tragically died during an operation for appendicitis. He had served with distinction in the Royal Navy in the First World War, and he left a widow and an infant daughter. But it was his brief connection with Wells that he was chiefly remembered for. Kiddell had been the young deckhand on board the *Excelsior*, and a local paper reported his death under the heading:

MATE TO MONTE CARLO WELLS: FALMOUTH TUG OFFICER'S DEATH.

For all his faults, Wells was admired by many of the people he met. Some appear to have been entranced, or even mesmerised, by him. This was certainly the case with the individuals he defrauded. But he cast a spell on others, too. Edward Abinger, who defended Wells at his trial for the patent frauds, wrote:

> I should say that he was not only one of the most successful gamblers of all time, but also a man of a highly fascinating personality. Like the Ancient Mariner immortalised by Coleridge, he would hold his victims with his glittering eye and to their wondering ears a tale unfold. He could –
> 'Dip into the future, as far as human eye could see,
> See the vision of the world, and all the wonder there would be ...

Ernest Nicholls, a former officer in the City of London Police (not to be confused with George Nicholls of Scotland Yard), described Wells as 'the most picturesque, the most interesting and certainly the most intriguing figure ... As a high-class crook he has had no equal.'

Prison Governor Basil Home Thomson devoted an entire chapter to Charles Wells in his autobiography. He, too, testified to Wells' enthusiastic, beguiling manner:

> 'Monte Carlo Wells,' who was in my charge at Dartmoor, was an example of the man who sins through sheer optimism ... Granted that many poor people suffered in their pockets from him; granted that he may have defrauded the widow and orphan by his specious promises: it is the motive that I would have judged him by, and his motives were always dictated by a pure-souled optimism. He intended to make all their fortunes – and his own ... If when I met him he had been a free man and I had had money to invest ... he would have defrauded even me, who have a fairly wide acquaintance among fraudulent company promoters: so great is the power of the man who believes in himself! ... he remained a memory of the pleasantest and the most unselfish of all the rascals that passed through my hands.

Apart from a stone tablet in a Marseille church, there are no monuments to remind us of Wells and his deeds; no statues adorn the places where he lived, nor is there a plaque bearing his name to mark the building where he died. Yet, in the south-coast town of Newhaven, legend has it that, after his Monte Carlo triumph, Wells and Jeannette were regular guests at the London and Paris Hotel. They are said to have held riotous parties which went on until the early hours of the morning, keeping the other visitors awake. The hotel management asked Wells to take his custom elsewhere, and he rented a nearby house in Fort Road – where the festivities continued. Whether the story is true, or simply a local legend, is uncertain, but when the author of this book visited Newhaven in about 2015 he found that the local council had signposted the house where Wells stayed as a place of historical interest. Several local people, when approached, knew of Wells and could point out the house where he had reputedly lived.

Most of Wells' victims were well-to-do people who could afford to lose some of their wealth. And none of his crimes involved physical violence. He obtained other people's money by advertising, by letter and by telegram. Not that these factors in any way excuse his actions. 'White-collar crime' (as we now know it) can have just as severe an effect on the victim as any other offence. But with his reputation for being 'exceptionally reserved', it suited his purposes to commit crime by remote control, as it were, rather than by direct confrontation. And the fact that he did not deal with the dupes in person made it even easier for him to behave in a cold and dispassionate manner towards them.

So what did become of his victims?

Miss Phillimore, who lost far more than probably anyone else, resumed her career as a writer with scarcely a pause following her dealings with Charles Wells. She went on to publish several further books, including an 1898 study of the Italian poet Dante Alighieri. In 1893, she opened a mission-house for vulnerable women in London's East End. Many years later this building became the setting for the popular TV series, *Call the Midwife*. She never married, and she died in 1929.

The Honourable William Cosby Trench seems to have recovered surprisingly quickly from his brush with financial disaster. In September 1893, just a few months after Wells was convicted for fraud, Trench married Frances Shawe-Taylor. They had four children. His experiences with Wells seem to have instilled in him a lifelong interest in legal matters. He became a Justice of the Peace and, in 1905, was appointed high sheriff of County Limerick. He died in 1944 at the age of 75. And there were others who survived into the second half of the twentieth century. His early 'client', Miss Frances Budd, served her country in the First World War by assisting at a branch of the YMCA in France. In the Second World War, having deducted no less than twelve years from her true age, she worked in the Department of the Official Censor. She died in a Bournemouth rest home in April 1952. One month later, Amy Elliott, who had invested in the Fishing and Trawling Syndicate passed away too. At the time of her death she had still occupied the small house in Goods Station Road, Tunbridge Wells; the house is there to this day.

It was Wells' smaller creditors who were, in general, less able to get over their losses. Frank Jupp, who had supplied the magnificent outfits for the crew of the *Palais Royal*, was bankrupted by his creditors and was still slowly paying off his debts some thirty years later.

Wells' own associates do not appear to have enjoyed particularly charmed lives, either. Aristides Vergis and Charles Wells never saw each other again following Wells' incarceration in 1893. Vergis died in 1895 while Wells was still in prison.

Henry Baker Vaughan, who had copied thousands of circulars, came to a particularly tragic end. His association with Wells seems to have cast a shadow over his subsequent career, and at one time the former legal clerk took a job as a dock labourer.

Finally he managed to secure a position as bookkeeper to a moneylender. But in 1906 the sum of £3 appeared to be missing from the office, and suspicion fell on him once again. The 49-year-old clerk was suspended while a close scrutiny of the ledgers was carried out. In a state of depression, he took a fatal dose of arsenic on Hampstead Heath just before Christmas. Vaughan's family had increased in size since his involvement with Wells, and he left a widow and eight children. An examination of the accounts later revealed that the money had not been missing after all.

Wells' partners in the Fishing and Trawling Syndicate fared little better. After his release from prison, the Reverend Vyvyan Henry Moyle was found begging in the streets: the police charged him with vagrancy and he was sent to an institution so that he should not starve. He died shortly afterwards, in 1908.

Alfred Emanuel, the former journalist, publisher, financial pundit and conman, is recorded in the 1911 census as a 'manufacturing chemist' specialising in the production of a proprietary hair restorer – but that's only half the story. A newspaper report of 1914 headed 'TRADING ON THE DEAD' explains how he adopted the practice of searching the 'Deaths' columns in newspapers. He then wrote to the executors enclosing a bill for hair stimulants which he falsely claimed to have supplied to the deceased person prior to their death. In this way he gained a regular income for himself until the day when he invoiced for recent purchases by a man who had already been dead for five years. He received a six-month jail sentence.

Wells' pride and joy, the *Palais Royal*, was sold to Henry Scown, a Plymouth scrap metal dealer, but was reprieved before being broken up. The ship was converted back into a cargo vessel and was – in the words of the official record – 'sold to foreigners', finishing up in the hands of a Turkish ship owner. On 30 October 1908 she collided with another vessel off Seraglio Point, Istanbul, and sank, thus ending a chequered career which had lasted for more than forty years.

The impressive business premises at 154–156 Great Portland Street, where Wells had operated his patents scam, were demolished around 1929 and, together with the adjoining property, were replaced by Yalding House. This building was for many years in the ownership of the British Broadcasting Corporation, and housed the studios of BBC Radio 1 between 1996 and 2012.

Fred Gilbert's song about Charles Wells enjoyed quite remarkable longevity. For at least half a century everyone from a toddler to a centenarian knew the words, and could whistle or hum the jaunty melody. Between 1904 and 1930, Charles Coborn released no fewer than five separate recordings of it, either on its own or as part of a medley. He toured the country's music halls constantly, and kept the number in his act year in, year out. If the unthinkable happened and he had omitted it, the audience would not have allowed him to escape until they had heard their perennial favourite. Coborn once claimed – rather wearily, it must be said – that he had sung it about a quarter of a million times. He continued to recite it almost until his death at the age of 93.* Today, 130-plus years after it was written, the song is still given an occasional airing. No album of music hall favourites would be complete without it, and it has been used in a variety of motion pictures – from *The Railway Children* to *Lawrence of Arabia* – to conjure up a bygone era.

The Casino at Monte Carlo has gone from strength to strength in the years since Charles Wells was last there, and until recently it was Monaco's primary source of income. It is still operated by the Société des Bains de Mer – the company established by François Blanc – but today the majority shareholders are the principality's government and royal family. Many architectural features of the building remain almost exactly as they were in Charles Wells' era.

---

* Coborn sang the song in the 1934 film *Say It With Flowers* and this performance can currently be viewed on YouTube.

As we have seen, Charles Wells' daughter, Marie Antoinette Florence Charlotte de Ville-Wells, had married Joseph Vayre in 1896. Vayre later became a playwright, then an impresario. Eventually, under the pen-name Charles Vayre, he embarked on a successful and prolific career as an author of popular fiction. Nearly all of his novels were collaborations with other writers, including over twenty books with Robert Florigni as his co-author. His themes included romance, adventure ... and crime.

Vayre and his wife once collaborated on a song (credited to 'Vayre - De Wills'). It is about a woman who has lost her lover, a ship-owner, and is clearly influenced by Charles Wells and his maritime exploits.

Vayre died on 29 January 1941 at the home he shared with Marie Antoinette at St Tronc, Marseille. Marie Antoinette died on 1 April 1944. The couple had no children, and consequently Charles Wells has no surviving descendants today.

Charles Wells' sister, Anna Maria, died aged 72 at the Carmelite Convent in Morlaix in 1903. The youngest sister, Florence, spent her life in a convent, and died in 1914. Emily Jane, the eldest sibling, had several children, however, and many of her descendants now live in Britain and Australia.

It was reported that after Wells' funeral, Jeannette and her maid, Mildred, left for France where Jeannette planned to start a business. I suspect that, on reaching Paris, Jeannette notified Monsieur Desbleumortier, the administrator, that Charles had died. This would explain why news of his death came not from London, but from Paris, creating the false impression that he had died in France.

For a long time, the present author tried unsuccessfully to discover what had become of Jeannette. Recently, however, members of the Pairis family found the answer. Jeannette had taken a job as a domestic servant at number 44, rue de la Pompe – an up-market street close to the Bois de Boulogne and popular with artists, writers and musicians.

She became ill and was admitted to the Boucicaut Hospital (a charitable institution for those unable to pay for their own medical treatment). On 13 November 1929 she died at the age of 60.

French records do not include the cause of death, but it seems likely that Jeanette's addiction to cigarettes may have been responsible for her early demise.

Arthur de Courcy-Bower, the other renowned bank-breaker, died in early January 1926. He had been living in reduced circumstances in a small flat in London. *The Times* printed a brief mention of his death – something they had omitted to do for Charles Wells. The article misleadingly asserted that it was Bower who was known as 'the man who broke the bank'.

Bower was, incidentally, buried in the same cemetery as Charles De Ville Wells. In fact, the two Monte Carlo bank-breakers lie not 50 yards apart.

As one gambler might have said to another, 'What are the odds against that?'

Notes

Abbreviations Used

BL   British Library
ODNB   *Oxford Dictionary of National Biography.*
POB   The Proceedings of the Old Bailey.
TNA   The National Archives (Kew, London).

References to Court Proceedings and Other Official Hearings

Reports in the *Proceedings of the Old Bailey* are shown in the following format: 'POB – 1893, Smith testimony'.

(The published proceedings were, contrary to what we might expect, neither complete nor very accurate. In most cases, supplementary information from newspapers is given with a separate reference.)

Other hearings are described in line with the following example: 'Bankruptcy hearing – 1893, Wells testimony'.

Prologue

9–10   See notes for Chapter 15.

1 – A Frenchman in the Making

17   For general background information on Charles Jeremiah
        Wells, see Tatchell, and Johnston.
        'While the bees … fishing.' – *The Academy*, 19 April 1879,
        p.350.
        Birth record, Charles Jeremiah Wells – London Parish Records
        (Ancestry).
        'Sparkling … humour.' – Rossetti & Charles Wells (essay
        by Theodore Watts-Dunton in foreword to Wells – C. J.,
        pp. xliv–xlv).
        Friendship with Keats – Tatchell, pp. 7–8.
18   'But when, O Wells … unquell'd.' – Keats, J., p. 135.
        Plays trick on Tom Keats – Johnston, pp. 79–80.
        Blamed for Tom's death – Johnston, p. 80.
        'That degraded Wells … possibly can' – Johnston, p. 80.
        'I wrote it … fault.' – Johnston, p. 81.
        'Used to get very drunk together' – Wu, p. 217; *Encyclopedia
        Britannica* (11th Edition).
19   'Boarding and day school' – *Hertfordshire Directory* 1838.
        'Would have been a really good … was up …' – Re-told by
        Richard Hengist Horne in *The Academy* 19 April 1879, p. 349.
20   James Deville – 1841 census (Ancestry).
        Wells overseer and Deville warden – Broxbourne Parish
        Records (Hertfordshire Archives).
        Family details: Civil and Parish Records – www.findmypast.
        co.uk and www.ancestry.co.uk. (See also family tree, p. 9).
        Britain's first census. To be precise, earlier censuses had been
        held, but this was the first to record individual names and
        personal details. Some individuals listed appear not to be
        family members, and are almost certainly servants.
        List of goods to be sold – *Hertford Mercury & Reformer*,
        12 June 1841.
23   'It is probable … over people' – Tatchell, p. 14.
        'He had only … anything' – Johnston, p. 77, (F.N.).

'I cannot recall … poets.' – Rossetti & Charles Wells (essay by Theodore Watts-Dunton in foreword to Wells, C. J., pp. lvii–lviii).

Census, 1841 (France) – Quimper Archives.

Anna Maria becomes a nun. – A law of 18 February 1809 decreed that at sixteen years of age novices could, with their parents' consent, take their vows and join for one year (Art. 7). At 21 they could join for five years (Art. 8).

24   Letter 'W' in French. The *Nouveau Dictionnaire de la Langue Française* of 1856 shows only four words beginning with W: Wagon, Whig, Whisky, Whist and Wiski. There are very many more today, mostly borrowed from English.

25   'A most dangerous … person.' – Johnston, p. 77.

26   Marseille as world's third largest port: London and Liverpool were the largest.

28   Wells' marriage and the birth of Marie Antoinette de Ville-Wells – marriage and birth records: Marseille Archives.

29   Messageries Maritimes – the original 'messageries' were a network of stagecoaches which later moved into the shipping business.

Compagnie Fraissinet – Wikipedia article, 'Fraissinet'.

Applies for French and British patents – the invention was patented in France (No. 83,451) in December 1868, and in Britain (No. 3200) in November 1869.

Test on steamship *Durance* – *Engineering*, 23 September 1870.

Wells works for Branicki – POB 1893, Jartoux testimony. See also Magocsi, p. 348, and Wikipedia (France) for articles on Branicki and on Bila Tserkva.

Henry Jartoux : he always used the English spelling – Henry (not *Henri*).

30   Engineer at lead mine – POB 1893, Jartoux testimony. Most of the lead imported into France came via Marseille: nearly all of it was from Spain. It may be significant that Henry Jartoux had lived in Spain in the mid-1870s, and in Armenia, which is also a lead-producing area. A figure of 1,000f per month is quoted in the official record as Wells' salary, but this must be an error: 1,000f per *year* would be a typical figure.

31   'Hygienic ice-cooled jug' – French patent 121,894.

Showgrounds, extent and location – The site was immediately opposite where the Eiffel Tower now stands. (It was built nine years afterwards for a subsequent Exposition). See also *The Engineer*, 1 March 1878, p. 148.

Telephone, phonograph, refrigerator etc. – Jones, p. 385. See also Wikipedia article on the Exposition.

31–2   Visits Paris *c.* 1878–9 – POB 1893, Jartoux testimony.

Boilers, engines, etc. – *The Engineer*, 10 May 1878, p. 321.

2 – With an Independent Air

33   Mother dies – death records, Marseille Archives. The 'large house' at 2 Montée des Oblats is still in existence.

Burns unpublished works – *ODNB*, entry for Charles Jeremiah Wells.

References to Milton and Shakespeare – Johnston, p.86.

34   'For a brief period … poet.' – *ODNB*, Charles Jeremiah Wells.

'I have the first … one year.' – Quoted in Tatchell, pp.16–17.

Death of Charles Jeremiah Wells – death records, Marseille Archives.

Inventions – drill bit and advertisement hoarding – French patents Nos 127,840 and 127,841 respectively.

35   Avenue des Tilleuls – since renamed Avenue Zola.

'The application … signs.' – French Patent No. 147,074.

36   Countess de Janville, baronesses Ordener and Saint-Amand – *L'Univers*, 13 January 1882.

37–8   'From the information … instead.' – *Le Temps*, 9 February 1882.

38   Charles Jeremiah Wells requests loan – British Library manuscripts ref. RP 794 (R. H. Horne).

'He had no industry … or others.' – *Ibid*.

38–9   Horne's loan to C.J. Wells – Johnston, p.83.

39   'The loss … time forward.' – British Library manuscripts ref. RP 794 (R. H. Horne).

29   'Nothing is more … create confusion.' – *Le Capitaliste*, 15 February 1882.

Banque des Arts et Manufactures – *Archives Commerciales de la France*, 18 June 1882.

Patent applications – French Patent Nos 147,636; 147,671; 147,672. These were granted in March 1882.

40   'To publish such … arrangements.' – *Le Capitaliste*,
        25 July 1882.
        'which is published … experience.' – *Le Figaro*, 29 July 1882.
        'magnificent apartment' – *La Justice*, 15 December 1892.
        Simon Philippart background – *La Grande Encyclopédie*.
41   'The biggest and most healthy' – publicity poster for
        Berck-sur-Mer (*c.*1880).
        'A drive of about … discomfort.' – *Pall Mall Gazette*,
        8 September 1882.
        Ship's captain buys shares – *Le Gaulois*, 22 December 1882.
41–2   Newspaper expresses doubt – *Le Capitaliste*, 14 February 1883.
        Arrest of Philippart – *Le Figaro*, 5 April 1883; *Le Journal de
        Fourmies*, 10 May 1883.
        Charles De Ville Wells disappears – *Gil Blas*, 21 January 1912.
        Philippart bankrupt – *Journal des Finances*, 9 February 1884.
42–3   'Misuse of funds' – the expression used in French is *abus de
        confiance*, sometimes translated as 'theft by bailee'.
43   18 Walker Terrace – the address given on British patent
        applications 1730–1733 of 1885.
44   'About £8,000 … ships &c.'; and paper manufacturing
        – Bankruptcy hearing, 1893, reported in *The Times*,
        13 July 1893, Wells testimony.
        Millbay Station, Brunel's railway etc. – see Wikipedia article,
        Millbay Station.
        Number of patent applications – Intellectual Property Office.
        See www.gov.uk.
48   'Nearly 100 patents' and 'practically exhausted his funds' –
        Morning Post, 12 July 1893. The actual number was probably in
        the region of 70.
        Wells' wife and daughter leave him – *Petit Parisien*,
        15 November 1912.

3 – A Patent Fraud

49   Wells lives in Fenchurch Street – Bow Street hearing, 1893,
        opening statements by C. Gill (prosecution lawyer).
49–50   Charles Jeremiah Wells' office in Fenchurch Street – his last
        entry at this address is in the *Law List* of 1831.

50   53 Charlotte Street was the address given on some patent applications, (for example the Musical Skipping Rope of December 1887). The street has since been re-named Hallam Street. It is not the same as the present-day Charlotte Street, which lies further to the east. The status of the area is confirmed by the Booth Poverty Map 1898–99.

51   Vaughan says he started in May or June, but does not specify the year. It is most likely to have been 1887. POB, 1893, Vaughan testimony (see also *The Times*, 15 February 1893).
Vaughan's family – various birth, marriage and death records and census records (www.ancestry.co.uk, www.findmypast.co.uk, www.freebmd.org.uk etc.).
Vaughan is paid 7s 6d – works for Wells several years – POB, 1893, Vaughan testimony (see also *The Standard*, 16 February 1893).
Patents: information from applications as follows: Goad (No. 4627, 1887); Pickburn; (No. 6108 of 1888).

52   Drake-Brockman (No. 6110 of 1888); Churchill-Shann (No. 13626 of 1888).
Musical skipping rope – Some other accounts say that the patent sold for £20, e.g. *Reynolds's Newspaper*, 29 January 1893.

53   Eschen's background / starts work for Wells – POB, 1893, Eschen testimony.
'Small business premises': POB, 1893, Trench testimony.
'Always busy … a hard working man' – POB, 1893, Eschen testimony.
Wells visits Eschen at home / people came to see models – POB, 1893, Langford testimony.

53–4   Loom-picking mechanism and inkstand – Patent Nos. 9758 and 13627 (both 1888); and Bow Street, 1893, Blake testimony.
Costs of models – POB, 1893, Eschen testimony.

54–5   Statistics on newspapers – *May's British & Irish Press Guide and Advertiser's Handbook & Dictionary*, 1889.

55–6   Frances Budd background – British Library (India Office): Madras Military Fund, Children's Pensions, BL L/ AG/21/30/10 and L/AG/21/30/13.

56–8   Willing's (formerly May's) – advertising agents and publishers of a press guide.

56   Emily Forrester's dealings with Wells – *Yorkshire Evening Post* 31 March 1892.

57   'Four Hundred Pounds' – Advertisement from *Morning Post*,
            9 September 1889.
            Advertising costs – Bow Street and Old Bailey, 1893, Young
            testimony.
58   Investment suitable for a lady – *Daily News*, 25 January 1893.
            Sir Walter Phillimore background – *ODNB*.
58–9   Catherine Mary Phillimore background – Kirk, p. 1231.
59–60   Letter, Wells to Phillimore, reproduced in *Truth*, 27 February
            1890.
60   Gains in efficiency of steam engines – Geels, pp. 131–2; Smith,
            E. C., p. 174.
61   Phillimore family owns land in Kensington – Abinger,
            pp. 89–90.
            Sir Walter Phillimore's estate – *ODNB*.

4 – The Certainty of a Fortune

62   Baroness Orczy at 162 Great Portland Street – Dugan, p.39
            F.N.
62–3   Miss Budd's concerns – Bow Street testimony.
63   Dr. White contacts lawyer and police – *Morning Post*, 1 March
            1893.
            Bartram background – Will of William Bartram; Census
            Records; The London Gazette, 31 July 1891; 7 August 1891;
            25 February 1898; National Archives, BT221.1997.
64   Labouchère's background – Wikipedia articles, Labouchère
            and *Truth*.
            'Armed at all points … no terrors.' – *Lancashire Evening Post*,
            6 December 1892.
            'It costs only £1 … "let Wells alone."' – *Truth*, 27
            February 1890.
65   'I never expose … in future.' – *Truth*, 6 March 1890.
            'So much frightened … had expired.'; 'I hear, however …
            public.' – *Truth*, 13 March 1890.
            'Not upon any account … attention.' – *Truth*, 27 March 1890.
67   'Speedily realise her desire.' – *Morning Post*, 25 January 1893.
            'Twenty-Five Thousand Pounds.' – Advertisement from *The
            Times*, 28 November and 2 December 1890.

68	Letter and other material sent by Wells to Trench – *The Standard*, 15 February 1893.
	'When a man saw … anxious.' – *Ibid.*
69–70	Further correspondence between Wells and Trench – *Ibid.*
70	Patents for steam engines – Nos 637; 1,044; 2,352 (all 1891).
	Patent for galvanic batteries – No. 884 of 1891.
	Patent for 'motive power from exhaust …' – No. 4,563 of 1891.
	Proportion of patents completed overall – *Encyclopedia Britannica*, 1911.
71	'A pretty pouting mouth' – *Lake's Falmouth Packet and Cornwall Advertiser*, 27 January 1912.
	'An artist's model from Chelsea' – Graves, p.90.
72	'Little ladies' – *Gil Blas*, 9 May 1911.
	Wells reports on business in France; Trench makes further investment – *The Standard*, 15 February 1893.
	Franco-Belgian company etc. – *Ibid.*
	Meeting between Wells and Trench – *Ibid.*
73	Wells states he will form one large company. Thibaud president – *Ibid.*
	I went on board … see them.' And 'I was satisfied … the trip.' – POB, 1893. Trench testimony; see also *The Times*, 13 March 1893.
73–4	Wells informs Trench about new company, agrees to take him to France – *The Standard*, 15 February 1893.
74	'Fifty Thousand Pounds' – Advertisement from *The Times*, 21 April 1891.
	154–156 Great Portland Street – this address is confirmed in British Phone Books 1891 (www.ancestry.co.uk).
	'nicely painted … appearance' – POB, 1893, Richards testimony.
75	Price of lease and ongoing rent – Bow Street, 1893, Trench testimony. This statement incorrectly refers to Great Titchfield Street, but at this date it is obvious that Great Portland Street was what Wells had intended to say.
	All details of yachts from *Lloyd's Register of Yachts*, 1890–93 and additional details Bankruptcy, 1893 (hearing of 13 July).
	Debt on a boat, £600 – *Freeman's Journal* (Dublin), 4 April 1893.
	'When people came … did not.' – POB, 1893, Eschen testimony.

75–6   Vergis' criminal record – Vergis' Trial, POB, hearings of
          27 June 1887; 24 October 1887.
          History of *Tycho Brahe*; routes and size of vessel – *Lloyd's
          Register of Shipping*. See also Heaton, p.110.
76   £3,500 paid for *Palais Royal* – Bankruptcy, 1893, Wells'
          statement of affairs (read out at initial hearing).

5 – Breaking the Bank

77   Information generally on Monte Carlo and the Casino – see
          Bethell; Corti; Dumont; Fielding; Graves; Herald and Radin;
          Kingston; Polovtsoff; Silberer; and Smith, A.
78   'As gorgeous … make it' – *The Times*, 11 April 1879.
          'Dazzling place … mirrors.' – Twain, p. 92.
78–9   Description of roulette table – Silberer, p. 32.
80   'With a recklessness … capital.' – Kingston, p. 164.
          Behaviour of onlookers – Dumont, especially pp. 283–287.
          'The worst thing … the other guests.' – Herald and Radin,
          p. 69.
          'In a few minutes … to the office for more.' – *The Elks
          Magazine*, January 1927.
81   Oppressive, stuffy atmosphere – *The Times*, 11 April 1879.
          Camille Blanc watches through peep-hole – website of the
          Monte Carlo Casino: casinodemonaco.com (retrieved August
          2014).
81–6   Background of Blanc brothers and casino – Corti, pp. 19–26.
82   Telegraph scam incorporated in *The Count of Monte Cristo*,
          Dumas, Chapter 60, '*The Telegraph*'.
83   Prince Bonaparte's win – Corti, pp. 93–99.
          Garcia's win – Corti, pp. 112–121.
          Cash reserve at table – according to *The Big Wheel* (Herald and
          Radin, p. 69) each roulette table's reserve was 50,000 fr. at
          the time of Wells' 1891 visit. At the trente-et-quarante tables,
          100,000 fr. is more likely to have been the reserve.
83–4   Blanc invents ceremony of 'breaking the bank' – Smith, A.
          p. 370.
84   'Only one visitor … five francs.' – Corti, p. 154.
          Contract between Prince of Monaco and Blanc, and payments
          to principality – Fielding, p. 89.
84–5   Share structure of 'Sea-bathing Company' – Smith, A., p. 334.

86   Restructuring of 'Sea-bathing Company'; Blanc family owns 87% – *Ibid*.

87   Distinguished visitors to the Casino – *The Times*, 5 February 1883; 23 January 1889.

'The harm this attractive … to do so.' – Queen Victoria's journal; RA VIC/MAIN/QVJ (W) 30 March 1882 (Princess Beatrice's copies).

88   'Another victim … critical condition.' – *The Times*, 8 December 1890.

Sarah Bernhardt suicide attempt – Sharpe, p. 88.

Payments for 'publicity' – *The Times*, 4 November 1890.

88–9   The Prince returns flowers – *Pall Mall Gazette*, 12 August 1891.

89   'I'd shut it up … the place.' – Edwards, p. 166.

Possible closure of Casino or move to Andorra or Liechtenstein – *Daily Independent*, 12 July 1891; *Western Daily Press*, 6 August 1891.

90   Wells wins £10,000, first day – Graves, p. 89.

Wells wins £40,000 during stay – POB, 1893, Trench testimony. Wells told Trench he had won this amount. Other versions state that he won 32,000 on this trip, and £28,000 on the next. Dundee Courier & Argus, 10 November 1891.

91   'Luck at Monte Carlo' – *Nottingham Evening Post*, 31 July 1891.

'Gambling at Monte Carlo' – *The Times*, 1 August 1891.

91–2   'Mr. Wells continues … his marvellous success.' – *Birmingham Daily Post*, 3 August 1891.

Large crowd … two secretaries – *Morning Post*, 3 August 1891.

6 – The Infallible System

96   'Couldn't have got through … turned up.' – *The Times*, 10 March 1893.

97   'My loan of £6,000 … again.' – POB, 1893, Phillimore testimony.

'The advertisement I answered … Monte Carlo.' – POB, 1893, Trench testimony.

Wells' letter to Trench – POB, 1893, Trench testimony; and *The Times*, 14 February 1893.

98   Left Monte Carlo to work on invention – *The Times*, 15 February 1893.

'I sent him no money … with.' – Bow Street, 1893, Trench
testimony and *The Standard*, 15 February 1893.

Large bank deposits – Bow Street, 1893, Green testimony.

99 Recipients forward letters to *Truth* magazine – *Truth*,
19 November 1891; and 27 October 1892.

Wells engages Capt. Smith – POB, 1893, Smith testimony.

Capt. Smith background – *Lloyd's Captains Register* (London
Metropolitan Archives); see also Masters' and Mates' Certificates
(Ancestry).

100 Smith's views – 'a mug' would spend so much; but ship
seaworthy: Bow Street, 1893, Smith testimony.

Wells renames the *Tycho Brahe* – the new name was not officially
registered with the Board of Trade until June 1892. TNA: BT
110/62/63.

The Palais Royal in Paris; background – Corti, p. 29.

John J. Marks had premises at 42 Grafton Street, Queen's Dock –
(Gore's Directory of Liverpool, 1892).

Wells and Marks on telephone – www.ancestry.co.uk (British
Phone Books, 1891, London, Liverpool).

100–1 Description of Palais Royal – Bow Street, 1893, Smith testimony.

Information in Table – Lloyd's Register of Yachts, 1892.

102 Wells did not drink alcohol – Bow Street, 1893, Smith testimony.

7 – Monte Carlo Wells

The account of Wells' November 1891 visit to Monte
Carlo is based principally on *The Times*, 6 November and
9 November 1891; see also *Pall Mall Gazette*, 9 November 1891.

103–4 Returning to be plucked … losing £4,000 – *Sheffield Evening
Telegraph & Star*, 3 November 1891.

104 'An excited crowd … 250,000f.' – *The Times*,
6 November 1891.

'Mr. "Bonne-Chance Wells" … Place du Casino.' – *Pall Mall
Gazette*, 9 November 1891.

104–5 Play on Saturday (7 November) – Fielding, p.94.

105 'All this naturally … enemy.' – *Pall Mall Gazette*,
9 November 1891.

106 'Because the physical … win again.' – *Ibid*.

'After watching … every coup.' – *The Times*,
9 November 1891.

106–7   Wells' comments to reporter: pestered for loans; dowry;
woman demands return of money; house always wins against
ordinary gamblers – *Ibid*.

107   Prince allows Casino to continue – Edwards, p. 166.
New salon opens after decorations completed – *The Times*,
31 October 1891.
'Rush to Monte Carlo … 2,000 francs.' – *Edinburgh Evening
News*, 18 November 1891.
'The hotels … season.' – *Hull Daily Mail*, 30 November 1891.

109   Wells wins 70,000fr. on 5 November – *The Times*,
6 November 1891.
'If it is worth … after year?' – *Truth*, 5 November 1891.
'Of a far worse … Wells.' – *Truth*, 19 November 1891.
'The Nice correspondent … system.' – *Truth*,
12 November 1891.

110   *Evening News* exposes Wells – 'Wells of Monte Carlo … my
Wells.' – *Truth*, 3 December 1891.
'Mr. Charles Hill Wells … lost it all?' – *Western Mail*,
21 November 1891.
Letters to Miss Phillimore – *Morning Post*, 25 January 1893.

111   Visit beginning 7 January – The section on this visit to Monte
Carlo by Wells is largely based on *The Standard* (London),
9 January 1892.
Wife and daughter present – Bankruptcy hearings, 1893, Wells'
testimony reported in *The Times*, 13 July 1893, and *Western
Gazette*, 14 July 1893.
The modern spelling is Saint-Roch (no 'e').
'With a big pile of notes' – *The Standard*, 9 January 1892

112   'Every movement … interest.' – *The Standard*, 9 January 1892.
Camille Blanc as *chef de partie* – Herald and Radin, p.71.
'Mr Wells started … pounds.' – *The Standard*, 9 January 1892.
'Before the dinner … building.' – *Ibid*.
'He has several … at the tables.' – *The Standard*,
11 January 1892.

113   Loss of £3,000 to £4,000 because wife and daughter distracted
him – Bankruptcy hearings, 1893, Wells' testimony.

113–4   The return of Mr Hill Wells … year by year.' – *The Times*,
11 January 1892.

114   'Was confined … menu card' – Kingston, p.168.
             Fred Gilbert background – Baker, p.235.

115   '[I] liked the tune … Hoxton.' – Coborn, p.227.
             Coborn buys rights to song – Coborn, pp.227–8.

116   'The supreme compliment' – Graves, pp.91–2. See also POB, 1893, Gill's closing speech. 'He was now known everywhere, even on the street organ, as "the man who broke the bank at Monte Carlo"'
             Coborn introduces the song – *The Era*, 13 February 1892 (however, Coborn himself said that he thought he first sang it in late 1891 – Coborn, p.228).

117   Discussion between Wells and Miss Phillimore. She sends £1,500 – Bow Street, 1893, Phillimore testimony.
             Discussion between Wells and Trench. Trench makes two payments – Old Bailey, 1893, Trench testimony. See also *Birmingham Daily Post*, 13 March 1893.

117–8   'There is now lying … a week.' – *Liverpool Mercury*, 6 February 1892.

119   'Many visitors … roulette.' – *Dover Express*, 16 December 1892.
             Trench views *Palais Royal*; 'receive company promoters … in her.' – POB, 1893, Trench testimony; see also *Birmingham Daily Post*, 13 March 1893.
             Fire on *Palais Royal* – *Liverpool Mercury*, 23 February 1892 and 24 February 1892; and *Aberdeen Journal*, 24 February 1892.
             Wells' letter to Miss Phillimore. He has lost £6,000, insurers to investigate – *The Times*, 24 January 1893 and 25 January 1893.
             'Sad disaster …' – *The Standard*, 15 February 1893.

119–20   Wells' letter to Trench promising £100,000 – *The Times*, 15 February 1893.

120   Mrs Forrester's action against Wells – *Yorkshire Evening Post*, 31 March 1892.

121   'Monte Carlo Wells' – first appearance in print – *Yorkshire Post*, 31 March 1892.

8 – The Biggest Swindler

122   'Now all is right … here.' – *The Times*, 13 March 1893.

Correspondence with Miss Phillimore – *The Times*, 25 January 1893.

122–3 Wells hides Monte Carlo activities by sending correspondence from other towns – casino admission cards dated May 1892 were found later at 154 Great Portland Street by Inspector Richards (see p. 136).

Apologetic letter from Miss Phillimore – *Morning Post*, 25 January 1893.

'Miserable amount' – *The Times*, 25 January 1893.

124 'Unless she had many millions' and 'Very scarce … law suit' and Wells has 'common sense' – *London Daily News*, 11 March 1893; *Morning Post*, 25 January 1893.

Wells' discussions with Vaughan – *The Standard*, 16 February 1893.

124–5 Trip to Paris with Vaughan – *Ibid*.

125 Wells claims Trench is liable; they meet at Drummond's Bank – Old Bailey, 1893, Trench testimony.

'I must explain … assure you.' – *Sheffield Evening Telegraph & Star*, 15 February 1893.

126 Trench threatens Wells – Gleadow goes to Paris; no trace of company: *The Times*, 15 February 1893.

127 'I asked him … then left.' – POB, 1893, Gleadow testimony.

Blake's sporting prowess – *Wikipedia: 1885 Men's tennis tour*.

127–8 Wells' dealings with Blake – Bow Street, 1893, Blake testimony.

128 'A man of position'; 'guaranteed a return of £50,000 …' – *Morning Post*, 22 February 1893

Wells' representations; Blake sends payment; 'Herewith I have … £3,000' – Bow Street, 1893, Blake testimony.

129 Wells requests £500, Blake refuses – Bow Street, 1893, Blake testimony.

Repairs to yacht and piano; 'to the tune of £69' – *Lloyd's Weekly Newspaper*, 5 March 1893.

Dispute between Wells and Capt. Smith – Bow Street and POB, 1893, Smith testimony.

Johnston takes command; vessel sails – Bow Street, 1893, Ferguson testimony.

Cost of uniforms – Bankruptcy, 1893, list of claims (Jupp).

130 Willoughby Brothers – *Edinburgh Evening News*, 5 December 1892.

Wells takes room in Paris, 35 Rue de Londres – *The Standard*, 22 February 1893.

Wells blackmails Blake – principally from *Morning Post*, 22 February 1893.

131   Loan on *Palais Royal* – TNA: BT 110/62/63.

131–2   'The Biggest Swindler … incredulity.' – *Truth*, 27 October 1892.

132–3   Harris versus Wells; and 'I think it should be known … Portland Street.' – *The Times*, 17 November 1892; and *The Standard*, 17 November 1892.

133   Wells withdraws £5,000 – *North-Eastern Daily Gazette*, 26 January 1893.

'Instructed the cabman … possible.' – *Morning Post*, 25 January 1893; Bow Street, 1893, Gill's opening remarks.

Workmen scramble – *Edinburgh Evening News*, 5 December 1892.

Workmen have no time to disembark – *Morning Post*, 25 January 1893; Bow Street, 1893, Gill's opening remarks.

Sails straight to France – *The Standard*, 22 February 1893.

'Wells said … Marseilles.' – Old Bailey, 1893, Ferguson testimony.

134   'We remained in Cherbourg … came.'. *Ibid*.

Extradition arrangements; crew's articles – *The Standard*, 22 February 1893.

'We could not go … Consul.' – POB, 1893, Ferguson testimony.

Great Portland Street premises searched – *The Times*, 22 February 1893 and *The Standard*, 22 February 1893.

134–5   Selling coal – *The Times*, 24 January 1893.

Detectives arrive – Polovtsoff , p. 164.

'Age 50 … black eye.' – Draft telegram, Scotland Yard to British Consul, Le Havre for onward transmission to French police (2 December 1892). TNA: HO 144/490/X38749.

'His French was … wrong man.' – *Yorkshire Herald*, 6 December 1892.

Arrest – *Le Temps*, 5 December 1892.

Admits true identity and says he broke the bank – *Pall Mall Gazette*, 5 December 1892.

Only 24 francs in pocket – British Consul, le Havre, to Home Office, 5 December 1892, TNA: HO 144/490/X38749.

135–6	'The magnificent … Cherbourg' and 'one of the richest …' – *Le Figaro*, 5 December 1892.
136	'Wells is the man … "Monte Carlo Fleet".' – *Le Gaulois*, 5 December 1892.
	'Charles Wells, the adventurous … *Palais Royal*.' – Penny Illustrated, 17 December 1892.
	'She is the daughter … died.' – *Le Gaulois*, 5 December 1892.
136–7	Background on Alsace generally is from *La Grande Encyclopédie*.
137	Family swears allegiance – *Déclarations de Citoyenneté, Alsace-Lorraine*, 1872 (Collection des Optants, www.ancestry.fr).
138	Out of all of Jeannette's family, it seems likely that her sister Léonie was the only one who knew anything approaching the truth about Jeannette's activities in connection with Charles Wells.

9 – The Darling of the Hour

139	'Sensational Arrest for Fraud' – *Daily Gazette*, Middlesbrough, 5 December 1892.
	'The Hero of Monte Carlo' – *Sunderland Daily Echo*, 5 December 1892.
139–40	'Perhaps Mr. Charles Wells … antagonist.' – *Lancashire Evening Post*, 6 December 1892.
141	'I recognise … captain.' – *Gil Blas*, 11 December 1892.
	'Since his arrest … suicide.' – *Le Temps*, 12 December 1892.
142	'Don't forget … pigeon-holes.' – Quoted from Wells' letter to Jeannette in communication from British Consul, le Havre, to Foreign Office, 6 December 1892: TNA: HO 144/490/X38749.
	Sea captain defrauded of 15,000f – *Le Figaro*, 15 December 1892.
142–3	Statute of limitations, France – *La Grande Encyclopédie*, Vol 27; p. 577.
143	'Only too glad …' – *The Times*, 10 March 1893.
	Palais Royal and Velléda – *Le Figaro*, 6 January 1893.
	Menier's background – https://fr.wikipedia.org/wiki/Henri_Menier.
	Fittings stripped out – *Financial Times*, 7 January 1893.

Bankruptcy petition – Register of Receiving Orders: TNA, B12/4.

143–4   Journey to England delayed – *Le Figaro*, 15 January 1893.

144   Wells aware of frauds, not larcenies – Bow Street, 1893, Dinnie testimony.

'Had nothing about it … Commerce.' – *Le Figaro*, 18 January 1893.

144–5   Dinnie background – *Te Ara Encyclopedia of New Zealand*. Donald Dinnie – Wikipedia. See also http://www.gordondinnie.com/FT1.html.

145   'Somewhat common-place … stout.' – *Western Mail*, 25 January 1893.

He was somewhat … lamely.' – *Reynolds's Newspaper*, 22 January 1893.

146   Bow Street hearing, in general – *Birmingham Daily Post*, 18 January 1893; *Western Mail*, 18 January 1893; *Belfast Newsletter*, 18 January 1893; *Leeds Mercury*, 18 January 1893; *Reynolds's Newspaper*, 22 January 1893; *Lloyd's Weekly*, 22 January 1893; *Western Mail*, 25 January 1893.

'He was firing … lived.' – *Leeds Times*, 21 January 1893.

'It was curious … accent.' – *Leeds Mercury*, 18 January 1893.

Shrug of the shoulders – *Western Mail*, 24 November 1892.

147   'Absolutely nothing but defraud people'; and Wells' claims about being established since 1868 as a civil engineer – Bow Street, 1893, Gill's opening comments.

149   Miss Phillimore; pieces of paper quote etc.; and 'Gentleman of youthful appearance' – *The Standard*, 15 February 1893.

Boats offered as security near-worthless – *Ibid*.

149–50 Trench asked no advice, had no experience – *Ibid*.

150   'Considerably improved … amusement.' – *Morning Post*, 22 February 1893.

Caroline Davison's testimony – *Ibid*.

151   Capt. Smith's testimony – *The Times*, 22 February 1893.

'I don't suppose … uncles.' – *The Standard*, 22 February 1893.

151–2   Ferguson's testimony – *The Times*, 22 February 1893; *Morning Post*, 22 February 1893; *Bristol Mercury & Daily Post*, 22 February 1893.

152–4   Miss Budd's testimony – *The Times*, 1 March 1893; Manchester Evening News, 29 February 1893; *Morning Post*, 1 March 1893.

'What was he doing? … didn't play.' – *Morning Post*, 1 March 1893.

10 – An Accomplished Scoundrel

155 'His trial … adventurer.' – *Derby Daily Telegraph*,
29 September 1928.

'Dapper, quick … clever' – Abinger, p. 88. Parts of the
following sequence are also based on Abinger's account,
pp. 87–95.

156 Quill pen – Abinger, p. 91.

'I never received … first and last.' – *London Daily News*,
11 March 1893.

'He didn't include judges … think not.' – *Birmingham Daily
Post*, 13 March 1893.

157 'I should say … what I have said.' – POB, 1893, Green
testimony.

'Wells of Monte Carlo … Old Bailey.' – *Lancashire Evening
Post*, 14 March 1893.

157–9 Eschen's testimony – POB; *The Times*, 14 March 1893;
Lancashire Evening Post, 14 March 1893; *Lancaster Gazette*,
15 March 1893.

158 'Fairly danced up and down … evidence.' – Abinger,
pp.90–91.

'Here comes a triple … size of engine.' – Based on a report in
the *Lancashire Evening Post*, 14 March 1893. The original article
attempted a mock-phonetic version of Eschen's evidence,
presumably making fun of his German accent.

'Inflammable balloon' and 'Then I will take it … skipping-
rope.' – *Manchester Courier & Lancashire General Advertiser*,
14 March 1893.

159 'You can do anything …' – Abinger, p. 92.

Prosecution's attempt to discredit Eschen: bribe regarding
warrant; Eschen and Wells very friendly; no extradition treaty
with Portugal – POB, 24 January 1893.

159–60 Hollingsworth background – 1891 Census, (www.ancestry.
co.uk).

160 'This case may last forever … it is over.' – *Western Daily Press*,
15 March 1893.

'There has been so much confusion … case.' – *Ibid.*

Vergis' criminal case – POB, 27 June 1887; 24 October 1887.

160–1   Langford testimony. 'He came on business … suppose.' – POB
         13 March, 1893.
161   Mynn testimony. – POB 13 March, 1893.
         'Where is the Isabella … all at sea?' – *Western Daily Press*,
         15 March 1893.
         Jartoux testimony – POB.
161–2   Abinger's concluding comments – *The Times*, 15 March 1893.
162–3   'The prisoner … not tell you.' – Abinger, pp. 92–4.
163   'Do you know … thought not.' – *Ibid*.
         Judge's summing-up. – *The Times*, 15 March 1893.
163–4   'It was easy … hear him.' – *Queensland Times*, 2 May 1893.
164   'I had been … sorry for him.' – Abinger, p. 94–5.
164–5   'He was a great advertiser … country fair.' – *London Daily
         News*, 15 March 1893.
165   'One of the most accomplished scoundrels … purposes.' –
         Dundee Courier & Argus, 15 March 1893.
         'Suppose Mr. Wells … falls on them.' – *Sheffield & Rotherham
         Independent*, 18 March 1893.
         'It is true … ought to avoid.' – *The Times*, 15 March 1893.
166   'Monte Carlo Wells … hurriedly.' – *Western Mail*,
         23 February 1893.
166–7   'It appears that the convict … literature.' – *Lichfield Mercury*,
         28 April 1893.
167   'Saturday … broken the bank.' – Peddie, J. (*How the Bank at
         Monte Carlo was Broken*).
         'Sole, soup, and fowl.' – *Western Mail*, 24 April 1893.
168   'Such music-hall … the Bank.' – *Western Mail*, 24 May 1893.
169–71   Bankruptcy hearing. This was, if anything, more widely
         reported than Wells' trial for fraud. See *The Times*, 27 January
         1893, 11 February 1893, 23 February 1893, 12 July 1893,
         13 July 1893. See also: *Yorkshire Evening Post*, 20 July 1893.
170   'Could your system … valuable asset.' – *The Times*,
         13 July 1893.
171   'Do you really mean … in trouble.' – *Yorkshire Evening Post*,
         20 July 1893.
         'So opposed to him'; and 'went about shabbily … satisfied.' –
         Cheltenham Chronicle, 22 July 1893.
172   'July 17th. 1893 … old uncle.' – Letter, Lizzie Ritchie to
         Queen Victoria. TNA: HO 144/490/X38749 .

11 – Hell Upon Earth

Most of the background information on prison life is from Balfour.

174–5 'My greatest wish … Charles Wells.' – *Hampshire Advertiser*, 1 September 1894.

175 '[His] affable manner … friends.' – Lloyd's Weekly, 9 April 1899.

175–6 'At one end … as ever.' – Liverpool Mercury, 9 October 1897.

177 'Louis Charles … in London.' – Marriage Register, Marseille Archives.

Joseph Vayre's letter to Home Office: – TNA: HO 144/490/X38749.

Wells plays organ in chapel: – *Lloyd's Weekly*, 9 April 1899.

'Persons coming forward … durance.' – *Ibid*.

Wells interviewed at London hotel – *Ibid*.

178 'He is by no means … indicates.' – *Belfast News Letter*, 10 April 1899.

'He has improved … of age.' – *St. Paul Globe*, 1 May 1899.

Jeannette's jobs – Graves, p. 91.

178–9 Zalma Bradley Lee background – Birth, marriage and death records, and 'England Select Marriages' (www.ancestry.co.uk).

179 'The divertissements of London' – *Evening World*, 29 August 1903.

'Widow fights for Lee's body' – *Ibid*.

Zalma awarded $1m – Evening World, 22 September 1903.

Jeannette owns restaurant – Graves, p. 91.

179–80 Bankruptcy Discharge Application, 1899 – *The Times*, 26 April 1899; *The Argus* (Melbourne, Australia.) 14 June 1899.

180 'Monte Carlo of Wells' – *Bristol Mercury & Daily Post*, 29 September 1899.

Encyclopedia Britannica (10th Edition, 1902: article on Charles Jeremiah Wells).

180–1 H.G. Wells mistaken for 'Monte Carlo Wells' – Wells, H.G., pp. 638–9.

181 Fred Gilbert's death – Probate Register, 1903. Baker (p. 235) gives the district of Gilbert's death as 'Eltham', whereas it was in fact Elham (Kent), the district in which Sandgate is situated.

Jeannette as governess – Graves, p. 91.

Settling in or near Paris (various districts) – *Sûreté* to
Metropolitan Police, 03.06.1911. TNA: MEPO 3/204.

182–3   Applies for various patents, France and Belgium – Letter,
Sûreté to Metropolitan Police, TNA: MEPO 3/204.

183–6   Charles and Jeannette in Ireland – *The Times*, 23 December
1905.

185   Boating incident – *Southern Star*, 24 February 1906.
Omnium Général established – Archives Commerciales de la
France, 05 December 1903.

185–6   Louis Servatel; claims birth in Martinique – Petit Parisien,
9 May 1911.

12 – A Royal Personage

1187   Naval, Shipping and Fisheries Exhibition – *The Times*,
27 April 1905.

187–8   Moyle background – *Truth*, 9 November 1905; *The Times*, 24
March 1873 and Thomson (The Criminal), pp. 68–70.

188   'Owe no man any thing.' *King James Bible* (Romans 13:8):
'Owe no man any thing, but to love one another: for he that
loveth another hath fulfilled the law'.

189   People who appeared to have died, and who had actually died
– POB 1906, Walton testimony (citing a letter allegedly from
Dr. Hart, M.D., U.S.A.,… etc.).
Wells takes office in Stamford Street – *Western Gazette*,
24 November 1905.

189–90   Purchase of Shanklin – *Daily Telegraph*, 20 November 1905.

190   'If you don't mind …' – Advertisement in *Daily Telegraph*,
(date unknown), quoted POB, 1906, Walton testimony.
Walton invests – *Ibid*.

190–1   Emanuel's earlier conviction, divorce etc. – Criminal Records,
1878 embezzlement conviction (Ancestry); *The Times*, 10 June
1901; Divorce Court Records 1882 (Ancestry); Old Bailey
Trial 24 November 1890; birth, marriage and death, census
records, criminal records etc. (Ancestry).

191   'The business … if any.' – POB, 1906, Walton testimony.
'Voluminous literature … style.' – *Truth*, 9 November 1905.
'One of the best … business.' – *The Times*, 20 November 1905.

192   'Respectable-looking … the cards.' – *Truth*, 9 November 1905.
       'Dear Sir … V.H. Moyle': *Ibid*.
193   Hugh Richard Dawnay – Wikipedia article on Lord Downe
       (Dawnay).
194   'Underpart of the Stern … of fuel.' – *Farm Life*, 2 September
       1905.
       Advertisement in *Penny Illustrated*, 7 October 1905.
       Jeannette negotiates hotel lease – *The Times*, 6 January 1906.
195–8 Letters, Charles to Jeannette – *Sheffield Evening Telegraph & Star*,
       6 January 1906.
197   'For the "Bouillabaisse à Nana" … successful' – *Sheffield
       Evening Telegraph & Star*, 6 January 1906.
198   Empty property – *Manchester Courier*, 30 October 1905.
       'We are fully prepared … writing.' – *Manchester Courier*,
       9 November 1905.
       'Everything that ingenuity … doing.' – *Truth*, 9 November
       1905
199   'What has that got … concern.' – *The Times*, 13 November
       1905.
       'Monte Carlo Wells … immortal.' – *Daily Mirror*,
       20 November 1905.
200   'Leaked badly … glass case.' – *The Times*, 20 November 1905.
       Case transfers to Old Bailey – POB, 1906, Walton testimony.
201   'They were practically … not quite' – POB, 1906, Elliott
       testimony and judge's summing-up.

13 – An Amusing Case

       Dartmoor Prison generally – Thomson (*The Criminal*) and
       Thomson (*Story of Dartmoor Prison*).
203   Thomson's background – *ODNB*.
203–4 'The contented … interesting books.' – Thomson (*The
       Criminal*), pp. 70–1.
204   'I have been looking … author, sir.' – *Ibid*. pp. 71–2.
       Prison library – Thomson (*Story of Dartmoor Prison*), pp. 268–9.
       'You will be discharged … again, Wells.' – Thomson (*The
       Criminal*).
205   Leaves for France 27 April 1899 – draft letter, Metropolitan
       Police to *Sûreté*, 21 July 1911, TNA MEPO 3/204.

Nearly all of the information about 'Cuvilier', including his trial, is from *Le Progrès* (Lyon), 22 June 1909.

Myriam d'Etigny / Marie Chalandre – see *Sûreté* leaflet. TNA: MEPO 3/204.

206   'Long prospectus with extraordinary phraseology' – *Petit Parisien*, 9 May 1911.

207   'By taking the journey … sights.' – Quoted in Fontaine, p. 290.

'The work of the … as a whole.' – *Le Progrès* (Lyon), 22 June 1909.

208   Marriage of Jeannette Pairis and James Burns – marriage certificate (General Register Office).

Their voyage to America – www.ancestry.co.uk/search/collections/2997/.

208–10   Description of trial – *Le Progrès* (Lyon), 22 June 1909 and *Le Matin*, 22 June 1909.

210   Taken to Clairveaux prison – *Gil Blas*, 21 January 1912.

211   'Absolutely penniless' – transcript of hearing 22 May 1912, p. 48; TNA: HO 144/1187/218989; and *L'Aurore*, 20 April 1911.

'A very correct … gentleman.' – *Le Matin*, 20 April 1911.

211–2   Rents office in Avenue de l'Opéra – *Le Matin*, 20 April 1911; *Petit Parisien*, 20 April 1911.

212   Two entrances to same building – *Petit Parisien*, 20 April 1911. See also map, p. 37.

'Revolutionise the world … business.' – *Le Matin*, 20 April 1911.

Advertisement – *Le Matin*, 3 September 1910.

212–3   'The profits are … cold and hunger.' – *Petit Parisien*, 22 April 1911.

213   'Naturally you will … fortune.' – *Le Matin*, 20 April 1911.

214   '1% Guaranteed …'. Advertisement – *Le Temps*, 10 December 1910.

Description of bank premises; extravagant office; many staff; Rivier smart in frock coat etc.– Petit Parisien, 20 April 1911 – *Ibid*.

215   Rivier's simple life-style – *Daily Mirror*, 22 January 1912.

Upper and lower investment limits – *Petit Parisien*, 20 April 1911.

Clergy as investors; staff worked to death – *Ibid*.; see also *Yorkshire Evening Post*, 22 January 1912.

216   500fr. note sent without covering letter – *Petit Parisien*,
21 April 1911; Le Stéphanois, 22 April 1911.

Jeannette moves back to London. According to *Le Matin*,
20 April 1911, she left the Rue Cherubini six months before
April 1911, i.e. about October 1910.

Excelsior Yachting and Trading Club Ltd. – TNA: BT
31/13538/114487.

217   Particulars of properties on which mortgages were secured –
TNA: HO 144/1187/218989.

Particulars of annuities – TNA: HO 144/1187/218989.

'A splendid affair … suspect.' – *Le Matin*, 20 April 1911.

218   'A blustering man … temper.' – Scotti, p. 42.

Background on elite squad of detectives, and on Roux
personally – *La Croix*, 24 July 1910, and *La Revue de Paris*,
July–August 1912, p. 141 etc.

Roux questions 'Rivier' who then informs Paul that he will be
out late – *Le Matin*, 20 April 1911.

14 – A Business Genius

219   'Rivier' has disappeared; his note found – *Le Matin*, 20 April
1911.

220   Rivier's successor does not arrive – *Petit Parisien*, 20 April 1911.

221   'perpetual Christmas box'. – Dickens, p. 419.

'Financier flees … liabilities.' – *Petit Parisien*, 20 April 1911.

222   '365 per cent … profit?' – *Le Matin*, 20 April 1911.

'For the whole of yesterday … angry.' – *Petit Parisien*,
21 April 1911.

'That bandit … owes me.' – *Petit Parisien*, 22 April 1911.

222–3   'I shouldn't have … scraping.' – *Ibid*.

223   'The big banks … honest man.' – And 'He'll be back … pay us
back.' Le Stéphanois, 22 April 1911.

'He was such a good … savings again.' – *L'Impartial*, 25 April
1911.

Poteau: 'It's a really admirable … implementing it.' –
Le Temps, 24 April 1911.

224   'He's a clever … crook!' – *Le Matin*, 20 April 1911.

'We all had absolute … lunch-break.' – Le Stéphanois, 22 April
1911.

224–5   'He had loads … let me down, then.' – *Le Matin*, 20 April 1911.
          'How could you not … genius.' – *Petit Parisien*, 22 April 1911.
225   'A passion for "little ladies"' – *Gil Blas*, 9 May 1911.
          'The man was a mystery … didn't.' – *Le Matin*, 20 April 1911.
          'No, the money … complained.' – *Ibid.*
226   '[Rivier's] dupes … swindler.' – *Le Radical*, 21 April 1911.
          'On many occasions … certain loss.' – *La Croix*, 25 April 1911.
          Comparison with casino; the only dupes were the latecomers –
          Journal des Finances, 6 May 1911.
          'Paid a large rent … London.' – *Yorkshire Evening Post*,
          22 January 1912.
226–7   Whereabouts of 'Mrs. Burns' – *Le Matin*, 20 April 1911.
227   Aftermath of the fraud, generally – *Petit Parisien*, 20 April
          1911; *Le Matin*, 20 April 1911; *L'Aurore*, 20 April 1911; *Le
          Stéphanois*, 21 April 1911; *Le Matin*, 21 April 1911; *La Lanterne*,
          22 April 1911.
227–8   'With a grave … financier' and wine merchant loses savings –
          Petit Parisien, 22 April 1911.
228   Malétras quantifies losses – *Petit Parisien*, 21 April 1911.
          Two million francs fraudulently obtained – *La Lanterne*,
          16 September 1912.
229   Rivier (victim of Servatel) – *Le Gaulois*, 9 May 1911.
230   Judge in Lyon – *Petit Parisien*, 9 May 1911.
          Judge asks for photograph and Roux and Mlle Clérico
          recognise picture – *Gil Blas*, 9 May 1911.
          Safe deposit box empty – *La Lanterne*, 11 May 1911.
230–1   Contents of Sûreté leaflet – 'This fraudster … origins': TNA:
          MEPO 3/204.
231   'Enquiries have been made … obtained.' – Letter:
          Metropolitan Police to *Sûreté* : TNA: MEPO 3/204.
          Rivier made bankrupt – *Le Figaro*, 23 May 1911.
232   Sûreté to Metropolitan Police – 'Rivier, alias Well … music
          hall-song.'
233–4   Nicholls background – 1911 census; London Parish Marriages
          (Ancestry).
          'Tall and unassuming' – *Derby Daily Telegraph*, 29 July 1929.
          'Splendid physique' – *Western Daily Mercury*, 23 January 1912.

15 – The French Captain

Mona Lisa theft, generally – see Scotti.

237–8   Hamard and Bertillon investigate at the scene – *Le Figaro*, 24 August 1911.

238   'Twelve days ... mystery deepens.' – *Le Figaro*, 2 September 1911.

'We have to accept ... is lost' – *Le Figaro*, 4 September 1911.

Wells' wife and daughter – *Sûreté* to Metropolitan Police. TNA: MEPO 3/204.

239   Registered letter: request for identity of sender – *Sûreté* to Metropolitan Police. *Ibid.*

240   Nicholls' reply to above – *Ibid.*

241   Background on Falmouth, generally – *Kelly's Directory* Cornwall, 1910.

'And all other conveniences ... cargoes.' – *Ibid.*

Cox background – *Ibid.*, and birth, marriage and death records.

His participation in shipwreck committee – see www.plimsoll. org.

241–2   Wells' orders placed with Falmouth firms – *Yorkshire Telegraph*, 22 January 1912.

242   'The French captain ... and enjoyment.' – *Lake's Falmouth Packet and Cornwall Advertiser*, 27 January 1912.

'Deville' good customer – 'I have plenty ... when I buy?' *Ibid.*

'Quite thirty years ... and hats.' – *Kalgoorlie Miner* (Australia), 12 March 1913.

'Lie down unobserved ... coast.' – *Daily Mirror*, 22 January 1912.

243   'The lines were ... with the line.' – *Ibid.*

'To make his little doll happy' – *Lake's Falmouth Packet and Cornwall Advertiser*, 27 January 1912.

'Jeannette's boudoir ... and comfort.' – *West Briton & Cornwall Advertiser*, 25 January 1912.

Crew's observations on the couple – *Lake's Falmouth Packet and Cornwall Advertiser*, 27 January 1912.

244   '30 June 1911 ... your Loulou.' – *West Briton & Cornwall Advertiser*, 11 March 1912; and *Daily News* (Perth, Australia), 16 April 1912.

'Not having had ... all the family.' – TNA: MEPO 3/204

244–5   'If you do not reply ... Léon.' – *Ibid.*

245   Christmas present for crew – *Lake's Falmouth Packet and Cornwall Advertiser*, 27 January 1912.

245–6   '20 December 1911 … it bears' – TNA: MEPO 3/204.

246   'I have … locate him.' – *Ibid*.

247   'Further enquiries … identify Wells.' – Nicholls memo. *Ibid*.
            'He is proceeding … be seized.' – *Ibid*.

249–50   Details of arrest generally –*Lake's Falmouth Packet and Cornwall Advertiser*, 27 January 1912; *Cornish Echo*, 26 January 1912.

249   'Time was given … toilette.' – *Yorkshire Evening Post*, 22 January 1912.
            'A large quantity … dapper and distinguished.' And note on his clothing: *Lake's Falmouth Packet and Cornwall Advertiser*, 27 January 1912.

249–50   'Keep the yacht clean … day or two.' – *Ibid*.

250   'One £20 Bank of England … purse.' Jewellery list made by police – TNA: MEPO 3/204.
            Contents of Wells' pockets – a gold watch etc. *Ibid*.
            'The accused … charge they were' – *Lake's Falmouth Packet and Cornwall Advertiser*, 27 January 1912.
            'The parties were allowed … of the town' – *Ibid*.

250–1   'They have had their meals … French.' – *Kalgoorlie Miner* (Australia), 12 March 1913.

251   'Another episode … has ever known.' – *Yorkshire Evening Post*, 22 January 1912.
            'The Sûreté put … million [francs].' – *Gil Blas*, 21 January 1912.
            Uncertainty over extradition – *L'Aurore*, 21 January 1912.

252   His nationality a mystery. He is multilingual, will make life difficult – *Le Figaro*, 21 January 1912.

16 – A Vast Roulette

253   'Pairis is a great … custody.' – *Lake's Falmouth Packet and Cornwall Advertiser*, 27 January 1912.
            'When Wells last arrested … corsets.' – Telegram, Scotland Yard to Nicholls. TNA: MEPO 3/204.
            Formalities and dialogue at police station, generally – *Lake's Falmouth Packet and Cornwall Advertiser*, 27 January 1912; *Cornish Echo*, 26 January 1912.

254   Chard and Cox investigated the sinking of the sailing ship *Ifor* in 1909 (see plimsoll.org).

'Not at all … Monte Carlo.' – *Lake's Falmouth Packet and Cornwall Advertiser*, 27 January 1912.

255   '6 pairs knickers … 3 shirts.' List of property on board *Harbinger* and forwarded to Scotland Yard by Cornwall Constabulary – TNA: MEPO 3/204.

255–6   Crutchett background – *Sunday Post*, 3 September 1922.
His part in the conviction of the Stratton brothers – www.capitalpunishmentuk.org.

256   'At that time … bogus concerns.' – *Sunday Post*, 3 September 1922.

Crutchett goes to Safety Deposit and banks – TNA: MEPO 3/204.

257   Crowds gather to see Wells leave; Charles and Jeannette send compliments to other crew – *Lake's Falmouth Packet and Cornwall Advertiser*, 27 January 1912.

'Short in stature … figure' – *Western Daily Mercury*, 23 January 1912; 'distinctly of French appearance' – *Lake's Falmouth Packet and Cornwall Advertiser*, 27 January 1912.

258   'Wells seemed … companion.' *Ibid*.

'Close to the door … the occupants.' *Ibid*.

'As comfortable … traveller'; and 'All five were … vivacious leader.' – *Ibid*.

259   'Those who saw … his appearance.' – *Cornish Echo*, 26 January 1912.

His companion … Scotland Yard.' – *Ibid*.

Cab full of papers – *Daily Herald* (Adelaide), 26 March 1912.

The unusual interest … particularly so.' – *Western Times*, 24 January 1912.

259–60   'Short, plump … eyelashes.' – *Daily Herald* (Adelaide), 26 March 1912.

'Little trace … in the song.' – *Lake's Falmouth Packet and Cornwall Advertiser*, 27 January 1912.

'A man whom age … withered' – *Ibid*.

'Rivier is sure … escaper' – *La Lanterne*, 23 January 1912.

'Rivier will plead … subjects.' – *La Lanterne*, 25 January 1912.

Jeannette smiles as Nicholls reads out list – *Daily Herald* (Adelaide), 26 March 1912; *Dominion* (New Zealand) 7 March 1912.

Jeannette takes little notice but Wells listens intently – *Ibid*.

261   Solicitor asks for small sum of money to be available – *Lake's Falmouth Packet* and *Cornwall Advertiser*, 27 January 1912; *The Times*, 24 January 1912.

'We have heard … other sources.' – *West Briton & Cornwall Advertiser*, 22 January 1912.

Led to cells, downcast: *Lake's Falmouth Packet and Cornwall Advertiser*, 27 January 1912.

262   'It is for the very … great kindness.' – Wells' note to Nicholls and Roux: Nicholls records in a subsequent memo that he did not pass it on: TNA: MEPO 3/204.

Subsequent paperwork, report etc. by Nicholls – *Ibid*.

Witness statements, Micklethwaite Road, etc. – *Ibid*.

263   Nicholls promoted –website: murderatthestar.wordpress.com.

Account of extradition hearing; 'We have been here … remand you.' – *Daily Mirror*, 15 March 1912.

264   'The money was not handed to him … got it' – *Morning Advertiser*, 21 March 1912.

'Don't trust him … swindler.' – *Ibid*.

'Many well-known banks … business.' – *Ibid*.

265   Barton background – Wikipedia article, and Churchill, W.S., p. 250 etc.

'I am C. Wells … other places.' – Wells' letter to Barton, TNA: HO 144/1187/218989.

'I do not know … effusions.' – Barton to Home Office. *Ibid*.

Zalma's friendship with Lt-Gen Sir Charles Barter – *Le Courrier de l'Oise*, 6 February 1921

Extradition via Boulogne – *Gil Blas*, 30 May 1912.

'The sum of one million … intends.' – *Ibid*.

266–7   Saint-Lazare prison; 'totally incapable … improvement.' – Petit, p. 138.

Wells' letter to E. Caen (lawyer), 11 August 1912 – TNA, BT221.1997.

Board of Trade memo regarding solitary confinement – 20 August 1912. *Ibid*.

267–8   Open questioning; Malétras indicates scope of fraud – *La Lanterne*, 16 September 1912.

Report on full criminal trial Petit Parisien, 14 September 1912; *La Lanterne*, 16 September 1912; *Nottingham Evening Post*, 16 September 1912.

268–9   Jeannette's involvement – *Le Matin*, 22 June 1912.
269   Possible fifteen-year sentence – *Sunday Morning Star* (Wilmington, Delaware, USA), 25 February 1912.
         Prospect of sentence; Wells amused; recitation of his life story – *L'Ouest-Éclair*, 15 November 1912.
         If daring bankers … features.' – *Le Matin*, 15 November 1912.
         'Romancier anglais' – *La Croix*, 15 November 1912.
         'He speaks with … millionaires?' – *Le Matin*, 15 November 1912.
270   A strange character … behaviour.' – *Le Rappel*, 16 November 1912.
         'He answers questions … her lover.' – *Ibid*.
         'Mlle. Pairis … innocence.' – *Le Matin*, 15 November 1912.
         'M. Malétras explained … promises.' – *Le Rappel*, 16 November 1912.
270–1   'Two million francs' – *La Croix*, 15 November 1912.
271   'A vast roulette … after all' – *Ibid*.
         'A professor … series.' – *Le Figaro*, 15 November 1912.
         'Yes, not once … system.' – *Evening News*, Sydney, 4 January 1913.
         'If I took flight … extradition.' – *La Croix*, 15 November 1912.
271–2   Jeannette denies involvement – *La Presse*, 15 November 1912.
         'I know it must … any way.' – *Evening News* (Sydney), 4 January 1913.
         'Buyer beware … knaves.' – *Timaru Herald* (New Zealand), 31 December 1912.
         Wells and Jeannette found guilty and sentenced – *Le Rappel*, 24 November 1912.
         'The promise of … their money?' – *Le Frou-Frou*, 8 December 1912.
273   Special Eighth Section; 'Close enquiry … bankers.' – *Financial Times*, 19 March 1912.
         Desbleumortier to act as Administrator – *Le Rappel*, 24 November 1912.
274   'I have come to this … obligations.' – TNA: TNA, HD 144/1187/218989.
275   'The carriage would not … pay it.' – Nicholls memo: TNA: MEPO 3/204.

Official Receiver holds annuities, Desbleumortier to certify that Wells still alive – *The Times*, 28 April 1913, and 30 June 1913; see also TNA: HD 144/1187/218989.

275–6 Bucknill says case might have gone to House of Lords – *The Times*, 30 June 1913.

276 Jeannette keeps £835 – *Sheffield Evening Telegraph & Star*, 28 June 1913.

Maison Cellulaire de Fresnes – Petit, p. 138.

276–7 Bower: 'officer in South-American state' – *The Standard*, 11 February 1903; wins at Monte Carlo: *The Cornishman*, 19 January 1911.

277–8 'There is a double … ports.' – *The Times*, 27 August 1914.

Mata Hari questioned. – TNA: KV2/1.

'Charles de Ville Wells … particulars.' – Warrell phone message. TNA: MEPO 3/204.

279 'Charles de Ville Wells … Morse, P.C.' – Report on Wells' non-arrival: *Ibid*.

280 Wells requests more money, creditors agree – *Le Matin*, 1 December 1920.

Wells receives further £4 per week. – TNA BT221/1997, 4 March 1916.

'Monte Carlo Wells … at Monte Carlo.' – *Daily Telegraph*, 25 July 1922.

281 'Nobody will be more sorry … creditors.' – *Hartlepool Mail*, 26 July 1922.

Wilson claims creditors received most of money owed: *Ibid*.

Story embellished with time: subsequently, other inaccuracies crept into the story. *Brewer's Rogues, Villains and Eccentrics* (Donaldson) shows his year of death as 1920; elsewhere 1926 is cited; an otherwise excellent book, *The Money Spinner* by Xan Fielding, says he passed away in 1929.

'He Broke Monte Carlo bank … years old.' – *Bourbon News*, (Paris, Kentucky), 16 September 1922.

282 Addresses of Charles and Jeannette in London, etc. – his death certificate, General Register Office; *Weekly Dispatch*, 30 July 1922.

Landlady's recollection – *Dundee Courier*, 31 July 1922.

Clothing shabby; landlady gave him cast-off clothes – *Northern Standard* (Darwin, Australia), 17 October 1922 .
'The end came … armchair.' – *Derby Daily Telegraph*, 20 September 1928.

283 'Monte Carlo Wells … perennial youth.' – Thomson (*The Criminal*), p. 73.

17 – How the Bank was Broken

284–5 Ritual of black cloth discontinued – Smith, A., p. 370.

285 Wells' ability to win multiple times – *Daily Mirror*, 23 November 1912

286 Joseph Jagger – Fletcher, A., especially pp. 107–19.
'If there were any possible … a croupier?' – *Daily Telegraph*, 3 March, 1891.

287 Blanc offers 1 million-franc prize – Jackson, pp. 42 and 68.
Wells sends winnings home – *The Standard*, 1 August 1891.

288 Dishonest croupiers and supervisors (San Remo) – *The Times*, 29 January 1981 and *The New York Times*, 10 June 1981.

289 Rival casino proposed for Cannes – *Eastbourne Gazette*, 12 August 1891.
Possible move to Andorra or Liechtenstein – *Daily Independent*, 12 July 1891, *Western Daily Press*, 6 August 1891.
Lavish ornamentation by designer – *The Times*, 31 October 1891 and 17 November 1891.

290 Wells channels winnings through Sloane Square bank – POB: Green testimony.
Millionaire sixty times over – *Le Petit Journal*, 4 June 1879.

290–1 Countess Kisselev and gambling – Corti, pp. 54–60.
Branicki guest at marriage of Blanc's daughter – Corti, p. 264.
Wells' self-promoting letter to Ms Phillimore – see p. 98 of this book.

293 Wells advertises for £75 loan – *The Times*, 27 July 1891.

294 'I did not believe … valuable advertisement' – , p. 232.

295 Croupiers help friends to win – Dumont, p. 265.
'… Six or seven deep … Wells backed.' – *The Elks Magazine*, January 1927.

18 – The Power of the Press

297   John Waller – News UK Archives and *Scoop!* (scoop-database. com).

298   'It is easy to understand … sober truth' – *The Globe*, 3 August 1891.

299   'On 8 November … good fortune themselves' – *The Times*, 8 November 1891.

             Work recommences on Salle Touzet – *The Times*, 31 October 1891 and 17 November 1891.

             'Why is this Wells … year after year?' – *Truth*, 5 November 1891.

300   'Not a leader or paragraph … at Monte Carlo' – Peddie, p. 6.

301   Salle Touzet re-opens – *The Times*, 31 October 1891.

302   Blanc and race-horses – see, for example, *The Australasian* (Melbourne), 26 December 1891.

302–3   Suspected of election rigging – *Time Magazine*, 21 April 1923.

303   Employees exist only on paper – *Ibid*.

             Mme. Chinon – *Ibid*.

304   'One result of … Casino' – *London Evening Standard*, 23 March 1892.

             Players … stand five deep … are English – *Manchester Times*, 25 March 1892.

             '1891 marked the turning point … of failure' – *The Elks Magazine*, January 1927.

19 – A High-Class Crook

306   Mustard sold in tubes – email correspondence with Unilever Archives.

307   Dinnie's later career – Grant, pp. 67, 83.

308   Det. Inspector Charles Richards' career – Bristow, p. 188.

             Crutchett's later career – *Sunday Post*, 3 September 1922

              'Wells was a really wonderful … gifts.' – *Ibid*.

             Nicholls' later career – *Evening Telegraph*, 4 July 1922; see also murderatthestar.wordpress.com.

             'Mate to Monte Carlo … death.' – *West Briton & Cornwall Advertiser*, 26 February 1923.

309	'I should say ... there would be.' – Abinger, p. 87. (The brief 'quotation within a quotation' is from Tennyson's Locksley Hall.)
	'The most picturesque ... no equal.' – Nicholls, p. 181.
	'Monte Carlo Wells ... my hands.' – Thomson (*The Criminal*), pp. 65–73.
311	William Cosby Trench's later career – *Who's Who and Who Was Who*, 2015.
	William Charles Gamble King – *Dover Express & East Kent News*, 26 January 1900.
	Jupp's bankruptcy – *The Standard*, 24 October 1896.
	Still paying long after – *London Gazette*, 28 March 1922.
	Death of Vergis – death certificate (General Register Office).
311–2	Henry Baker Vaughan – *Essex Newsman*, 08 December 1906.
312	Moyle's final years – Nicholls, p. 191.
	Alfred Emanuel's later career – 'Trading on the dead': *Oamaru Mail*, 31 January 1914.
312–3	*Palais Royal*'s fate – TNA: BT 110/62/63; and tynebuiltships.co.uk.
313	Coborn's multiple recordings – Rust.
	The SBM today – Wikipedia entry for Monte Carlo Casino.
314	Charles Vayre's later career – author profile, Bibliothèque Nationale de France (data.bnf.fr/10337131/charles_vayre/).
	Death of Charles and Marie Antoinette Vayre – information kindly provided by the Société des Gens de Lettres de France.
	Song ('Consolations') by Vayre – De Wills (published in 1913 by Georges Ondet, Paris).
314–5	Jeannette's death – Register of deaths, Paris, 1929.
315	Arthur De Courcey-Bower's death – *The Times*, 4 January 1926.

Sources

Books – General Reference

Annuaire de la Presse Française.
Encyclopedia Britannica (10th edn, 1902; 11th edn., 1911).
Gore's Directory of Liverpool (1892).
Grande Encyclopédie, la (1885–1902).
Kelly's Post Office Directory (various places and years).
Law List (various years).
Lloyd's Captains Register.
Lloyd's Register of Shipping (London: various years).
Lloyd's Register of Yachts (London: various years).
May's British & Irish Press Guide and Advertiser's Handbook & Dictionary (London: various editions).
Nouveau Dictionnaire de la Langue Française, 3rd edn (Paris: Larousse, 1856).
ODNB (*Oxford Dictionary of National Biography*) (2013).
Te Ara Encyclopedia of New Zealand (Blackwell, 2008).
Who's Who and *Who Was Who?* (London: A&C Black, 2015).
Willing's (late May's) British & Irish Press Guide (London: various editions).

Books – Other

Abinger, E., *Forty Years at the Bar* (London: Hutchinson & Co., 1930).
Allier, P., *Les Rues de Quimper* (Quimper: Éditions France-Bretagne, 1950).

Baker, R.A., *British Music Hall: an Illustrated History* (Barnsley: Pen & Sword, 2014).

Balfour, J., *My Prison Life* (London: Chapman & Hall, 1907).

Bethell, V., *Monte Carlo Anecdotes and Systems of Play* (London: William Heinemann, 1901).

Bethell, V., *Ten Days at Monte Carlo at the Bank's Expense* (London: William Heinemann, 1898).

Bristow, J, *Oscar Wilde on Trial* (Yale University Press, 2023).

Churchill, W.S., *London to Ladysmith via Pretoria* (London: Longmans Co., 1900).

Coborn, C., *The Man Who Broke the Bank at Monte Carlo* (London: Hutchinson, *c.*1928).

Corti, Count, *The Wizard of Homburg and Monte Carlo* (Thornton Butterworth, 1934).

Dickens, C., *Martin Chuzzlewit* (Wordsworth, 1994).

Donaldson, W., *Brewer's Rogues, Villains and Eccentrics* (London: Cassell, 2002).

Dugan, Dr S., *Baroness Orczy's* The Scarlet Pimpernel*: A Publishing History* (Farnham: Ashgate, 2012).

Dumas, A., *The Count of Monte Cristo* (Paris: Journal des débats, 1846)

Dumont, P., *Monte-Carlo. Le Prince Rouge et Noir et sa Cour* (Paris: Dumont, 1892).

Edwards, A., *The Grimaldis of Monaco* (London: Harper Collins, 1992).

Fielding, X., *The Money Spinner: Monte Carlo Casino* (Weidenfeld & Nicolson, 1977).

Fontaine, G., *La Culture du Voyage à Lyon de 1820 à 1930* (Lyon: Presses Universitaires de Lyon, *c.*2003).

Geels, F.W., *Technological Transitions and System Innovations* (Cheltenham: Edward Elgar, 2005).

Gilbert, D., *Lost Chords* (New York: Cooper Square, 1970).

Graves, C., *The Big Gamble: The Story of Monte Carlo* (Hutchinson, 1951).

Grundy, E., Borough of Southall, Annual Report of the Medical Officer of Health (1937).

Heaton, P.M., *Lamport & Holt* (Pontypool: Heaton, 1986).

Herald, G.W., and E.D. Radin, *The Big Wheel* (London: Robert Hale, 1965).

Jackson, S., *Inside Monte Carlo* (New York: Stein and Day, 1975)

Johnston, P., *Keats-Shelley Journal*, Vol. 26 (Keats-Shelley Association of America, Inc., 1977).

Jones, C., *Paris: Biography of a City* (London: Allen Lane, 2004).

Keats, J., *The Poetical Works of John Keats* (Part 1) (New York: Wiley & Putnam, 1846).

Kingston, C., *The Romance of Monte Carlo* (London: John Lane, Bodley Head, 1925).

Kirk, J.F., *Supplement to Allibone's Critical Dictionary of English Literature and British and American Authors* (Vol. 2) (Philadelphia: Lippincott, 1902).

Lax, R., and F. Smith, *The Great Song Thesaurus* (New York: Oxford University Press, 1984).

Magocsi, P.R., *A History of Ukraine* (Toronto; London: University of Toronto Press, 1996).

Maxim, Sir H.S., *Monte Carlo Facts and Fallacies* (London: Grant Richards, 1904).

Nicholls, E., *Crime Within the Square Mile* (London: John Long, 1935).

Peddie, J., *All About Monte Carlo. Extraordinary Career of Charles Wells, the Man who Broke the Bank at Monte Carlo etc.* (London: 'The Comet' Publishing Co., 1893).

Peddie, J., *How the Bank at Monte Carlo was Broken* (London: Edmund Seale, 1896).

Petit, J.G., *Histoire des Prisons en France* (Toulouse: *c.*2002).

Polovtsoff, P., *Monte Carlo Casino* (Paul, 1937).

Rust, B., *British Music Hall on Record* (Harrow: General Gramophone Publications, 1979).

Scotti, R.A., *The Lost Mona Lisa* (London: Bantam, 2009).

Sharpe, G., *Gambling's Strangest Moments* (London: Robson, 2005).

Silberer, V., *The Games of Roulette and Trente-et-Quarante as Played at Monte Carlo* (London: Harrison & Sons, 1910).

Smith, A., *Monaco and Monte Carlo* (London: Grant Richards, and Philadelphia: Lippincott, 1912).

Smith, E.C., *A Short History of Naval and Marine Engineering* (Cambridge: University Press, 1938).

Tatchell, M., *Keats-Shelley Memorial Association*, Bulletin No. XXII (London: Keats-Shelley Memorial Association, 1971).

Thomson, Sir B., *The Criminal* (Hodder & Stoughton, 1925).

Thomson, Sir B., *The Story of Dartmoor Prison* (London: Heinemann, 1907).

Twain, M., *The Innocents Abroad, or The New Pilgrims' Progress* (Leipzig: Tachnitz, 1879).

Wells, C.J., *Joseph and his Brethren* (1908).

Wells, H.G., *Experiment in Autobiography* (Vol. 2) (London: Gollancz, 1934).

Williams, G.L., *The Proof of Guilt: Study of the English Criminal Trial* (London: Stevens & Sons, 1955).

Wu, D., *William Hazlitt: The First Modern Man* (Oxford: Oxford University Press, 2008).

Index